MW01698097

OUR DAILY BREAD®

To: ____________________

From: ____________________

rbc ministries®

ACKNOWLEDGMENTS

COVER PHOTO: *Vine, Santiago, Chile,* Alex Soh, © RBC Ministries.

POEM CREDITS:

Feb. 25, by John W. Peterson. © Renewal 1980. John W. Peterson Music Company.
Feb. 27, by Civilla Martin. © Renewal 1958. Hope Publishing.
Feb. 28, by Bertha Lillenas. ©1934 Homer A. Rodeheaver.
Mar. 19, by C. Austin Miles. © Renewal 1940. The Rodeheaver Co.
Apr. 3, by Helen Frazee-Bower. © 1956 Helen Frazee-Bower.
Apr. 5, by Alfred Ackley. © Renewal 1961. The Rodeheaver Co.
Apr. 16, by Annie Johnson Flint. © Renewal 1969. Lillenas Publishing.
Apr. 24, by H. H. Lemmel. © Renewal 1950. H. H. Lemmel.
Apr. 30, by John Wesley. © 1951 Singspiration.
May 23, by William Martin. © Renewal 1938. The Rodeheaver Co.
June 2, by John W. Peterson. © 1958 Singspiration.
June 6, by Sidney Cox. © Renewal 1979 Singspiration.
June 12, by Ralph C. Carmichael. © 1958 SpiritQuest Music.
June 18, by Haldor Lillenas. © Renewal 1945 Haldor Lillenas. Assigned to Hope Publishing.
July 9, by St. Francis of Assisi, translated by William H. Draper. © 1968 Singspiration.
July 10, by H. S. Lehman. © 1924 H. S. Lehman.
July 19, by Rhea F. Miller. © Renewal 1950. Chancel Music.
July 27, by Albert S. Reitz. © Renewal 1946. Hope Publishing.
Aug. 9, by Norman J. Clayton. © Renewal 1966. Norman J. Clayton.
Nov. 11, by Thomas Chisholm. © Renewal 1951. Hope Publishing.
Nov. 21, by William J. Gaither. © 1970 William J. Gaither.
Nov. 26, by John W. Peterson. © 1968 John W. Peterson Music Co. All rights reserved. Used by permission.
Dec. 1, by Oswald Smith. © 1939 The Rodeheaver Co.
Dec. 10, by Margaret Clarkson. © 1966 Hope Publishing.
Dec. 14, by J. Wilbur Chapman. © Renewal 1938. The Rodeheaver Co.
Dec. 23, by Thomas Chisholm. © Renewal 1973. Lillenas Publishing.

ARTICLE CREDITS:

Jan. 10, *Meet the Bible: A Panorama of God's Word in 366 Daily Readings and Reflections,* by Philip D. Yancey and Brenda Quinn; Nov. 8, *Grace Notes,* by Philip D. Yancey, © 2009 Zondervan. Published by permission of Zondervan; Dec. 14, *The Jesus I Never Knew,* by Philip D. Yancey. © 1995 Zondervan. Published by permission of Zondervan.

Internet address: www.rbc.org • Email: rbc@rbc.org
Printed in China.

ISBN: 978-1-60485-857-0

CONTENTS

Introduction

We are glad you picked up a copy of the 2015 Annual Gift Edition of *Our Daily Bread*. We pray that it will help you draw near to our wonderful Lord.

In the center of this edition is a special feature article by Mart DeHaan, senior advisor of ministry content at RBC Ministries. He discusses common concerns that people have about forgiveness, including *How can we be sure we have not made ourselves unforgivable in the eyes of God?* Mart says, "The answer is found in the extent to which God has gone to bear the pain and punishment of what we deserve." Our desire is that Mart's article will help you find a freedom that will compel you to tell others about the gracious forgiveness of God.

Consider sharing this book with loved ones or friends who can use it in their personal quiet time with God.

If we can serve you, please contact us.

—The staff at *Our Daily Bread*

Decision Time

Since Jesus' day, kings, governments, and empires have come and gone. But the King who set Himself apart from all other kings by dying in our place remains. He alone can meet our deepest needs. Jesus doesn't want to be merely our King—He wants to be our Lord and Savior. He offers us a life of unimaginable significance and purpose if we will accept His forgiveness.

Jesus' friend and disciple John the apostle wrote, "As many as received Him [Jesus], to them He gave the right to become children of God, to those who believe in His name" (John 1:12). But what does that mean? The explanation comes from Jesus Himself.

Jesus told the religious leader Nicodemus this encouraging news: "God did not send His Son into the world to condemn the world, but that the world through Him might be saved" (John 3:17).

That sounds great, doesn't it? But this salvation is not automatic. Jesus continued, "He who believes in Him is not condemned; but he who does not believe is condemned already, because he has not believed in the name of the only begotten Son of God" (v.18). A little later in His ministry, Jesus would reveal to a desperate woman that He was indeed the long-awaited Messiah (John 4:25-26).

If you've never done so before, are you ready to put your trust in the One who can give us real forgiveness of sins and the right to enter into His kingdom as His child?

Allow your heart to be changed by inviting the King of kings to His rightful place in your life.

January 1
Thursday

THE GOOD LIFE

READ:
Psalm 73:21-28

It is good for me to draw near to God.
—Psalm 73:28

THE BIBLE IN ONE YEAR:
■ Genesis 1–3
■ Matthew 1

Beauty, wealth, power, love, marriage, and pleasure are good things, but they're not the best. The best is loving God and taking in His love—bringing Him glory and making Him our friend for life. That leads to the best possible life because it gives us satisfaction and joy now (John 10:10), and it's what Christians are going to be doing forever.

That's why we should make time for God and rest in His love—the love that made you and me. It is the reason for our existence and the means by which we will make the most of our lives.

I like the way the psalmist put it: "It is good for me to draw near to God; I have put my trust in the Lord GOD, that I may declare all Your works" (Ps. 73:28). In other words, the good life is drawing close to the One who loves us like no other.

And how can we "draw close" to Him? Here's a practice I began many years ago: Take a few minutes every morning to read some verses from the Gospels (Matthew, Mark, Luke, John) and note what Jesus said or did. After all, He came to show us what God is like (Heb. 1:1-3). Put yourself in the story—in the place of the leper He healed with His loving touch, for example (Mark 1:40-45). Think about how much He loves you and then thank Him! —David Roper

Perfect submission, all is at rest,
I in my Savior am happy and blest;
Watching and waiting, looking above,
Filled with His goodness, lost in His love. —*Crosby*

The wonder of it all—
just to think that Jesus loves me!

January 2
Friday

T-Ball Faith

Read:
Luke 15:1-7

The joy of the Lord is your strength.
—Nehemiah 8:10

The Bible In One Year:
- **Genesis 4–6**
- **Matthew 2**

Whoever dreamed up T-ball is a genius: Every kid on the field gets a taste of the fun and joy of the game before they taste the disappointment of striking out.

In T-ball, a baseball is placed on a rubber tee about waist-high to the 5- and 6-year-old batters. Players swing until they hit the ball and then run. On my first night as a coach, the very first batter hit the ball far into the outfield. Suddenly *every* player from *every* position ran to get the ball instead of staying where they were supposed to. When one of them reached it, there was nobody left in the infield for him to throw it to! All the players were standing together—cheering with unrestrained exuberance!

Those who have recently come to know Jesus as Savior have an unrestrained joy that is a delight to be around as well. We rejoice with them, and so do the angels in heaven! (Luke 15:7). New Christians are in love with God and excited about knowing Him and learning from His Word.

Those who've been Christians for a long time may get discouraged with the struggles of the Christian life and forget the joy of new-found faith. So take the opportunity to rejoice with those who've come to faith. God can use them to inspire you to renew your own commitment to Jesus. —Randy Kilgore

Rejoice, O soul, your debt is paid,
For all your sins on Christ were laid;
We've been redeemed, we're justified—
And all because the Savior died. —*D. DeHaan*

Restore to me the joy of Your salvation.
—Psalm 51:12

January 3
Saturday

Getting Along

Read:
Philippians 2:1-11

Fulfill my joy by being like-minded, having the same love.
—Philippians 2:2

The Bible In One Year:
- **Genesis 7–9**
- **Matthew 3**

I love being with people . . . most of the time. There is a special joy that resonates in our hearts when we are with people we enjoy. But unfortunately we are not always with those we like to be around. Sometimes people can be prickly, which may be why someone has said, "The more I get to know people, the more I love my dog!" When we don't find joy in a relationship, we tend to blame the other person; then we excuse ourselves as we exit to be with people we like.

The apostle Paul asks us to lovingly engage with our brothers and sisters in Christ. In fact, he calls all of us to be "of one accord," to look out "for the interests of others," and to "let this mind be in you which was also in Christ Jesus" (Phil. 2:2-5). Think about it. Jesus gave up His own prerogatives and privileges for us; He chose to live as a servant and paid the ultimate sacrifice that He might bring us into a joy-filled relationship with Him (see Heb. 12:2). And He did all that in spite of our prickliness (see Rom. 5:8).

So next time you are with someone who is not easy to get along with, ask Jesus to help you find a way to extend His love. In time, you might be surprised by how God can change your attitude about people. —Joe Stowell

Lord, thank You that while I was still offensive to You, You saved me with Your sacrificial love. Give me the same courage and grace to extend to others the love that You have so graciously extended to me.

The key to getting along with others is having the mind of Christ.

January 4
Sunday

HELP YOURSELF

READ:
Psalm 146

Happy is he who has the God of Jacob for his help, whose hope is in the LORD his God.
—Psalm 146:5

THE BIBLE IN ONE YEAR:
- **Genesis 10–12**
- **Matthew 4**

Recently, I saw a television ad for a restaurant chain that made a dramatic claim. At those restaurants, the ad said you could "Help Yourself to Happiness." Wouldn't it be nice if a helping of potatoes or meat or pasta or dessert would be all that was needed to provide happiness? Unfortunately, no restaurant can fulfill that promise.

Happiness is an elusive thing—as we can see in almost every area of life. Our pursuit of happiness may involve food or a host of other things, but, in the end, happiness continues to escape our grasp.

Why? In large measure it's because the things we tend to pursue do not touch the deepest needs of our hearts. Our pursuits may provide moments of enjoyment, distraction, or pleasure, but the cry of our hearts goes unheard—the cry for help and hope. That is why the psalmist points us to a better way when he says, "Happy is he who has the God of Jacob for his help, whose hope is in the LORD his God" (Ps. 146:5).

Help yourself? Yes—if we are seeking the happiness found in the Lord. It is only when we entrust ourselves to God and His care that we can find the happiness we seek. Our hope and help are found only in trusting Him. —Bill Crowder

Father, draw me to Yourself. Remind me that only in You will I know the real joy and satisfaction that my heart longs for. Help me to look beyond the surface things of life to what really matters.

The one who puts God first will have happiness that lasts.

January 5
Monday

Time Out

Read:
Acts 11:19-26; 13:1-3

Then, having fasted and prayed, and laid hands on them, they sent them away.
—Acts 13:3

The Bible In One Year:
- Genesis 13–15
- Matthew 5:1-26

El Bulli restaurant, 2 hours north of Barcelona, is so popular that customers must reserve a table 6 months in advance. But noted Spanish chef Ferran Adrià decided to close the doors of his award-winning restaurant for 2 years so he and his staff could have time to think, plan, and innovate. Adrià told *Hemispheres Magazine*, "If we are winning all the prizes, why change? Working 15 hours a day leaves us very little time to create." In the midst of great success, they took time out for what is most important to them.

The first-century church in Antioch experienced a time of exciting growth when "a great number believed and turned to the Lord" (Acts 11:21). As a result, Barnabas and Saul came to teach the new believers (vv.25-26). But along with the hard work, they took time to seek the Lord through prayer and fasting (13:2-3). Through this, God revealed His plan for taking the gospel into Asia.

Few people can take 2 years off to think and plan. But all of us can build time into our schedule to seek the Lord earnestly through prayer. As we open our hearts and minds to God, He will be faithful to reveal the steps of life and service that honor Him. —David McCasland

There is a blessed calm at eventide
That calls me from a world of toil and care;
How restful, then, to seek some quiet nook
Where I can spend a little time in prayer. —*Bullock*

Prayer is as important as breathing.

January 6
Tuesday

What Is That To You?

Read:
John 21:15-22

What is that to you? You follow Me.
—John 21:22

The Bible In One Year:
- **Genesis 16–17**
- **Matthew 5:27-48**

When you attend a children's choir concert, you're not surprised when the children look everywhere but at the director. They wiggle, squirm, and poke each other. They stand on tiptoes to search for parents in the audience. They raise their hands to wave when they see them. Oh, yes, and they occasionally sing. We smile at their antics. The behavior is cute in children. It's not so cute when adult choir members don't watch the conductor. Good music depends on singers who pay attention to the director so they can stay together as they sing.

Christians sometimes are like singers in a children's choir. Instead of looking at Jesus, the great Conductor of the symphony of life, we are busy squirming or looking at each other or watching the audience.

Jesus admonished Peter for such behavior. After He told him what would be required of him, Peter pointed to John and asked, "What about him?" Jesus answered with a question: "What is that to you? You follow Me" (John 21:22).

Sometimes we are distracted by what others are doing. We think God's plan for their life is better than His plan for ours. But God's plan for each of us is the same: Follow Jesus. When we watch Him intently, we'll not be distracted by God's plan for anyone else. —Julie Ackerman Link

My times are in my Father's hand;
How could I wish or ask for more?
For He who has my pathway planned,
Will guide me till my journey's o'er. —*Fraser*

Every child of God has a special place in His plan.

January 7
Wednesday

FULLY EQUIPPED

READ:
2 Timothy 3:14-17

All Scripture is given by inspiration of God . . . that the man of God may be complete, thoroughly equipped for every good work.
—2 Timothy 3:16-17

THE BIBLE IN ONE YEAR:
■ **Genesis 18–19**
■ **Matthew 6:1-18**

Karl Elsener, a Swiss designer of surgical equipment in the 19th century, worked for years on perfecting a military knife. Today his Swiss Army Knife is associated with excellence in blades and a variety of utilities. One model includes knife blades, a saw, scissors, a magnifying glass, a can opener, a screwdriver, a ruler, a toothpick, a writing pen, and more—all in one knife! If you are out camping in the wild, this one item can certainly make you feel equipped for survival.

We need something to equip us to survive spiritually in this sinful world. God has given us His Word, a kind of spiritual knife for the soul. Paul writes: "All Scripture is given by inspiration of God, and is profitable for doctrine, for reproof, for correction, for instruction in righteousness, that the man of God may be complete, thoroughly equipped for every good work" (2 Tim. 3:16-17).

The word translated *equipped* means to "furnish or fit completely." How does the Bible equip us for life's journey? It provides spiritual truth in *doctrine*; *reproof* in showing our imperfections; *correction* by revealing our sinful failures; and *instruction* in living a righteous life. There's not a more valuable tool than God's Word to make us fully equipped for spiritual survival and personal growth. —Dennis Fisher

Lord, thank You for equipping us with Your inspired Word. You've given us the tools we need to live for You. Help us to take time to read it and to follow what You tell us. Amen.

The Bible contains the nutrients we need for a healthy soul.

January 8
Thursday

Where Sinners Go

Read:
Romans 5:6-15

God demonstrates His own love toward us, in that while we were still sinners, Christ died for us. —Romans 5:8

The Bible In One Year:
- Genesis 20–22
- Matthew 6:19-34

My friend was having a conversation with a man who didn't have much good to say about the Christian faith. My friend knew that if he were to sound too "religious," he would jeopardize any chance to witness. So, in the middle of their discussion, he said, "Hey, Bob, do you know where sinners go?"

"That's easy," he replied. "You're going to tell me they go to hell."

"No," my friend responded. "They go to church."

Bob was speechless. That wasn't what he expected. He wasn't ready to hear from a Christian who realized he wasn't perfect. My friend had a chance to share that Christians understand their sinfulness and their need for continual spiritual restoration. He was able to explain grace—the unmerited favor we have with God despite our sinfulness (Rom. 5:8-9; Eph. 2:8-9).

Perhaps we don't give those outside the church a clear picture of what's happening inside. They may not understand that we're there to praise our Savior for providing "redemption through His blood, the forgiveness of sins" (Col. 1:14).

Yes, sinners go to church. And sinners—forgiven ones—go to heaven because of God's grace. —Dave Branon

We're far from perfection, yet perfect forever,
For Christ is our righteousness, Lord, and our Savior;
No justification for sin can we offer,
Yet sanctified fully, we're now His forever. —*Lee*

A church is a hospital for sinners, not a club for saints.

January 9
Friday

Making It Right

Read:
Luke 19:1-10

If I have taken anything from anyone by false accusation, I restore fourfold. —Luke 19:8

The Bible In One Year:
- Genesis 23–24
- Matthew 7

It was a perfect day for our garage sale—bright and warm. People rummaged through clothing, paperbacks, and mismatched dishes. I noticed a young woman looking at a string of white beads. A few minutes later, the necklace vanished along with its admirer. I spotted her in the street, jogged the length of my driveway, and discovered the missing jewelry nestled in her palm. As we faced each other with the knowledge of what had happened, she volunteered to pay for the stolen item.

Zacchaeus, the tree-climbing tax collector, met Jesus and was changed. He vowed to repay four times the amount of money he had dishonestly taken from others (Luke 19:8). In those days, tax collectors frequently overcharged citizens and then pocketed the extra funds. Zacchaeus' eagerness to pay back the money and to donate half of what he owned to the poor showed a significant change of heart. He had once been a taker, but after meeting Jesus he was determined to make restoration and be a giver.

Zacchaeus' example can inspire us to make the same kind of change. When God reminds us about items we have taken, taxes left unpaid, or ways we have wronged others, we can honor Him by making it right. —Jennifer Benson Schuldt

Help me, dear Lord, to be honest and true
In all that I say and all that I do;
Give me the courage to do what is right
To bring to the world a glimpse of Your light. —*Fasick*

A debt is never too old for an honest person to pay.

January 10
Saturday

Spiritual Sight

Read:
Ephesians 1:15-21

In Him we have redemption through His blood, the forgiveness of sins, according to the riches of His grace.
—Ephesians 1:7

The Bible In One Year:
- **Genesis 25–26**
- **Matthew 8:1-17**

A prisoner who survived 14 years in a Cuban jail told how he kept his spirits up and his hope alive: "I had no window in my cell, and so I mentally constructed one on the door. I 'saw' in my mind a beautiful scene from the mountains, with water tumbling down a ravine over rocks. It became so real to me that I would visualize it without effort every time I looked at the cell door."

Ironically, some of the most hopeful books of the Bible—Philippians, Colossians, and Ephesians—come out of Paul's house arrest in Rome. The letter to the Ephesians gives a hint as to what the apostle Paul saw when he thought about life beyond his place of confinement.

First he saw the spiritual growth in the churches he left behind. This book opens with a burst of thanksgiving for the vitality of the Ephesian church (Eph. 1:15-16). Then he sought to open the eyes of their hearts to even more exalted sights: the "exceeding riches" of God's grace (2:7). When Paul cranks up the volume to express God's plan of love, not one low, mournful note sneaks in.

If you feel discouraged or question whether the Christian life is worth it, Ephesians proves to be a great tonic. It prescribes the riches in Christ available to all. —Philip Yancey

Heavenly Father, thank You for the staggering good news of the riches of Your infinite grace. Thank You for the encouragement and hope we find in Ephesians. Amen.

No one is hopeless whose hope is in God and His Word.

January 11
Sunday

Eyewitness Account

Read:
1 John 1

Truly our fellowship is with the Father and with His Son Jesus Christ. —1 John 1:3

The Bible In One Year:
- Genesis 27–28
- Matthew 8:18-34

When the *Day of Discovery* television crew interviews people for a biography, we especially enjoy talking with those who knew the person whose life-story we are telling. Over the years, we've talked with a man who roomed with Eric Liddell in an internment camp in China; a woman who as a teenager lived in the home of C. S. Lewis during World War II; and a man who chauffeured Dr. George Washington Carver on a speaking tour throughout the southern US. They all spoke freely and openly about the special person they knew.

When John, one of Jesus' 12 disciples, was an old man, he wrote a letter in which his opening words established him as an eyewitness and close companion of Jesus: "The life was manifested, and we have seen, and bear witness, and declare to you that eternal life which was with the Father and was manifested to us" (1 John 1:2). His goals in writing were "that you also may have fellowship with us; and truly our fellowship is with the Father and with His Son Jesus Christ" (v.3) and "that your joy may be full" (v.4).

The eyewitness accounts of Jesus' disciples help lead us to faith in Christ. Even though we have not seen Him as they did, we have believed. —David McCasland

Thank You, Father, for the reliable eyewitness
accounts of Jesus' life that we can read in Your
Word. And thank You for people in our lives
who know Him. They help us believe too.

Blessed are those who have not seen and yet have believed. —Jesus

January 12
Monday

The Gift Of Sleep

Read:
Psalm 121

It is vain for you to rise up early, to sit up late . . . ; for so He gives His beloved sleep.
—Psalm 127:2

The Bible In One Year:
- **Genesis 29–30**
- **Matthew 9:1-17**

Sleep is essential for good health. Scientists don't know exactly why we need it but they know what happens when we don't get enough. We put ourselves at risk of premature aging, weight gain, and diseases ranging from colds and flu to cancer. What God accomplishes in our bodies while we drift off to dreamland is nothing short of miraculous. While we do nothing, God replenishes our energy, rebuilds and restores our cells, and reorganizes information in our brains.

The reasons for not getting enough sleep are many, and some we can't solve, but the Bible indicates that overwork should not be one of them (Ps. 127:2). Sleep is a gift from God that we should receive with gratitude. If we're not getting enough, we need to find out why. Are we rising early and staying up late to earn money to acquire things we don't need? Are we involved in ministry efforts that we think no one else is capable of doing?

I'm sometimes tempted to believe that the work I do when I'm awake is more important than the work God does while I sleep. But refusing God's gift of sleep is like telling Him that my work is more important than His.

God does not want anyone to be a slave to work. He wants us to enjoy His gift of sleep. —Julie Ackerman Link

The love of God is my pillow,
Soft and healing and wide,
I rest my soul in its comfort,
And in its calm I abide. —*Long*

If we do not come apart and rest awhile, we may just plain come apart. —Havner

January 13
Tuesday

Already Settled

Read:
1 John 5:10-15

These things I have written to you who believe in the name of the Son of God, that you may know that you have eternal life.
—1 John 5:13

The Bible In One Year:
- Genesis 31–32
- Matthew 9:18-38

I love watching soccer, and I am a fan of the Liverpool Football Club in England's Premier League. When the Reds are playing, it is an anxiety-filled experience for me. Because one goal or one misplay can change the game's outcome, I feel a constant tension as I watch. That is part of what makes the games enjoyable. Recently, though, I saw a tape-delayed replay of one of Liverpool's games. I was surprised how much calmer I felt seeing the replay. Why? Because I already knew the outcome, and as a result I was able to relax and enjoy the action.

Life is often like observing live sporting events. There are shocks and surprises, frustrations and fears, because we are unsure of the outcome. Followers of Christ can draw comfort, however, from the fact that though many of life's situations are uncertain, our eternal outcome is settled by the work of Jesus Christ on the cross.

The apostle John wrote, "These things I have written to you who believe in the name of the Son of God, that you may know that you have eternal life" (1 John 5:13). Life may present us with surprises along the way, but because of Christ's work we can have peace. He has already settled our eternal outcome. —Bill Crowder

Faith looks beyond this transient life
With hope for all eternity—
Not with some vague and wistful hope,
But with firm trust and certainty. —*D. DeHaan*

Peace rules the day when Christ rules the heart.

January 14
Wednesday

God Must Love Me More

Read:
Job 12:1-10

A [disaster] is despised in the thought of one who is at ease; it is made ready for those whose feet slip.
—Job 12:5

The Bible In One Year:
- Genesis 33–35
- Matthew 10:1-20

During a difficult recession, I organized a support group for fellow Christians to help them cope with unemployment. We provided resumé reviews, networking, and prayer support. One problem emerged: Whenever someone got a job, he or she almost never returned to the group to offer encouragement. That increased the loneliness and isolation of those left in the group.

Worse, though, were comments from those who had never experienced a job loss. They mirrored the accusations of Job's friends in his suffering: "If you were pure and upright, surely now [God] would awake for you, and prosper [you]" (8:6). By chapter 12, Job is starting to express things in terms modern workers can understand. He says that he feels despised by those whose life is easy (v.5).

When things are going well for us, we may start to think that we who don't have troubles are better somehow, or are more loved by God, than those who are struggling. We forget that the effects of this fallen world are indiscriminate.

We are all loved by the Lord and we all need Him—in good times and bad. The successes, abundance, and positions that God has given to us are tools to help us encourage others in their time of need. —Randy Kilgore

Give us the humility, Lord, not to act like Job's friends who accused him of sin because of his trials. Show us how to help those who are struggling so that we might give the kind of encouragement You have given us.

Humility toward God makes us gentle toward others.

January 15
Thursday

There's Power

Read:
James 5:13-18

The effective, fervent prayer of a righteous man avails much.
—James 5:16

The Bible In One Year:
- **Genesis 36–38**
- **Matthew 10:21-42**

When my sister found out she had cancer, I asked my friends to pray. When she had surgery, we prayed that the surgeon would be able to remove all of the cancer and that she wouldn't have to undergo chemotherapy or radiation. And God answered yes! When I reported the news, one friend remarked, "I'm so glad there's power in prayer." I responded, "I'm thankful that God answered with a yes this time."

James says that "the effective, fervent prayer of a righteous man avails much" (5:16). But does "effective" and "fervent" mean the harder we pray, or the more people we ask to pray, the more likely God is to answer with a yes? I've had enough "no" and "wait" answers to wonder about that.

Prayer is powerful, but it's such a mystery. We're taught to have faith, to ask earnestly and boldly, to persevere, to be surrendered to His will. Yet God answers in His wisdom and His answers are best. I'm just thankful that God wants to hear our hearts and that no matter the answer, He is still good.

I like Ole Hallesby's words: "Prayer and helplessness are inseparable. Only those who are helpless can truly pray. . . . Your helplessness is your best prayer." We can do helplessness quite well. —Anne Cetas

Lord, I've been taught many things about prayer—be specific, be bold, be surrendered, be strong in faith, be persistent. Today I recognize my helplessness and Your power as I share my heart with You. Amen.

Prayer is the child's helpless cry to the Father's attentive ear.

January 16
Friday

Upside Down

Read:
Isaiah 55:6-13

My thoughts are not your thoughts, nor are your ways My ways. —Isaiah 55:8

The Bible In One Year:
- Genesis 39–40
- Matthew 11

There are a lot of things that intrigue me about Jesus. One of the aspects of His ministry that has always produced jaw-dropping, head-scratching responses is His upside-down teaching about life.

As we journey through life, we may get to the point where we think we've got it figured out and our thought patterns and responses for navigating through life are deeply engrained. Yet Jesus interrupts us in the midst of our routines and calls us to a new and better way. But beware! This encounter with the ways of Jesus will be challenging.

Consider these paradoxical propositions: to live you must die (Mark 8:35); to gain you must give (Matt. 19:21); "blessed are those who mourn" (5:4); to rule you must serve (Luke 22:26); and suffering has purpose (Matt. 5:10-11).

It is pronouncements like these that make people think Christ is strangely out of touch. But we are the ones out of touch. He is not upside down, we are! We're like children who think they know better than their parents what is best.

No wonder God has told us, "My thoughts are not your thoughts, nor are your ways My ways" (Isa. 55:8). So, rather than relying on our mixed-up instincts, let's ask Him to help us reflect His ways. —Joe Stowell

Lord, You know what is best, and You desire to lead us in paths that are right and good. Give us the courage to trust and to follow You in the ways of righteousness for Your name's sake. Amen.

What may seem upside down to us is right side up to God.

January 17
Saturday

TROUBLE

READ:
John 16:25-33

In the world you will have tribulation; but be of good cheer, I have overcome the world.
—John 16:33

THE BIBLE IN ONE YEAR:
- **Genesis 41–42**
- **Matthew 12:1-23**

I was glad to see the final days of the year draw to a close. It had held so much sorrow, sickness, and sadness. I was ready to welcome January with its very own brass band!

But as the first month of the new year arrived, so did one bit of sad news after another. Several friends lost their parents. My dad's brother slipped away in his sleep. Friends discovered they had cancer. A colleague's brother and a friend's son both died tragically and abruptly. Rather than the sad times ceasing, the new year seemed to bring a whole new tsunami of sorrow.

John 16:33 tells us, "In the world you *will* have tribulation." Even God's children are not promised a life of ease, of prosperity, nor of good health. Yet we are never alone in our trouble. Isaiah 43:2 reminds us that when we pass through deep waters, God is with us. Although we don't always understand God's purposes in the trials we experience, we can trust His heart because we know Him.

Our God is a God of abundant love and "neither death nor life. . . nor things present nor things to come [will ever] separate us from the love of God which is in Christ Jesus our Lord" (Rom. 8:38-39). When trouble comes, His presence is His promise. —Cindy Hess Kasper

Swift cometh His answer, so clear and so sweet;
"Yea, I will be with thee, thy troubles to meet;
I will not forget thee, nor fail thee, nor grieve;
I will not forsake thee, I never will leave." —*Flint*

Faith is believing that God is present
when all we hear is silence.

January 18
Sunday

You're Necessary

Read:
1 Corinthians 12:14-26

But God composed the body, having given greater honor to that part which lacks it.
—1 Corinthians 12:24

The Bible In One Year:
■ Genesis 43–45
■ Matthew 12:24-50

The story has been told about a conductor who was rehearsing his orchestra. The organ was giving a beautiful melody, the drums were thundering, the trumpets were blaring, and the violins were singing beautifully. But the conductor noticed something missing—the piccolo. The piccolo player had gotten distracted and hoped his instrument wouldn't be missed. The conductor reminded him: "Each one of us is necessary."

This was essentially the same message Paul communicated to the Corinthian believers in his first letter to them (12:4-7). Every Christian plays an important role in the body of Christ. Paul gave a list of gifts of the Spirit and compared their use to the functioning of the various parts of the human body for the good of the whole (vv.8-10). The Corinthian believers may have had different cultural backgrounds, gifts, and personalities, but they were filled with the same Spirit and belonged to the same body of Christ. Paul made special mention of the parts of the body that were weak and obscure, and taught that all believers play a necessary and significant role. No one part was more necessary than any other.

Remember, Jesus has given you a significant part to play and will use you to build up His people. —Marvin Williams

The church, a living body, containing all the parts—
It lives, it moves, it functions, and touches many hearts;
When each part is committed to do the Savior's will,
His members are united, His purpose they fulfill. —*Fitzhugh*

As a member of the body of Christ,
you are a necessary part of the whole.

January 19
Monday

READY FOR GLORY

READ:
Philippians 1:12-23

Precious in the sight of the LORD is the death of His saints.
—Psalm 116:15

THE BIBLE IN ONE YEAR:
- **Genesis 46–48**
- **Matthew 13:1-30**

On March 1, 1981, preacher and Bible commentator D. Martyn Lloyd-Jones lay on his deathbed. From 1939 to 1968, he had served as the pastor of London's Westminster Chapel. Now at the end of his life, Lloyd-Jones had lost the ability to speak. Indicating that he did not want any more prayers for his recovery, he wrote on a piece of paper: "Do not hold me back from glory."

Because life is precious, it can be hard to let our loved ones go when the time comes for them to depart this earth and go to heaven. And yet God has set a time when He plans to call us home. Psalm 116:15 tells us, "Precious in the sight of the LORD is the death of His saints."

When Paul saw that death was near, he was encouraged by what awaited him in heaven: "Finally, there is laid up for me the crown of righteousness, which the Lord, the righteous Judge, will give to me on that Day, and not to me only but also to all who have loved His appearing" (2 Tim. 4:8).

No matter where Christians are in life's journey, their ultimate destination is to "be with Christ, which is far better" (Phil. 1:23). This should give us confidence in facing life's challenges and comfort when other believers leave us for that glorious home Christ has prepared. —Dennis Fisher

The glories of heaven await
All those who believe in God's Son;
The trials of this life will fade
When we see the Heavenly One. —*Sper*

Life's greatest joy is the sure hope of heaven.

January 20
Tuesday

A Song To Remember

Read:
Deuteronomy 31:16-22

Ascribe greatness to our God. He is the Rock, His work is perfect.
—Deuteronomy 32:3-4

The Bible In One Year:
- **Genesis 49–50**
- **Matthew 13:31-58**

I was delighted when I received a free gift in the mail—a CD of Scripture set to music. After listening to it several times, some of the melodies took root in my mind. Before long, I could sing the words to a couple of verses in the book of Psalms without the help of the recording.

Music can help us recall words and ideas we might otherwise forget. God knew that the Israelites would forget Him when they entered the Promised Land (Deut. 31:20). They would forsake Him, turn to idols, and trouble would follow (vv.16-18). Because of this, He asked Moses to compose a song and teach it to the Israelites so they could remember their past closeness with Him and the sin that hurt their relationship (31:19-22). Perhaps most important, God wanted His nation to recall His character: "[God] is the Rock, His work is perfect; for all His ways are justice, a God of truth and without injustice; righteous and upright is He" (32:4).

Consider what God might want you to remember about Him today. Is it His power, His holiness, His love, or His faithfulness? Can you think of a song that celebrates God's character? Sing it in your heart to the Lord (Eph. 5:19).
—Jennifer Benson Schuldt

Give me a spirit of praise, dear Lord,
That I may adore Your name,
Sing praises from the depths of a grateful heart
To the One who is always the same. —*Dawe*

Remembering God's goodness puts a song in your heart.

January 21
Wednesday

Open Arms

Read:
Luke 15:11-24

When he was still a great way off, his father saw him and had compassion, and ran and fell on his neck and kissed him. —Luke 15:20

The Bible In One Year:
- Exodus 1–3
- Matthew 14:1-21

At the funeral of former US First Lady Betty Ford, her son Steven said, "She was the one with the love and the comfort, and she was the first one there to put her arms around you. Nineteen years ago when I went through my alcoholism, my mother . . . gave me one of the greatest gifts, and that was how to surrender to God, and to accept the grace of God in my life. And truly in her arms I felt like the prodigal son coming home, and I felt God's love through her. And that was a good gift."

Jesus' parable about a young man who asked for and squandered his inheritance and then in humiliation returned home leaves us amazed at his father's response: "When he was still a great way off, his father saw him and had compassion, and ran and fell on his neck and kissed him" (Luke 15:20). Instead of a lecture or punishment, the father expressed love and forgiveness by giving him a party. Why? Because "this my son was dead and is alive again; he was lost and is found" (v.24).

Steven Ford concluded his tribute with the words, "Thank you, Mom, for loving us, loving your husband, loving us kids, loving the nation, with the heart of God."

May God enable us to open our arms to others, just as His are open wide to all who turn to Him. —David McCasland

Lord, help me be kind and forgiving—
Your loving forgiveness You've shown
To me for the sins I've committed;
Lord, grant me a love like Your own. —*Anon.*

Forgiven sinners know love and show love.

January 22
Thursday

Choose Your God

Read:
Joshua 24:14-18

Choose for yourselves this day whom you will serve . . . . But as for me and my house, we will serve the Lord.
—Joshua 24:15

The Bible In One Year:
- Exodus 4–6
- Matthew 14:22-36

I recently saw a commercial for an online game based on Greek mythology. It spoke about armies, mythological gods, heroes, and quests. What got my attention was the description of how to get the game started. You go online to register, choose your god, then build your empire.

Wow! "Choose your god." Those words, though presented casually in the ad, struck me as being characteristic of one of the most dangerous things about our world. In a game, it may be insignificant what "god" you choose; but in the real world that choice has eternal consequences.

To a generation of Israelites surrounded by the gods of their day, Joshua declared that they must choose their god—but it must not be done in a cavalier way. He set the example as he said, "Choose for yourselves this day whom you will serve, whether the gods which your fathers served that were on the other side of the River, or the gods of the Amorites, in whose land you dwell. But as for me and my house, we will serve the Lord" (Josh. 24:15).

Today, as in the days of Joshua, there are many options. But there is only one wise choice—the true God. Joshua made the right choice. "We will serve the Lord." —Bill Crowder

The gods of this world are empty and vain,
They cannot give peace to one's heart;
The living and true One deserves all our love—
From Him may we never depart. —*D. DeHaan*

Nothing can fill the emptiness in your heart except God.

January 23
Friday

WHOLESOME WORDS

READ:
Ephesians 4:25-32

Let no corrupt word proceed out of your mouth, but what is good for necessary edification, that it may impart grace to the hearers.
—Ephesians 4:29

THE BIBLE IN ONE YEAR:
- Exodus 7–8
- Matthew 15:1-20

A while back, an Emmy award-winning actress took a courageous stand and walked out in the middle of the Annual American Music Awards ceremony. Her reason? She grew increasingly upset and disappointed by what she described as "an onslaught of lewd jokes and off-color remarks" and raw and raunchy comments by presenters, performers, and hosts. She said the evening was an affront to anyone with a shred of dignity and self-respect.

Unwholesome speech was a problem even in the apostle Paul's day. He reminded the Christians at Ephesus that they should put away vulgarity, lewdness, slander, and obscene talk from their lives (Eph. 5:4; Col. 3:8). These were expressions of their old lives (1 Cor. 6:9-11), and it was now out of place with their new identity in Christ. Instead, their lives were to be characterized by wholesome speech. Their good or wholesome words would give grace to the hearers (Eph. 4:29). The Holy Spirit would help guard their speech, convict of any filthy talk, and help them to use words to benefit others (John 16:7-13).

We are called to reflect God with all we are, and that includes our words. May our mouths be filled with thanksgiving and words that benefit others. —Marvin Williams

Holy Spirit, we need Your help. Guard our hearts and minds today. Help us control our thoughts and words so that we might lift others up and show them who You are and what You've done in us. Amen.

Wholesome words flow out of a life made new.

January 24
Saturday

LIKE JESUS

READ:
1 John 2:5-11

He who says he abides in [Jesus] ought himself also to walk just as He walked. —1 John 2:6

THE BIBLE IN ONE YEAR:
- Exodus 9–11
- Matthew 15:21-39

During a children's church service, the teacher talked about the first of the Ten Commandments: "You shall have no other gods before Me" (Ex. 20:3). She suggested some ways for the kids to keep this command. She said, "Nothing should come before God—not candy, not schoolwork, not video games." She told them that putting God first meant that time with Him reading the Bible and praying should come before anything else.

An older child in the group responded with a thought-provoking question. She asked if being a Christian was about keeping rules or if instead God wanted to be involved in all areas of our life.

Sometimes we make the mistake of viewing the Bible as a list of rules. Certainly obeying God (John 14:21) and spending time with Him are important, but not because we need to be rule-keepers. Jesus and the Father had a loving relationship. When we have a relationship with God, we desire to spend time with Him and obey Him so we can become more like Jesus. John said, "He who says he abides in [Jesus] ought himself also to walk just as He walked" (1 John 2:6). He's the example we can follow.

When we want to understand how to love, or how to be humble, or how to have faith, or even how to set our priorities, we can look at Jesus and follow His heart. —Anne Cetas

Lord, as I look ahead to another day, I give myself to be led by Your Spirit. Give discernment in priorities, but most of all a sensitive heart to live like Jesus did—filled with Your love and power. Amen.

Jesus calls us to follow Him.

January 25
Sunday

Guest List

Read:
Luke 14:7-14

When you give a feast, invite the poor, the maimed, the lame, the blind. And you will be blessed.
—Luke 14:13-14

The Bible In One Year:
- Exodus 12–13
- Matthew 16

Qumran was a first-century Jewish community that had isolated itself from outside influences to prepare for the arrival of the Messiah. They took great care in devotional life, ceremonial washings, and strict adherence to rules of conduct. Surviving documents show that they would not allow the lame, the blind, or the crippled into their communities. This was based on their conviction that anyone with a physical "blemish" was ceremonially unclean. During their table fellowship, disabled people were never on their guest lists.

Ironically, at that same time the Messiah of Israel was at work in the cities and villages of Judea and Galilee. Jesus proclaimed His Father's kingdom, brought teaching and comfort, and worked mighty miracles. Strikingly, He proclaimed: "When you give a feast, invite the poor, the maimed, the lame, the blind. And you will be blessed" (Luke 14:13-14).

The contrast between Jesus' words and the guest list of the Qumran "spiritual elite" is instructive to us. Often we like to fellowship with people who look, think, and act like us. But our Lord exhorts us to be like Him and open our doors to everyone. —Dennis Fisher

The gospel must be shared with all,
Not just with those like you and me;
For God embraces everyone
Who turns to Him to set them free. —*Sper*

The inclusive gospel cannot be shared by an exclusive people. —George Sweeting

January 26
Monday

Story Time

Read:
2 Corinthians 3:1-11

You are an epistle of Christ . . . written not with ink but by the Spirit of the living God, not on tablets of stone but on tablets of flesh, that is, of the heart.
—2 Corinthians 3:3

The Bible In One Year:
- **Exodus 14–15**
- **Matthew 17**

As a child, I loved it when my mom read to me. I would sit on her lap and listen to every word. As she read, I examined the details of every picture and waited eagerly to hear what was on the next page.

Have you ever thought about the idea that our lives tell a story? In every situation—good, bad, or indifferent—people around us are watching and listening to the story we are telling. Our story is communicated not only through our words but also through our attitudes and actions as we respond to life's buffetings and blessings. Our children and grandchildren, spouses, neighbors, and coworkers can all observe the story we're telling.

Paul reminds us that as followers of Jesus, our lives are like letters "known and read by all men; . . . an epistle of Christ . . . written not with ink but by the Spirit of the living God" (2 Cor. 3:2-3).

What is the story that those around us are reading through the letter of our lives? Stories of forgiveness? Compassion? Generosity? Patience? Love?

If you've experienced the joy of a grace-filled life that comes from the Spirit of God in you, then welcome to the joy of being one of God's great storytellers! —Joe Stowell

Dear Lord, we love You. We want our lives to
tell the story of Your goodness and grace.
May we be a bold witness of You.
Use us in ways we never thought possible.

Let your life tell the story of Christ's love and mercy to the world around you.

January 27
Tuesday

THE MARK OF LEADERSHIP

READ:
Mark 10:35-45

Whoever of you desires to be first shall be slave of all. —Mark 10:44

THE BIBLE IN ONE YEAR:
- **Exodus 16–18**
- **Matthew 18:1-20**

While visiting the campus of Purdue University on a frigid winter day, I came upon two young men chipping away thick ice on the sidewalk next to a fraternity house. Thinking they must be underclassmen who had been assigned the tough job by older fraternity brothers, I said, "They didn't tell you about this when you joined, did they?" One looked up with a smile and said, "Well, we're both upperclassmen. I'm the fraternity vice-president and my friend here is the president." I thanked them for their hard work and went on my way having been reminded that serving others is the mark of a true leader.

When two of Jesus' disciples asked Him for positions of honor in His coming kingdom, the Lord gathered His twelve closest followers and told them, "Whoever desires to become great among you shall be your servant. And whoever of you desires to be first shall be slave of all" (Mark 10:43-44). If there was any doubt about what Jesus meant, He reminded them that He had not come to be served but to serve others and to give His life to ransom them from the power of sin (v.45).

The mark of true, godly leadership is not power and privilege, but humble service. God gives us strength to follow Jesus' example and to lead His way. —David McCasland

The paths of leadership are trod
By those who humbly walk with God,
Their gracious spirit holds a sway
That makes you want to go their way. —*D. DeHaan*

A qualified leader is one who has learned to serve.

January 28
Wednesday

THE GOOD OLD DAYS

READ:
Psalm 143:1-6

**I remember the days of old.
—Psalm 143:5**

THE BIBLE IN ONE YEAR:
■ Exodus 19–20
■ Matthew 18:21-35

Sometimes our minds run back through the years and yearn for that better time and place—the "good old days."

But for some, the past harbors only bitter memories. Deep in the night, they ponder their own failures, disillusionments, and fantasies, and think of the cruel hand life has dealt them.

It's better to remember the past as David did, by contemplating the good that God has done, to "meditate on all [His] works; . . . muse on the work of [His] hands" (Ps. 143:5). As we call to mind the lovingkindness of the Lord, we can see His blessings through the years. These are the memories that foster the highest good. They evoke a deep longing for more of God and more of His tender care. They transform the past into a place of familiarity and fellowship with our Lord.

I heard a story about an elderly woman who would sit in silence for hours in her rocking chair, hands folded in her lap, eyes gazing off into the far distance. One day her daughter asked, "Mother, what do you think about when you sit there so quietly?" Her mother replied softly with a twinkle in her eye, "That's just between Jesus and me."

I pray that our memories and meditations would draw us into His presence. —David Roper

I have promised you My presence
With you everywhere you go;
I will never, never leave you
As you travel here below. —*Rose*

Fellowship with Christ is the secret of happiness now and forever.

January 29
Thursday

Red Tape

Read:
Romans 5:1-8

Through [Jesus] also we have access by faith into this grace in which we stand, and rejoice in hope of the glory of God. —Romans 5:2

The Bible In One Year:
- **Exodus 21–22**
- **Matthew 19**

The expression "red tape" describes the annoying way that bureaucracy prevents things from getting done. Originally, the phrase referred to the common practice of binding official documents with red ribbon. In the early 1800s, the term was popularized by the writings of Scottish historian Thomas Carlyle, who was protesting governmental foot-dragging. Following the American Civil War, the problem of "red tape" resurfaced as war veterans struggled to receive their benefits. The term denotes frustration and disappointment because of the burdensome hurdles it erects to accomplishing goals.

Bureaucratic red tape is almost legendary, but there is one place in the universe where it's never an issue—the throne of God. In Romans 5:2, Paul speaks of Christ, "through whom also we have access by faith into this grace in which we stand." When our hearts are broken or our lives are troubled, there is no red tape hindering our access to God. Jesus Christ has paved the way so that we can have access to enter boldly into the presence of the King of heaven (Heb. 4:16).

Remember, when your heart is hurting, you don't have to cut through a lot of red tape to present your needs to God. Through Christ, we have full and immediate access. —Bill Crowder

Thank You, Father, that access to Your throne
has been secured for us by Jesus Christ. We
know that You will not ignore us. Thank You for
the confidence we can have that You care.

God's throne is always accessible to His children.

January 30
Friday

Unstoppable

Read:
Numbers 22:10-34

The Lord opened Balaam's eyes, and he saw the Angel of the Lord standing in the way. —Numbers 22:31

The Bible In One Year:
- Exodus 23–24
- Matthew 20:1-16

"Under it. Over it. Around it. Through it. Nothing will stop me from doing it." I often hear people express this kind of attitude when they get an idea or see an opportunity that seems good or profitable. They devote all of their resources to getting it done.

As evidence that this way of thinking may be flawed, I call as my witness a donkey—a donkey belonging to a man named Balaam.

Balaam was offered a profitable assignment from a neighboring king, and he inquired of God for permission to accept it (Num. 22). When God said no, the king's representatives made a better offer. Thinking God might change His mind, Balaam asked again. God granted permission for Balaam to go with them but with strict conditions. God knew Balaam's heart and was not pleased with him, so He placed His Angel in the way. Balaam couldn't see the Angel but his donkey could. When the donkey refused to continue, Balaam became angry with the animal for blocking his progress.

Balaam's story teaches us that not every obstacle is meant to be overcome. Some are placed by God to keep us from doing something foolish. When our plans are hindered, we shouldn't assume that it's Satan trying to stop us. It might be God trying to protect us. —Julie Ackerman Link

Let Your wisdom guide me ever,
For I dare not trust my own;
Lead me, Lord, in tender mercy,
Leave me not to walk alone. —*Reed*

**God is always protecting us—
even when we don't realize we need it.**

January 31
Saturday

RESCUED

READ:
1 Corinthians 15:1-4, 20-25

Believe on the Lord Jesus Christ, and you will be saved.
—Acts 16:31

THE BIBLE IN ONE YEAR:
- Exodus 25–26
- Matthew 20:17-34

Manuel Gonzalez was the first rescue worker to reach the 33 miners trapped for 69 days in a Chilean mine explosion in 2010. At great risk to his own life, he went underground more than 2,000 feet to bring the trapped men back to the surface. The world watched in amazement as one by one each miner was rescued and transported to freedom.

The Bible tells us of an even more amazing rescue. Because of Adam and Eve's disobedience, all of mankind is trapped in sin (Gen. 2:17; 3:6,19; Rom. 5:12). Unable to break free, everyone faces certain death—physically and eternally. But God has provided a Rescuer—Jesus Christ, the Son of God. Everyone who accepts the free gift of salvation offered through His death and resurrection is freed from sin's grip and its resulting death penalty (Rom. 5:8-11; 10:9-11; Eph. 2:1-10).

Jesus Christ is the "firstfruits of those who have fallen asleep" (1 Cor. 15:20). He was the first to be raised from the dead, never to die again. Likewise, all will be given life who put their faith in Christ (Rom. 8:11).

Are you still trapped in your sins? Accept Jesus' gift of salvation and enjoy the freedom of life in Christ and eternity with Him (Acts 16:31; Eph. 2:1; Col. 2:13). —C. P. Hia

THINKING IT OVER

What keeps you from calling out to God for spiritual rescue? Do you fear that you are too bad for God's grace? Read and think about Romans 3:23-26.

Through His cross, Jesus rescues and redeems.

February 1
Sunday

HEART ATTITUDE

READ:
Ephesians 6:5-9

Not with eyeservice, as men-pleasers, but as bondservants of Christ, doing the will of God from the heart. —Ephesians 6:6

THE BIBLE IN ONE YEAR:
■ Exodus 27–28
■ Matthew 21:1-22

I love watching the skill and passion of great athletes as they give their all on the field. It shows their love for the game. Conversely, when a long season is winding down and a team is already eliminated from any opportunity for championship or playoff games, sometimes it seems that the players are merely "going through the motions." Their lack of passion can be disappointing to fans who have paid to watch a good game.

Passion is a key aspect of our personal lives as well. Our heart attitude toward the Lord is revealed in how we serve Him. The apostle Paul said that our service includes the way we go about our daily work. In Ephesians 6:6-7, we read that we are to approach our work, "not with eyeservice, as men-pleasers, but as bondservants of Christ, doing the will of God from the heart, with goodwill doing service, as to the Lord, and not to men."

For me, the key in that verse is "from the heart." I have a heavenly Father who loves me deeply and sacrificed His Son for me. How can I do anything less than give my very best for Him? The passion to live for God that comes "from the heart" provides our best response to the One who has done so much for us. —Bill Crowder

Father, every day offers opportunities for me to express my love for You. May the passion with which I live, work, serve, and relate to others be a fitting expression of my gratitude for Your love for me. In Jesus' name, amen.

The love of God motivates us to live for God.

February 2
Monday

New Eyes

Read:
Ephesians 1:15-21

The eyes of your understanding being enlightened; that you may know . . . the riches of the glory of His inheritance. —Ephesians 1:18

The Bible In One Year:
- **Exodus 29–30**
- **Matthew 21:23-46**

A college student I met had recently placed her faith in Christ. She described her initial life-change this way: "When I trusted Christ for salvation, it felt like God reached down from heaven and placed a new set of eyes in my eye sockets. I could understand spiritual truth!"

It was moving to hear how her encounter with the Savior brought new spiritual perception. But her experience is not unique. Everyone is endowed with spiritual sight when they trust Christ as their Savior. Yet, at times a "fog" rolls in and our spiritual vision becomes cloudy and unclear. That happens when we neglect our relationship with Him.

In Paul's fervent prayer for believers' spiritual sight, we see how important it is to fully appreciate all that God has done and will do for us through Christ. He prayed that the eyes of our understanding would be enlightened that we "may know what is the hope of His calling, what are the riches of the glory of His inheritance in the saints" (Eph. 1:18).

Each believer has been given new eyes to discern spiritual truth. As we keep our hearts tuned to God, He will help us to see with our spiritual eyes all that He has given to us in Christ. —Dennis Fisher

My soul within me yearns for Thee
Till Christ be fully formed in me;
Let love divine enlarge my heart,
Then all Thy fullness, Lord, impart. —*Stewart*

I once was blind but now I see!

February 3
Tuesday

SAVOR THE FLAVOR

READ:
Nehemiah 8:1-12

All the people went their way to eat and drink . . . and rejoice greatly.
—Nehemiah 8:12

THE BIBLE IN ONE YEAR:
- **Exodus 31–33**
- **Matthew 22:1-22**

In a fast-paced culture of "eat and run," few people make time to enjoy a leisurely meal in the company of friends. Someone has even remarked that the only way to enjoy a seven-course meal today is to get it all between two pieces of bread!

After many of the Israelite exiles in Babylon returned to Jerusalem to rebuild the temple and the walls of the city, they gathered to hear Ezra read from the Book of the Law given by God through Moses (Neh. 8:1). They listened to God's Word for hours, while teachers among them "gave the sense, and helped them to understand the reading" (v.8).

When they wept because of their shortcomings, Ezra, along with Nehemiah the governor, told them this was not a time for sorrow but a time for rejoicing. The people were told to prepare a feast and share it with those who had nothing, "for the joy of the LORD is your strength" (v.10). Then "all the people went their way to eat and drink, to send portions and rejoice greatly, because they understood the words that were declared to them" (v.12).

The spiritual banquet God has prepared for us in His Word is a cause for great joy. It is worth taking time to savor. —David McCasland

Lord, give us a hunger and a thirst to know You more
that can be satisfied only by time spent with You in Your
Word. Help us to savor that time and, as we do,
to grow more in love with You each day.

Christ the Living Bread
satisfies our spiritual hunger through the Living Word.

February 4
Wednesday

JUST ENOUGH

READ:
Matthew 6:25-34

Seek first the kingdom of God and His righteousness, and all these things shall be added to you.
—Matthew 6:33

THE BIBLE IN ONE YEAR:
- Exodus 34–35
- Matthew 22:23-46

I love writing for *Our Daily Bread.* I confess, however, that sometimes I whine to my friends about how difficult it is to communicate everything I would like to say in a short devotional. If only I could use more than 220 words.

This year when I came to the book of Matthew in my Bible-reading schedule, I noticed something for the first time. As I was reading about the temptation of Christ (Matt. 4:1-11), I noticed how short it was. Matthew used fewer than 250 words to write his account of one of the most pivotal events in all of Scripture. Then I thought of other short yet powerful passages: the 23rd Psalm (117 words) and the Lord's prayer in Matthew 6:9-13 (66 words).

Clearly, I don't need more words, I just need to use them well. This also applies to other areas of life—time, money, space. Scripture affirms that God meets the needs of those who seek His kingdom and His righteousness (Matt. 6:33). The psalmist David encourages us, "Those who seek the LORD shall not lack any good thing" (Ps. 34:10).

If today you're thinking, "I need just a little bit more" of something, consider instead the possibility that God has given you "just enough." —Julie Ackerman Link

I would be quiet, Lord, and rest content,
By grace I would not pine or fret;
With You to guide and care, my joy be this:
Not one small need of mine will You forget! —*Bosch*

He is rich who is satisfied with what he has.

February 5
Thursday

THE LESSON

READ:
Romans 12:14-21

Do not be overcome by evil, but overcome evil with good.
—Romans 12:21

THE BIBLE IN ONE YEAR:
- **Exodus 36–38**
- **Matthew 23:1-22**

One summer I was at a gathering of old high school acquaintances when someone behind me tapped me on my shoulder. As my eyes drifted over the woman's name tag, my mind drifted back in time. I remembered a tightly folded note that had been shoved through the slot on my locker. It had contained cruel words of rejection that had shamed me and crushed my spirit. I remember thinking, *Somebody needs to teach you a lesson on how to treat people!* Although I felt as if I were reliving my adolescent pain, I mustered up my best fake smile; and insincere words began coming out of my mouth.

We began to converse. A sad story of a difficult upbringing and of an unhappy marriage began to pour out of her. As it did, the words "root of bitterness" from Hebrews 12:15 popped into my head. *That's what I'm feeling,* I thought. After all these years, I still had a deep root of bitterness hidden within me, twisting around and strangling my heart.

Then these words came to my mind: "Do not be overcome by evil, but overcome evil with good" (Rom. 12:21).

We talked. We even shared some tears. Neither of us mentioned the long-ago incident. God taught someone a lesson that afternoon—a lesson of forgiveness and of letting go of bitterness. He taught it to me. —Cindy Hess Kasper

Dear Lord, please help me not to harbor resentment
and bitterness in my heart. Through the power
of the Holy Spirit, enable me to let go of my
bitterness and forgive those who have hurt me.

Revenge imprisons us; forgiveness sets us free.

February 6
Friday

By Our Deeds

Read:
Matthew 23:23-31

Even a child is known by his deeds, whether what he does is pure and right.
—Proverbs 20:11

The Bible In One Year:
- Exodus 39–40
- Matthew 23:23-39

One night a clergyman was walking to church when a thief pulled a gun on him and demanded his money or his life. When he reached in his pocket to hand over his wallet, the robber saw his clerical collar and said: "I see you are a priest. Never mind, you can go." The clergyman, surprised by the robber's unexpected act of piety, offered him a candy bar. The robber said, "No thank you. I don't eat candy during Lent."

The man had given up candy as a supposed sacrifice for Lent, but his lifestyle of stealing showed his real character! According to the writer of Proverbs, conduct is the best indicator of character. If someone says he is a godly person, his words can only be proven by consistent actions (20:11). This was true of the religious leaders in Jesus' day as well. He condemned the Pharisees and exposed their sham for professing godliness but denying that profession with sin in their lives (Matt. 23:13-36). Appearances and words are deceiving; behavior is the best judge of character. This applies to all of us.

As followers of Jesus, we demonstrate our love for Him by what we do, not just by what we say. May our devotion to God, because of His love for us, be revealed in our actions today. —Marvin Williams

Spiritual words are mere distractions
If not backed up by our godly actions,
And all our good and beautiful creeds
Are nothing without God-honoring deeds. —Williams

Conduct is the best proof of character.

February 7
Saturday

STRANDED

READ:
Genesis 39:19-23

The LORD was with Joseph and showed him mercy.
—Genesis 39:21

THE BIBLE IN ONE YEAR:
- Leviticus 1–3
- Matthew 24:1-28

Traveling by bus from Memphis, Tennessee, to St. Louis, Missouri, typically takes about 6 hours—unless the bus driver leaves you stranded at a gas station. This happened to 45 passengers aboard a bus who waited 8 hours overnight for a replacement driver after the original driver abandoned them. They must have felt frustrated by the delay, anxious about the outcome, and impatient for rescue.

Joseph probably shared those feelings when he landed in prison for a crime he didn't commit (Gen. 39). Abandoned and forgotten by any human who might help him, he was stranded. Still, "the LORD was with Joseph and showed him mercy, and He gave him favor" (v.21). Eventually, the prison warden promoted Joseph to oversee fellow inmates, and whatever Joseph did, "the LORD made it prosper" (v.23). But despite God's presence and blessing, Joseph remained incarcerated for years.

You may be stranded in a hospital room, a jail cell, a country far from home, or your own inner prison. No matter where you are, or how long you've been there, God's mercy and kindness can reach you. Because He is God Almighty (Ex. 6:3) and present everywhere (Jer. 23:23-24), He can protect, promote, and provide for you when it seems no one else can help. —Jennifer Benson Schuldt

Dear God, help us to remember
Your presence and power even when
we are not where we want to be in life. Remind us
to reach for You when no one else can reach us.

God is present—even when we feel He is absent.

February 8
Sunday

Mysterious Truth

Read:
John 17:20-26

Precious in the sight of the Lord is the death of His saints.
—Psalm 116:15

The Bible In One Year:
- **Leviticus 4–5**
- **Matthew 24:29-51**

Sometimes when the infinite God conveys His thoughts to finite man, mystery is the result. For example, there's a profound verse in the book of Psalms that seems to present more questions than answers: "Precious in the sight of the Lord is the death of His faithful servants" (116:15 NIV).

I shake my head and wonder how that can be. I see things with earth-bound eyes, and I have a tough time seeing what is "precious" about the fact that our daughter was taken in a car accident at the age of 17—or that any of us have lost cherished loved ones.

We begin to unwrap the mystery, though, when we consider that what is precious to the Lord is not confined to earthly blessings. This verse examines a heaven-based perspective. For instance, I know from Psalm 139:16 that Melissa's arrival in God's heaven was expected. God was looking for her arrival, and it was precious in His eyes. And think about this: Imagine the Father's joy when He welcomes His children home and sees their absolute ecstasy in being face to face with His Son (see John 17:24).

When death comes for the follower of Christ, God opens His arms to welcome that person into His presence. Even through our tears, we can see how precious that is in God's eyes. —Dave Branon

Lord, when sorrow grips our hearts as we think about the death of one close to us, remind us of the joy You are experiencing as our loved one enjoys the pleasures of heaven. Please allow that to give us hope and comfort.

A sunset in one land is a sunrise in another.

February 9
Monday

Divine Diversions

Read:
Matthew 1:18-25

And he called His name Jesus. —Matthew 1:25

The Bible In One Year:
- **Leviticus 6-7**
- **Matthew 25:1-30**

I tend to get stuck in my ways, so anything that diverts me from my routines and plans can be very annoying. Worse yet, life's diversions are sometimes unsettling and painful. But God, who said, "My thoughts are not your thoughts, nor are your ways My ways" (Isa. 55:8), knows that He often needs to divert us in order to make more of our lives than we would have if we had stuck to our original plans.

Think of Joseph. God diverted him to Egypt to prepare him to rescue God's chosen people from starvation. Or of Moses, who was diverted from the luxurious lifestyle of Pharaoh's house to meet God in the wilderness in preparation to lead God's people toward the Promised Land. Or of Joseph and Mary to whom the angel announced the most significant diversion of all. Mary would be with child, and this child would be called "Jesus, for He will save His people from their sins" (Matt. 1:21). Joseph believed in the bigger purpose that God had for him, surrendered to the diversion, and obediently "called His name Jesus" (v.25). The rest is wonderful history!

We can trust God's greater plans as He does His far better work in the history of our lives. —Joe Stowell

Lord, teach us to be willing to adjust our plans to conform to Yours. You have greater things in store for us than we could ever dream, so help us to patiently wait for You to work in the circumstances of our lives.

Let God direct—or redirect—your steps.

February 10
Tuesday

GREEK FIRE

READ:
James 3:1-12

The tongue is a fire, a world of iniquity. The tongue is so set among our members that it defiles the whole body, and sets on fire the course of nature; and it is set on fire by hell.
—James 3:6

THE BIBLE IN ONE YEAR:
- Leviticus 8–10
- Matthew 25:31-46

Greek fire was a chemical solution that was used in ancient warfare by the Byzantine Empire against its enemies. According to one online source, it was developed around AD 672 and was used with devastating effect, especially in sea warfare because it could burn on water. What was Greek fire? Its actual chemical composition remains a mystery. It was such a valuable military weapon that the formula was kept an absolute secret—and was lost to the ravages of history. Today, researchers continue to try to replicate that ancient formula, but without success.

One source of catastrophic destruction among believers in Christ, however, is not a mystery. James tells us that the source of ruin in our relationships is often a very different kind of fire. He wrote, "The tongue is a fire, a world of iniquity. The tongue is so set among our members that it defiles the whole body" (James 3:6). Those strong words remind us how damaging unguarded words can be to those around us.

Instead of creating the kind of verbal "Greek fire" that can destroy relationships, families, and churches, let's yield our tongue to the Holy Spirit's control and allow our words to glorify the Lord. —Bill Crowder

It seems, Father, that sometimes we are our own worst enemies. Forgive us for speaking destructively to fellow Christians, and teach us to use wise words that can encourage and build their walk with You.

To bridle your tongue, give God the reins of your heart.

February 11
Wednesday

NUMBERED DAYS

READ:
Psalm 90:7-17

Teach us to number our days, that we may gain a heart of wisdom.
—Psalm 90:12

THE BIBLE IN ONE YEAR:
- **Leviticus 11–12**
- **Matthew 26:1-25**

In the aftermath of a devastating tornado, a man stood outside what was left of his home. Scattered somewhere among the rubble inside were his wife's jewelry and his own valuable collectibles. But the man had no intention of going inside the unstable house to search for them. "It's not worth dying for," he said.

In times of crisis, our sense of what is truly important in life often comes into clearer focus.

In Psalm 90, "A Prayer of Moses," this man of God looks at life from beginning to end. In light of the brevity of life (vv.4-6) and the realization of God's righteous anger (vv.7-11), Moses makes a plea to God for understanding: "Teach us to number our days and recognize how few they are; help us to spend them as we should" (v.12 TLB).

Moses continues this psalm with an appeal to God's love: "Have compassion on Your servants. Oh, satisfy us early with Your mercy" (vv.13-14). He concludes with a prayer for the future: "Let the beauty of the LORD our God be upon us, and establish the work of our hands for us" (v.17).

Our numbered days and the brevity of life call us to embrace God's eternal love and, like Moses, to focus on the most important things. —David McCasland

What a God we have to worship!
What a Son we have to praise!
What a future lies before us—
Everlasting, love-filled days! —*Maynard*

Our numbered days point us to God's eternal love.

February 12
Thursday

THE BEST LIFE

READ:
John 1:35-42

[Andrew] first found his own brother Simon, and said to him, "We have found the Messiah." —John 1:41

THE BIBLE IN ONE YEAR:
- Leviticus 13
- Matthew 26:26-50

A few months ago, I had to travel to Florida and back on business. On my flight home, I was pleasantly surprised to find that I had a seat with lots of leg room. It felt so good not to be scrunched into a small area. Plus, I had an empty seat beside me! The makings of a good nap.

Then I remembered those around me in their not-as-comfortable seats. I invited several others I knew to join me in a better spot but was surprised they all wanted to stay in their own seats for various reasons: They didn't want to be inconvenienced with a move or felt fine where they were.

As believers in Christ, we have a much more significant invitation to extend: We've received a new life of faith in Jesus and want others to experience it too. Some will want to do so, and others won't. In John 1:40 we read that Andrew had begun to follow Jesus. The first thing Andrew did was to find his brother Simon and invite him to meet Jesus, the Messiah, too (v.41). Jesus offered them a wonderful new way of life of knowing Him and enjoying His promises: His forgiveness (Rom. 3:24), continual presence (Heb. 13:5), hope (Rom. 15:13), peace (John 14:27), and a forever future in His presence (1 Thess. 4:17).

Won't you join in? Jesus gives the best life. —Anne Cetas

If we commit ourselves to Christ
And follow in His way,
He'll give us life that satisfies
With purpose for each day. —Sper

If you want someone to know what Christ will do for him, let him see what Christ has done for you.

February 13
Friday

The Power Of Demonstration

Read:
1 Corinthians 2:1-5

The kingdom of God is not in word but in power.
—1 Corinthians 4:20

The Bible In One Year:
- **Leviticus 14**
- **Matthew 26:51-75**

For 2 decades, ecologist Mike Hands has worked to help farmers in Central America adopt more effective methods of growing their crops. It's difficult, however, for them to abandon their long tradition of "slash and burn" agriculture, even though they know it destroys the soil and pollutes the air.

So instead of merely talking to them, Mike shows them a better way. In the documentary film *Up in Smoke*, he says: "It has to be demonstrated. You cannot preach it. You can't describe it. People have got to be able to get their hands on it and see it."

Paul took a similar approach to sharing the gospel of Jesus Christ. He wrote to the believers in Corinth, "My speech and my preaching were not with persuasive words of human wisdom, but in demonstration of the Spirit and of power, that your faith should not be in the wisdom of men but in the power of God" (1 Cor. 2:4-5). Later in his letter, Paul told them again, "The kingdom of God is not in word but in power" (4:20).

As you live each day, ask God to help you accompany your words with actions. When we allow God to show Himself through us, it's a powerful demonstration of His grace and love. —David McCasland

Allow us, Lord, to demonstrate
Our faith by what we do,
So that the gospel can be seen
By those who seek for You. —*Sper*

Our words need actions behind them.

February 14
Saturday

Second Best?

Read:
Genesis 29:16-30

While we were still sinners, Christ died for us. —Romans 5:8

The Bible In One Year:
■ Leviticus 15–16
■ Matthew 27:1-26

Leah must have laid awake all night thinking of the moment when her new husband would awaken. She knew that it was not her face he expected to see, but Rachel's. Jacob had been a victim of deception, and when he realized that a "bait and switch" had occurred, he quickly made a new deal with Laban to claim the woman he had been promised (Gen. 29:25-27).

Have you ever felt insignificant or second-best? Leah felt that way. It's seen in the names she chose for her first three sons (vv.31-35). *Reuben* means "See, a Son"; *Simeon* means "Heard"; and *Levi* means "Attached." Their names were all plays on words that indicated the lack of love she felt from Jacob. With each son's birth, she desperately hoped she would move up in Jacob's affections and earn his love. But slowly Leah's attitude changed, and she named her fourth son *Judah*, which means "Praise" (v.35). Though she felt unloved by her husband, perhaps she now realized she was greatly loved by God.

We can never "earn" God's love, because it's not dependent on what we do. In truth, the Bible tells us that "while we were still sinners, Christ died for us" (Rom. 5:8). In God's eyes, we are worth the best that heaven could offer—the gift of His precious Son. —Cindy Hess Kasper

Love sent the Savior to die in my stead.
Why should He love me so?
Meekly to Calvary's cross He was led.
Why should He love me so? —*Harkness*

Nothing speaks more clearly of God's love than the cross.

February 15
Sunday

Crying Out To God

Read:
Psalm 142

By prayer and supplication . . . let your requests be made known to God.
—Philippians 4:6

The Bible In One Year:
- Leviticus 17–18
- Matthew 27:27-50

After all these years, I still don't fully understand prayer. It's something of a mystery to me. But one thing I know: When we're in desperate need, prayer springs naturally from our lips and from the deepest level of our hearts.

When we're frightened out of our wits, when we're pushed beyond our limits, when we're pulled out of our comfort zones, when our well-being is challenged and endangered, we reflexively and involuntarily resort to prayer. "Help, Lord!" is our natural cry.

Author Eugene Peterson wrote: "The language of prayer is forged in the crucible of trouble. When we can't help ourselves and call for help, when we don't like where we are and want out, when we don't like who we are and want a change, we use primal language, and this language becomes the root language of prayer."

Prayer begins in trouble, and it continues because we're always in trouble at some level. It requires no special preparation, no precise vocabulary, no appropriate posture. It springs from us in the face of necessity and, in time, becomes our habitual response to every issue—good and bad—we face in this life (Phil. 4:6). What a privilege it is to carry everything to God in prayer! —David Roper

What a Friend we have in Jesus,
All our sins and griefs to bear!
What a privilege to carry
Everything to God in prayer. —*Scriven*

God's help is only a prayer away.

February 16
Monday

Godspeed!

Read:
2 John 1:1-11

If anyone comes to you and does not bring this doctrine, do not receive him into your house nor greet him.
—2 John 1:10

The Bible In One Year:
- **Leviticus 19–20**
- **Matthew 27:51-66**

In 1962, John Glenn made history as the first American to orbit the Earth. As the rocket ascended, ground control said, "Godspeed, John Glenn." "Godspeed" comes from the expression, "May God prosper you."

Though we don't often hear this word today, the apostle John used it in his second epistle: "If there come any unto you, and bring not this doctrine, receive him not into your house, neither bid him Godspeed" (2 John 1:10 KJV).

John has been referred to as "the apostle of love," so why would he warn believers against pronouncing a blessing on others? Traveling evangelists were dependent on the hospitality of Christians to provide them with room and board. John was telling the believers that biblical truth is important. If itinerant missionaries were not preaching doctrine consistent with apostolic teaching, believers were not to bless their work by providing lodging or financial assistance.

This is also true for believers today. We are to treat everyone with kindness because God is kind to us. But when asked to financially support an endeavor, it's important to always ask Him for wisdom. The Spirit who guides us into truth (John 16:13) will show us when it is appropriate to bid Godspeed to those we encounter. —Dennis Fisher

Dear Lord, You know my heart. I love You
and want Your kingdom to prosper.
Give me Your wisdom to know where You want
me to take part and how. Thank You.

God's Spirit through His Word gives wisdom to discern truth from error.

February 17
Tuesday

Gifted To Serve

Read:
Romans 12:3-13

There are diversities of activities, but it is the same God who works all in all.
—1 Corinthians 12:6

The Bible In One Year:
- Leviticus 21–22
- Matthew 28

It occurred to me one day that my right foot does all the pedal work when I'm driving my automatic transmission car. It alone works the accelerator and the brake. The left foot is idle. What happens if I decide that to be equitable, my left foot ought to replace my right foot half the time when I am driving? If you have never done so, please don't try it!

If we don't require such equality of the members of our own body, why is it that we sometimes expect it of people in the church? That seems to be an issue that the first-century church at Rome faced. Some were thinking more highly of themselves than they ought (Rom. 12:3) just because they were doing some things others were not doing. But Paul reminds us that "all members do not have the same function" (v.4). We've been gifted according to God's grace (v.6). He gave us those gifts to serve others, not ourselves (vv.6-13). Our service is to be marked by diligence and fervor, for we are serving the Lord, not man (v.11).

So, let's not look over our shoulders to see what others are doing or not doing. Look at how God may be able to use you in His kingdom today. He has gifted you just as He has pleased (v.3). —C. P. Hia

Lord, lead me today as You see best. Use the gifts You
have given me to encourage others on their journey.
Help me not to compare myself with others
but to be content with who You have made me to be.

We can't all play the same part in God's band of service, but we should all play in harmony.

February 18
Wednesday

A Small Sacrifice

Read:
Mark 10:17-27

With God all things are possible. —Mark 10:27

The Bible In One Year:
■ **Leviticus 23–24**
■ **Mark 1:1-22**

As we anticipate the coming celebration of Easter, I begin thinking about the sacrifice Jesus made so that I could be reconciled to God. To help me focus on all that He gave up for me, I make a small sacrifice of my own. When I fast from something I normally enjoy, every craving for that food or drink or pastime reminds me of how much more Jesus gave up for me.

Because I want to be successful, I tend to give up something that isn't a big temptation for me. Yet even then I fail. My inability to be perfect in such a small thing reminds me of why Easter is so important. If we could be perfect, Jesus would not have had to die.

The rich young man whom Jesus encountered along a Judean road was trying to earn eternal life by being good. But Jesus, knowing the man could never be good enough, said, "With men [salvation] is impossible, but not with God" (Mark 10:27).

Although giving up something does not make anyone good, it does remind us that no one is good except God (v.18). And that's important to remember, for it is the sacrifice of a good and perfect God that makes our salvation possible. —Julie Ackerman Link

I gave My life for thee;
My precious blood I shed,
That thou might ransomed be
And quickened from the dead. —*Havergal*

Jesus sacrificed His life for ours.

February 19
Thursday

WAIT

READ:
1 Samuel 13:7-14

Samuel said to Saul, "You have done foolishly. You have not kept the commandment of the LORD your God, which He commanded you." —1 Samuel 13:13

THE BIBLE IN ONE YEAR:
- Leviticus 25
- Mark 1:23-45

In an act of impatience, a man in San Francisco, California, tried to beat traffic by swerving around a lane of cars that had come to a stop. However, the lane he pulled into had just been laid with fresh cement, and his Porsche 911 got stuck. This driver paid a high price for his impatience.

The Scriptures tell of a king who also paid a high price for his impatience. Eager for God to bless the Israelites in their battle against the Philistines, Saul acted impatiently. When Samuel did not arrive at the appointed time to offer a sacrifice for God's favor, Saul became impatient and disobeyed God's command (1 Sam. 13:8-9,13). Impatience led Saul to think he was above the law and to take on an unauthorized position of priest. He thought he could disobey God without serious consequences. He was wrong.

When Samuel arrived, he rebuked Saul for his disobedience and prophesied that Saul would lose the kingdom (vv.13-14). Saul's refusal to wait for the development of God's plan caused him to act in haste, and in his haste he lost his way (see Prov. 19:2). His impatience was the ultimate display of a lack of faith.

The Lord will provide His guiding presence as we wait patiently for Him to bring about His will. —Marvin Williams

Tune your anxious heart to patience,
Walk by faith where sight is dim;
Loving God, be calm and trustful
And leave everything to Him. —*Chambers*

Patience means awaiting God's time and trusting God's love.

February 20
Friday

Rerouting . . . Rerouting

Read:
Proverbs 3:1-8

In all your ways acknowledge Him, and He shall direct your paths. —Proverbs 3:6

The Bible In One Year:
- Leviticus 26–27
- Mark 2

"Don't worry. I know right where I'm going," I said to my passengers. Then an almost-human voice ratted me out: "Rerouting . . . rerouting." Now everyone knew I was lost!

These days, millions of drivers recognize those words, or others like them, as a sign they've gone off track or missed a turn. The GPS device not only recognizes when a driver is off course, but immediately begins plotting a new path to get back on track.

Sometimes followers of Jesus need help to get back on track spiritually. We may intentionally veer off course because we think we know best, or drift away slowly, failing to notice we're moving further and further from the walk God wants with us.

God has not left us on our own, however. He has given all believers the Holy Spirit (John 14:16-17; 1 Cor. 3:16), who convicts us of our sin (John 16:8,13). When we're going off course, He sounds the alarm and triggers our conscience (Gal. 5:16-25). We may ignore the warning, but we do so to our own detriment (Isa. 63:10; Gal. 6:8).

What comfort to know that God is at work in our lives through the convicting work of the Holy Spirit! (Rom. 8:26-27). With God's help and guidance, we can continue on a path that is pleasing to Him. —Randy Kilgore

Holy Spirit, we would hear
Your inner promptings, soft and clear;
And help us know Your still, small voice
So we may make God's will our choice. —D. DeHaan

We're never without a helper, because we have the Spirit within.

February 21
Saturday

JARS OF CLAY

READ:
2 Corinthians 4:7-15

We have this treasure in earthen vessels, that the excellence of the power may be of God and not of us.
—2 Corinthians 4:7

THE BIBLE IN ONE YEAR:
■ Numbers 1–3
■ Mark 3

When you buy a nice piece of jewelry, it is often tucked into a setting of black- or dark-colored velvet. I think it's designed that way so that your attention is immediately drawn to the beauty of the jewelry. If the packaging were highly decorated, it would compete with the beauty of the treasure.

It reminds me of Paul's comments about the ministry of Jesus through us, when he said, "We have this treasure in jars of clay" (2 Cor. 4:7 NIV). It's easy to forget that we are the packaging and His work is the treasure. So we adorn our jars of clay, taking credit for the things we do to serve Christ. We seek to bring glory to ourselves when we've forgiven someone, or shown mercy, or given generously. The problem is, when we start seeking affirmation and praise for good deeds, we compete with the brilliance of the treasure of God working through us.

When we do things for Christ, it's not about us but about His glory. The less obvious we are, the more brilliant He becomes. Which is why, Paul says, the treasure has been put in jars of clay so that God would be the one to be glorified. Besides, since when are jars of clay significant? It's what's inside that counts! —Joe Stowell

Help us not to cloud God's glory
Nor with self His light to dim;
May each thought to Christ be captive,
Emptied to be filled with Him. —*Anon.*

Let the brilliance of the treasure of Christ shine through you as you live for Him.

February 22
Sunday

Crowned With Glory

Read:
Psalm 8

What is man that You are mindful of him?
—Psalm 8:4

The Bible In One Year:
■ Numbers 4–6
■ Mark 4:1-20

The *Voyager 1* spacecraft, which was launched in 1977, is on the outer edge of our solar system more than 10 billion miles away. In February 1990, when *Voyager 1* was almost 4 billion miles from us, scientists turned its camera toward Earth and took some pictures that revealed our planet as an almost imperceptible blue dot on a vast sea of empty space.

In the immense reaches of our universe, Earth is just a minuscule speck. On this seemingly insignificant pebble in the ocean of galactic objects live more than seven billion people.

If this makes you feel insignificant, God has some good news. Tucked into one of David's psalms is a rhetorical question that can allow you to step out into the night air, look up at the sky, and rejoice. Psalm 8:3-5 tells us that we are superstars in God's eyes: "When I consider Your heavens, the work of Your fingers, . . . what is man that You are mindful of him? . . . You have crowned him with glory and honor." Soak that in! God—who spoke into existence a universe so vast that the Hubble telescope hasn't found the end of it—created you, and He cares deeply for you. He cared enough to ask Jesus to leave heaven to die for you.

Look up in wonder at God's creation and praise Him that He crowned you with glory through His Son Jesus. —Dave Branon

We praise You, Father, for Your creation which reaches beyond our imagination, for the spellbinding night sky with its vast array of lights, and for loving each of us enough to send Jesus to be our personal Savior.

We see the power of God's creation; we feel the power of His love.

February 23
Monday

No Simple Recipe

Read:
Hebrews 4:11-16

For we do not have a High Priest who cannot sympathize with our weaknesses, but was in all points tempted as we are, yet without sin. —Hebrews 4:15

The Bible In One Year:
- Numbers 7–8
- Mark 4:21-41

For our grandson's birthday, my wife baked and decorated a gigantic chocolate chip cookie to serve at his party. She got out her cookbook, gathered the ingredients, and began to follow the simple steps involved in making cookies. She followed a simple recipe and everything turned out well.

Wouldn't it be nice if life was like that? Just follow a few easy steps and then enjoy a happy life.

But life is not so simple. We live in a fallen world and there is no easy recipe to follow that will ensure a life free of pain, loss, injustice, or suffering.

In the midst of life's pain, we need the personal care of the Savior who lived in this world and experienced the same struggles we face. Hebrews 4:15 encourages us: "For we do not have a High Priest who cannot sympathize with our weaknesses, but was in all points tempted as we are, yet without sin." Christ, who died to give us life, is completely sufficient to carry us through our heartaches and dark experiences. He has "borne our griefs and carried our sorrows" (Isa. 53:4).

Jesus knows there is no simple "recipe" to prevent the heartaches of life, so He entered into them with us. Will we trust Him with our tears and grief? —Bill Crowder

When the trials of this life make you weary
And your troubles seem too much to bear,
There's a wonderful solace and comfort
In the silent communion of prayer. —*Anon.*

The Christ who died to give us life will carry us through its heartaches.

February 24
Tuesday

God's Lighthouse

Read:
Matthew 5:1-14

You are the light of the world. A city that is set on a hill cannot be hidden.
—Matthew 5:14

The Bible In One Year:
- Numbers 9–11
- Mark 5:1-20

The Mission Point Lighthouse was built in 1870 on a peninsula in Northern Michigan to warn ships of sand bars and rocky shores along Lake Michigan. That lighthouse got its name from another kind of lighthouse, a mission church, which was built 31 years earlier.

In 1839, Rev. Peter Dougherty answered the call to become pastor of a church in Old Mission that was made up of Native Americans who lived farther south on the same peninsula. Under his leadership, a thriving community of farmers, teachers, and craftsmen worked side by side to build a better life for the community.

When believers in Christ work together in unity, their fellowship of faith provides spiritual light in the world's darkness (Phil. 2:15-16). Jesus said, "You are the light of the world. A city that is set on a hill cannot be hidden. . . . Let your light so shine before men, that they may see your good works and glorify your Father in heaven" (Matt. 5:14-16).

The Mission Point Lighthouse warned ships of danger, but the original Old Mission Church provided spiritual direction to all who would listen. Believers do the same individually and through our churches. We are God's lighthouse because Jesus lives in us. —Dennis Fisher

You are called with a holy calling
The light of the world to be;
To lift up the lamp of the Savior
That others His light may see. —*Anon.*

Believers help the lost to find their way home when their life shines brightly.

February 25
Wednesday

Always Accepted

Read:
John 1:6-13

He came to His own, and His own did not receive Him.
—John 1:11

The Bible In One Year:
- Numbers 12–14
- Mark 5:21-43

Financial expert Warren Buffet, one of the richest people in the world, was rejected by Harvard's Business School at age 19. After a failed admissions interview, he recalls a "feeling of dread," along with concern over his father's reaction to the news. In retrospect, Buffet says, "[Everything] in my life . . . that I thought was a crushing event at the time has turned out for the better."

Rejection, though undeniably painful, does not have to hold us back from accomplishing what God wants us to do. The citizens of Jesus' hometown denied that He was the Messiah (John 1:11), and many of His followers later rejected Him (6:66). Just as Jesus' rejection was part of God's plan for His Son (Isa. 53:3), so was Jesus' continued ministry. Enduring earthly rejection and knowing that the Father would turn away from Him at Calvary (Matt. 27:46), Jesus went on to cure the sick, cast out demons, and preach good news to the masses. Before His crucifixion, Jesus said, "[Father], I have finished the work which You have given Me to do" (John 17:4).

If rejection has become a hindrance to the work God has given you to do, don't give up. Remember that Jesus understands, and those who come to Him will always be accepted by Him (6:37). —Jennifer Benson Schuldt

No one understands like Jesus
When the days are dark and grim.
No one is so near, so dear as Jesus;
Cast your every care on Him. —*Peterson*

No one understands like Jesus.

February 26
Thursday

GIVING THANKS

READ:
John 11:32-44

Jesus lifted up His eyes and said, "Father, I thank You that You have heard Me."
—John 11:41

THE BIBLE IN ONE YEAR:
- Numbers 15–16
- Mark 6:1-29

A tragedy left a family with a void that nothing could fill. A toddler chasing a cat wandered into the road and was run over by a delivery truck. A 4-year-old watched in shocked silence as her parents cradled the lifeless body of her little sister. For years, the cold emptiness of that moment encased the family in sadness. Feelings were frozen. The only comfort was numbness. Relief was unimaginable.

Author Ann Voskamp was the 4-year-old, and the sorrow surrounding her sister's death formed her view of life and God. The world she grew up in had little concept of grace. Joy was an idea that had no basis in reality.

As a young mother, Voskamp set out to discover the elusive thing the Bible calls joy. The words for joy and grace come from the Greek word *chairo,* which she found out is at the center of the Greek word for thanksgiving. *Could it be that simple?* she wondered. To test her discovery, Voskamp decided to give thanks for 1,000 gifts she already had. She started slowly but soon gratefulness was flowing freely.

Just as Jesus gave thanks before, not after, raising Lazarus from the dead (John 11:41), Voskamp discovered that giving thanks brought to life feelings of joy that had died along with her sister. Joy comes from thanksgiving. —Julie Ackerman Link

Lord, I thank You that You have the power
to raise the dead. May the feelings of joy
that arise from our thanksgiving be seeds of
grace to those who are afraid to feel.

The joy of living comes from a heart of thanksgiving.

February 27
Friday

Grandpa Snucked Out

Read:
Psalm 16

My heart is glad, and my glory rejoices; my flesh also will rest in hope. —Psalm 16:9

The Bible In One Year:
- **Numbers 17–19**
- **Mark 6:30-56**

My cousin Ken fought a courageous 4-year battle with cancer. In his final days, his wife, three children, and several grandchildren were in and out of his room, spending time with him and sharing special goodbyes. When everyone was out of the room for a moment, he slipped into eternity. After the family realized that he was gone, one young granddaughter sweetly remarked, "Grandpa snucked out." One moment the Lord was with Ken here on earth; the next moment Ken's spirit was with the Lord in heaven.

Psalm 16 was a favorite psalm of Ken's that he had requested to be read at his memorial service. He agreed with the psalmist David who said that there was no treasure more valuable than a personal relationship with God (vv.2,5). With the Lord as his refuge, David also knew that the grave does not rob believers of life. He said, "You will not leave my soul in Sheol [the grave]" (v.10). Neither Ken nor anyone else who knows Jesus as Savior will be abandoned in death.

Because of Jesus' own death and resurrection, we too will rise one day (Acts 2:25-28; 1 Cor. 15:20-22). And we will find that "at [God's] right hand are pleasures forevermore" (Ps. 16:11). —Anne Cetas

"In the Beloved" accepted am I,
Risen, ascended, and seated on high;
Saved from all sin through His infinite grace,
I am accorded in heaven a place. —*Martin*

God is our treasure now, and being with Him in heaven will bring pleasures forever.

February 28
Saturday

Pack Up Your Sorrows

Read:
Isaiah 53:1-6

Surely He has borne our griefs and carried our sorrows.
—Isaiah 53:4

The Bible In One Year:
- Numbers 20–22
- Mark 7:1-13

During the turbulent years of the 1960s, popular music in America was a strange mixture of protest and patriotism. Some songs lashed out against war, greed, and injustice in society, while others affirmed duty to country and traditional values. But "Pack Up Your Sorrows," written by Richard Farina and Pauline Baez Marden, seemed to fit all of the categories with its focus on the quest for personal peace. The refrain said the following:

Well, if somehow you could pack up your sorrows, / And give them all to me / You would lose them, I know how to use them, / Give them all to me.

Perhaps everyone hoped that someone really could bring them peace.

The good news is that there is Someone who can! Isaiah 53 is a prophetic picture of Israel's promised Messiah. Christians see its fulfillment in the death and resurrection of Jesus Christ. "Surely He has borne our griefs and carried our sorrows . . . . He was wounded for our transgressions, He was bruised for our iniquities; the chastisement for our peace was upon Him, and by His stripes we are healed" (vv.4-5).

Jesus took our sins and sorrows on Himself so that we could be forgiven and have peace with God. Will you give Him your sorrows today? —David McCasland

Never a burden that He does not carry;
Never a sorrow that He does not share;
Whether the days may be sunny or dreary,
Jesus is always there. —*Lillenas*

No sorrow is too heavy for our Savior to bear.

March 1
Sunday

Expect Great Things

Read:
Hebrews 11:32-40

Who through faith . . . out of weakness were made strong.
—Hebrews 11:33-34

The Bible In One Year:
- Numbers 23–25
- Mark 7:14-37

William Carey was an ordinary man with an extraordinary faith. Born into a working-class family in the 18th century, Carey made his living as a shoemaker. While crafting shoes, Carey read theology and journals of explorers. God used His Word and the stories of the discovery of new people groups to burden him for global evangelism. He went to India as a missionary, and not only did he do the work of an evangelist but he learned Indian dialects into which he translated the Word of God. Carey's passion for missions is expressed by his words: "Expect great things from God; attempt great things for God." Carey lived out this maxim, and thousands have been inspired to do missionary service by his example.

The Bible tells of many whose faith in God produced amazing results. Hebrews tells of those "who through faith subdued kingdoms, worked righteousness, obtained promises, stopped the mouths of lions, quenched the violence of fire, escaped the edge of the sword, out of weakness were made strong" (11:33-34).

The list of heroes of the faith has grown through the ages, and we can be a part of that list. Because of God's power and faithfulness, we can attempt great things for God and expect great things from God. —Dennis Fisher

If God can hang the stars on high,
Can paint the clouds that drift on by,
Can send the sun across the sky,
What can His power do through you? —Jones

When God is your partner, you can make your plans large!

March 2
Monday

A Good Man

Read:
Romans 3:10-18

By grace you have been saved through faith, and that not of yourselves; it is the gift of God.
—Ephesians 2:8

The Bible In One Year:
■ Numbers 26–27
■ Mark 8:1-21

Jerry was a good man," the pastor said at Jerald Stevens' memorial service. "He loved his family. He was faithful to his wife. He served his country in the armed services. He was an excellent dad and grandfather. He was a great friend."

But then the pastor went on to tell the friends and family gathered that Jerry's good life and good deeds were not enough to assure him a place in heaven. And that Jerry himself would have been the first to tell them that!

Jerry believed these words from the Bible: "All have sinned and fall short of the glory of God" (Rom. 3:23) and "the wages of sin is death" (6:23). Jerry's final and eternal destination in life's journey was not determined by whether he lived a really good life but entirely by Jesus dying in his place to pay sin's penalty. He believed that each of us must personally accept the free gift of God, which is "eternal life in Christ Jesus our Lord" (6:23).

Jerry *was* a good man, but he could never be "good enough." And neither can we. It is only by grace that we can be saved through faith. And that has absolutely nothing to do with our human efforts. "It is the gift of God" (Eph. 2:8).

"Thanks be to God for His indescribable gift!" (2 Cor. 9:15). —Cindy Hess Kasper

Christ's work for my salvation is complete!
No work of mine can add to what He's done;
I bow to worship at the Master's feet,
And honor God the Father's only Son. —*Hess*

We are not saved by good works, but by God's work.

March 3
Tuesday

Refreshing Candor

Read:
John 4:7-26

He who looks into the perfect law of liberty and continues in it, . . . this one will be blessed in what he does. —James 1:25

The Bible In One Year:
- Numbers 28–30
- Mark 8:22-38

Of the many things I love about my mom, chief among them may be her candor. Many times I have called to ask her opinion on a matter and she has consistently responded, "Don't ask my opinion unless you want to hear it. I'm not going to try to figure out what you want to hear. I'll tell you what I really think."

In a world where words are carefully parsed, her straightforwardness is refreshing. It is also one of the characteristics of a true friend. Real friends speak the truth to us in love—even if it isn't what we want to hear. As the proverb says, "Faithful are the wounds of a friend" (Prov. 27:6).

This is one of the reasons Jesus is the greatest of friends. When He encountered the woman at the well (John 4:7-26), He refused to be pulled into a tug-of-war over secondary issues but instead drove to the deepest issues and needs of her heart. He challenged her about the character of the Father and lovingly spoke to her of her broken dreams and deep disappointments.

As we walk with our Lord, may we allow Him to speak candidly to the true condition of our hearts through the Scriptures—that we might turn to Him and find His grace to help us in our times of need. —Bill Crowder

Father, thank You for sending Your Son to be my Savior and the greatest of friends. Help me to learn from Him how loving honesty can make a difference in helping the hurting people around me.

Jesus always tells us truth.

March 4
Wednesday

They're Watching

Read:
Titus 3:1-8

Speak evil of no one, . . . be peaceable, gentle, showing all humility to all men. —Titus 3:2

The Bible In One Year:
■ Numbers 31–33
■ Mark 9:1-29

It's been several decades since a high school event devastated me. Playing sports was hugely important to me. I zeroed in on basketball and spent hundreds of hours practicing my game. So when I didn't make the varsity team in my last year after being on the team since junior high, I was crushed.

Disappointed and confused, I carried on. I became a stats guy for the team, going to games and keeping track of my friends' rebounds and shots as they got within one game of the state championship without me. To be honest, I never thought of how they were viewing my response. I just muddled through. That's why I was surprised recently to hear that several of my classmates told my brother that they saw in my response a lesson in Christianity—a picture of Christ. My point is not to tell you to do as I did, because I'm not sure what I did. My point is this: Whether we know it or not, people are watching us.

In Titus 3:1-8, Paul explains the life God enables us to live—a life of respect, obedience, and kindness that results from being reborn through Jesus and renewed by the Holy Spirit who has been poured out on us.

As we live a Spirit-guided life, God will show the reality of His presence to others through us. —Dave Branon

Dear Father, You know how inadequate I am.
Please equip me through the Spirit to show love
and respect in my life so that others will see
through me and see You.

A Christian is a living sermon whether or not he preaches a word.

March 5
Thursday

Forced Leisure

Read:
Zephaniah 3:14-20

The Lord your God in your midst, the Mighty One, will save; He will rejoice over you with gladness, He will quiet you with His love, He will rejoice over you with singing. —Zeph. 3:17

The Bible In One Year:
- **Numbers 34–36**
- **Mark 9:30-50**

Just before Christmas one year, a friend was diagnosed with leukemia and was told she must begin chemotherapy immediately. Just a few weeks earlier, Kim had told friends how blessed and content she felt with a loving family, a comfortable home, and a new grandson. As she entered the hospital, Kim asked Jesus to make His presence known to her and to stay close.

The next 7 months of treatments followed by recovery in partial isolation became a season she calls "forced leisure." She says she learned how to slow down, reflect quietly, and rest in God's goodness, love, and perfect plan—regardless of whether or not she would be healed.

One of God's promises to His people Israel became personal to Kim: "The Lord your God . . . will save; He will rejoice over you with gladness, He will quiet you with His love, He will rejoice over you with singing" (Zeph. 3:17).

Kim is in remission after a journey she says changed her life for the better. Now back in her busy routine, she often pauses to recapture the lessons of "forced leisure."

How important that we—in good times or times of challenge—draw near to God's loving heart to hear His voice and place our lives in His hands. —David McCasland

A troubled heart, a wearied mind
Are burdens hard to bear;
A lack of peace, a heavy load
Are lifted by God's care. —*Fitzhugh*

People are at the heart of God's heart.

March 6
Friday

Bumper Cars

Read:
Matthew 18:23-35

Lord, how often shall my brother sin against me, and I forgive him? Up to seven times?
—Matthew 18:21

The Bible In One Year:
- **Deuteronomy 1–2**
- **Mark 10:1-31**

Life is a lot like "bumper cars" at an amusement park. You get in your car, knowing that you will get hit . . . you just don't know how hard. And when you get hit, you step on the gas pedal, chase the one who has hit you, and hope to bump that person harder than they have bumped you.

That may be a fun strategy for bumper cars, but it's a terrible strategy for life. When you get bumped in life, bumping back only escalates matters and in the end everyone suffers damage.

Jesus had a better strategy: Forgive those who have "bumped" us. Like Peter, we may wonder how many times we have to forgive. When Peter asked Jesus, "Up to seven times?" Jesus answered "Up to seventy times seven" (Matt. 18:21-22). In other words, there are no limits to grace. We should always extend a spirit of forgiveness. Why? In the story of the forgiving master, Jesus explained that we forgive not because our offenders deserve it but because we've been forgiven. He says, "I forgave you . . . because you begged me. Should you not also have had compassion on your fellow servant, just as I had pity on you?" (vv.32-33).

Since we are among those who've been forgiven much, let's stop the damage and share that blessing with others.
—Joe Stowell

Lord, remind us of how deeply we have offended You and how often You have extended the grace of forgiveness to us. Teach us to forgive others and to trust You to deal with those who sin against us.

Forgiveness is God's grace in action through us.

March 7
Saturday

On The Fringe

Read:
Philippians 4:10-20

God shall supply all your need according to His riches in glory by Christ Jesus.
—Philippians 4:19

The Bible In One Year:
- **Deuteronomy 3–4**
- **Mark 10:32-52**

When butterflies hatch at Frederik Meijer Gardens in Grand Rapids, Michigan, they do so in an indoor tropical paradise perfectly suited to meet their every need. The temperature is perfect. The humidity is perfect. The food is a perfect balance of calories and nutrition to keep them healthy. No need to go elsewhere. Yet some butterflies see the bright blue sky outside the conservatory and spend their days fluttering near the glass ceiling far away from the plentiful food supply.

I want to say to those butterflies, "Don't you know everything you need is inside? The outside is cold and harsh, and you will die within minutes if you get what you are longing to have."

I wonder if that is the message God has for me. So I ask myself, Do I look longingly at things that would harm me? Do I use my energy to gain what I don't need and shouldn't have? Do I ignore God's plentiful provision because I imagine that something just beyond my reach is better? Do I spend my time on the fringes of faith?

God supplies all our needs from His riches (Phil. 4:19). So instead of striving for what we don't have, may we open our hearts to gratefully receive everything we've already been given by Him. —Julie Ackerman Link

All that I want is in Jesus;
He satisfies, joy He supplies;
Life would be worthless without Him,
All things in Jesus I find. —Loes

Our needs will never exhaust God's supply.

March 8
Sunday

Jesus' Team

Read:
Luke 5:27-35

He . . . saw a tax collector named Levi . . . . And He said to him, "Follow Me." —Luke 5:27

The Bible In One Year:
- Deuteronomy 5–7
- Mark 11:1-18

In 2002 the Oakland Athletics built a winning baseball team in an unorthodox way. They had lost three top players after 2001, and the team didn't have money to sign any stars. So Oakland's general manager, Billy Beane, used some often-neglected statistics to assemble a group of lesser-known players either "past their prime" or seen by other teams as not skilled enough. That ragtag team ran off a 20-game winning streak on the way to winning their division and 103 games.

This reminds me a little of the way Jesus put together His "team" of disciples. He included rough Galilean fishermen, a zealot, and even a despised tax collector named Levi (Matthew). This reminds me that "God has chosen the weak things of the world to put to shame the things which are mighty" (1 Cor. 1:27). God used those dedicated men (minus Judas) to ignite a movement that affected the world so dramatically it has never been the same.

There's a lesson here for us. Sometimes we seek out the familiar, the influential, and the rich. And we tend to ignore people with less status or those with physical limitations.

Jesus put some of society's less desirable people on His team—treating everyone the same. With the Spirit's power and guidance, we too can honor all people equally. —David Egner

In Jesus Christ we all are equal,
For God's Spirit makes us one;
As we give each other honor,
We give glory to His Son. —*Fitzhugh*

There are no unimportant people in the body of Christ.

March 9
Monday

PRAYING FRIENDS

READ:
1 Thessalonians 3:6-13

Brethren, pray for us.
—1 Thessalonians 5:25

I met my friend Angie for lunch after having not seen her for several months. At the end of our time together, she pulled out a piece of paper with notes from our previous get-together. It was a list of my prayer requests she had been praying for since then. She went through each one and asked if God had answered yet or if there were any updates. And then we talked about her prayer requests. How encouraging to have a praying friend!

The apostle Paul had a praying relationship with the churches he served, including the one at Thessalonica. He thanked God for the faith, love, and hope of the people (1 Thess. 1:2-3). He longed to see them, and asked God "night and day" that he might be able to visit them again (3:10-11). He requested that the Lord would help them "increase and abound in love to one another and to all" (v.12). He also prayed that their hearts would be blameless before God (v.13). They must have been encouraged as they read about Paul's concern and prayers for them. Paul knew too his own need for God's presence and power and pleaded, "Brethren, pray for us" (5:25).

THE BIBLE IN ONE YEAR:
- Deuteronomy 8–10
- Mark 11:19-33

Loving Father, thank You for wanting us to talk with You. Teach us all to be praying friends. —Anne Cetas

I need the prayers of those I love
While traveling on life's rugged way,
That I may true and faithful be,
And live for Jesus every day. —*Vaughn*

The best kind of friend is a praying friend.

March 10
Tuesday

Extravagant Gifts

Read:
Luke 21:1-4

All these out of their abundance have put in offerings for God, but she out of her poverty put in all the livelihood that she had. —Luke 21:4

The Bible In One Year:
- Deuteronomy 11–13
- Mark 12:1-27

When I was pastoring a small church, we faced a huge crisis. Unless we could complete the extensive renovations necessary to bring our building up to the proper safety codes, we would lose our place of worship. A desperate time of fund-raising ensued to pay for those renovations; but of all the money given, one gift captured our leadership's attention.

An elderly woman in the church donated several hundred dollars to the project—money we knew she could not spare. We thanked her for her gift but wanted to return it, feeling that her needs were greater than the church's. However, she refused to take the money back. She had been saving for years in order to buy a stove and was cooking on a hot plate in the meantime. Yet she insisted that she needed a place to worship with her church family more than she needed a stove. We were astounded by her extravagant gift.

When our Lord observed a widow putting two mites (the smallest of coins) into the temple offerings, He praised her for her extravagance (Luke 21:3-4). Why? Not because of how much she gave, but because she gave all she had. It's the kind of gift that not only honors our God, but also reminds us of the most extravagant of gifts to us—Christ. —Bill Crowder

What can I give Him, poor as I am?
If I were a shepherd, I would bring a lamb;
If I were a wise man, I would do my part;
Yet what can I give Him—give my heart. —*Rossetti*

Gratitude of heart can often be seen in a generous spirit.

March 11
Wednesday

Thankful In All Things

Read:
1 Thessalonians 5:12-22

In everything give thanks.
—1 Thessalonians 5:18

The Bible In One Year:
- **Deuteronomy 14–16**
- **Mark 12:28-44**

My daughter is allergic to peanuts. Her sensitivity is so acute that eating even the tiniest fragment of a peanut threatens her life. As a result, we scrutinize food package labels. We carry a pre-filled syringe of medicine (to treat allergic reactions) wherever we go. And, when we eat out, we call ahead and quiz the wait staff about the restaurant's menu items.

Despite these precautions, I still feel concerned—both for her current safety and for her future safety. This situation is not something I would naturally be thankful about. Yet, God's Word challenges: "In everything give thanks; for this is the will of God in Christ Jesus for you" (1 Thess. 5:18). There's no getting around it. God wants us to pray with thanksgiving when the future is uncertain, when heartbreak hits, and when shortfalls come.

It's hard to be grateful in difficulties, but it's not impossible. Daniel "prayed and gave thanks" (Dan. 6:10), knowing that his life was in danger. Jonah called out "with the voice of thanksgiving" (Jonah 2:9) while inside a fish! These examples, coupled with God's promise that He will work all things together for our good and His glory (Rom. 8:28), can inspire us to be thankful in all things. —Jennifer Benson Schuldt

Thanks for roses by the wayside,
Thanks for thorns their stems contain.
Thanks for homes and thanks for fireside
Thanks for hope, that sweet refrain! —*Storm*

In all circumstances, we can give thanks that God has not left us on our own.

March 12
Thursday

Riches Of The Soul

Read:
Proverbs 30:1-9

Give me neither poverty nor riches—feed me with the food allotted to me.
—Proverbs 30:8

The Bible In One Year:
- **Deuteronomy 17–19**
- **Mark 13:1-20**

With the hope of winning a record jackpot of $640 million, Americans spent an estimated $1.5 billion on tickets in a multistate lottery in early 2012. The odds of winning were a staggering 1 in 176 million, but people stood in lines at grocery stores, gas stations, and cafes to buy a chance to become rich. Something inside us makes us think more money will solve our problems and improve our lives.

A man identified in the Bible as Agur had a different perspective on riches when he asked God to grant him two requests before he died.

First, he said, "Remove falsehood and lies far from me" (Prov. 30:8). Integrity is a key to living without anxiety. When we have nothing to hide, we have nothing to fear. Deceit enslaves; honesty liberates. Second, he said, "Give me neither poverty nor riches—feed me with the food allotted to me" (v.8). Contentment springs from trusting God as our supplier and gratefully accepting what He provides. Agur said of the Creator that He "established all the ends of the earth. . . . He is a shield to those who put their trust in Him" (vv.4-5).

Integrity and contentment are riches of the soul that are available to all. Our Lord is pleased to give these treasures to everyone who asks. —David McCasland

Contentment does not come from wealth—
It's not something you can buy;
Contentment comes to give you peace
When you depend on God's supply. —*Branon*

Discontentment makes us poor while contentment makes us rich!

March 13
Friday

Living Testament

Read:
2 Timothy 2:1-10

Remember that Jesus Christ, of the seed of David, was raised from the dead according to my gospel.
—2 Timothy 2:8

The Bible In One Year:
- **Deuteronomy 20–22**
- **Mark 13:21-37**

Watchman Nee was arrested for his faith in Christ in 1952, and he spent the rest of his life in prison. He died in his jail cell on May 30, 1972. When his niece came to collect his few possessions, she was given a scrap of paper that a guard had found by his bed. On it was written his life's testimony:

"Christ is the Son of God who died for the redemption of sinners and was resurrected after three days. This is the greatest truth in the universe. I die because of my belief in Christ—Watchman Nee."

Tradition says that the apostle Paul also was martyred for his faith in Christ. In a letter written shortly before his death, Paul exhorted his readers: "Remember that Jesus Christ, of the seed of David, was raised from the dead according to my gospel, for which I suffer trouble . . . ; but the Word of God is not chained" (2 Tim. 2:8-9).

We may not be called upon to be martyred as witnesses to the reality of Christ—as millions of His followers through the centuries have been—but we are all called to be a living testament of Jesus' work on our behalf. No matter the outcome, from a heart of gratitude for God's gracious gift we can tell others what Jesus has done for us. —Dennis Fisher

The Christ of God to glorify,
His grace in us to magnify;
His Word of life to all make known—
Be this our work, and this alone. —Whittle

Let your life as well as your lips speak for Christ.

March 14
Saturday

Black Boxes

Read:
1 Corinthians 10:1-11

These things happened to them as examples, and they were written for our admonition.
—1 Corinthians 10:11

The Bible In One Year:
- **Deuteronomy 23–25**
- **Mark 14:1-26**

Commercial aircraft carry two flight-data recorders called "black boxes." One logs the performance and condition of the aircraft in flight, and the other records the conversation of the crew with air-traffic controllers on the ground. These boxes are insulated to protect against extreme temperatures and are fitted with underwater locator beacons that emit sounds to the surface. After an airplane crash, these boxes are retrieved and the data carefully analyzed to determine the cause of the crash. Air safety experts want to learn from past mistakes, among other things, so they won't be repeated.

As Christians, we too should look at mistakes from the past and learn from them. Paul, for example, alluded to some of the mistakes the Israelites made in their journey from Egypt to Canaan. He wrote that because God was not pleased with them, many died in the wilderness (1 Cor. 10:5). Paul went on to explain that "these things happened to them as examples for us. They were written down to warn us who live at the end of the age" (v.11 NLT).

The inspired Word of God is written for our instruction for living (2 Tim. 3:16-17). Thank You, Lord, for the guidance of Your Word. —C. P. Hia

For Your holy Book we thank You;
May its message be our guide,
May we understand the wisdom
Of the truth Your laws provide. —*Carter*

God's warnings are to protect us, not to punish us.

March 15
Sunday

Jesus' Eyes

Read:
Mark 5:1-20

[Jesus] was moved with compassion for them, because they were weary and scattered, like sheep having no shepherd.
—Matthew 9:36

The Bible In One Year:
- **Deuteronomy 26–27**
- **Mark 14:27-53**

We were in line at the ice cream store when I noticed him. His face bore the marks of too many fights—a crooked nose and some scars. His clothes were rumpled, though clean. I stepped between him and my children, using my back to erect a wall.

The first time he spoke, I didn't hear him clearly and so just nodded to acknowledge him. I scarcely made eye contact with him. Because my wife wasn't with me, he thought I was a single parent and gently said, "It's hard raising them alone, isn't it?" Something in his tone made me turn to look at him. Only then did I notice his children, and I listened to him tell me how long his wife had been gone. His soft words contrasted with his hard exterior.

I was duly chastened! Once again I had failed to see beyond outward appearances. Jesus encountered people whose outward appearance could have turned Him away, including the demon-possessed man in our reading for today (Mark 5:1-20). Yet He saw the heart-needs and met them.

Jesus never fails to see us with love, even though we have scars of sin and a rumpled nature that shows in our stutter-step faithfulness. May God help us to replace our haughtiness with Jesus' heart of love. —Randy Kilgore

Father, may the focus of our lives never disrupt
our ability to see others with the same eyes that
Jesus sees them. Grant us Your heart.
May we yearn to introduce others to You.

If you look through the eyes of Jesus,
you'll see a needy world.

March 16
Monday

BROKEN BONES

READ:
Psalm 51:1-13

Make me hear joy and gladness, that the bones You have broken may rejoice.
—Psalm 51:8

THE BIBLE IN ONE YEAR:
- Deuteronomy 28–29
- Mark 14:54-72

Years ago, I played collegiate soccer as a goalkeeper. It was more fun than I can describe here, but all that fun came at a hefty price—one I continue to pay today. Being a goalie means that you are constantly throwing your body into harm's way to prevent the other team from scoring, often resulting in injuries. During the course of one season, I suffered a broken leg, several cracked ribs, a separated shoulder, and a concussion! Today, especially on cold days, I am visited by painful reminders of those broken bones.

David also had reminders of broken bones, but his injuries were spiritual, not physical. After David's moral collapse involving an affair with Bathsheba and the murder of her husband, God firmly disciplined him. But then David turned to Him in repentance and prayed, "Make me hear joy and gladness, that the bones You have broken may rejoice" (Ps. 51:8).

God's chastening was so crushing that David felt like his bones were broken. Yet he trusted that the God of grace could both repair his brokenness and rekindle his joy. In our own failure and sin, it's a comfort to know that God loves us enough to pursue and restore us with His loving discipline.
—Bill Crowder

Father, open my eyes to see my failings, open my heart to receive Your discipline, and open my will to embrace Your loving purposes. When I fall, I pray that You will make me whole and restore my joy in You.

God's hand of discipline is a hand of love.

March 17
Tuesday

Who Owns My Lips?

Read:
Psalm 12

Let the words of my mouth and the meditation of my heart be acceptable in Your sight, O Lord.
—Psalm 19:14

The Bible In One Year:
- **Deuteronomy 30–31**
- **Mark 15:1-25**

The difference between a compliment and flattery is often motive. A compliment offers genuine appreciation for a quality or action seen in another person. The goal of flattery is usually self-advancement through gaining the favor of someone else. Compliments seek to encourage; flattery attempts to manipulate.

In Psalm 12, David lamented his society in which godly, faithful people had disappeared and been replaced by those who speak deceitfully "with flattering lips and a double heart" (v.2). They had said, "With our tongue we will prevail; our lips are our own; who is lord over us?" (v.4).

The question "Who owns my lips?" is a good one to ask ourselves when we're tempted to use insincere praise to get what we want. If my lips are my own, I can say what I please. But if the Lord owns my lips, then my speech will mirror His words, which the psalmist described as "pure words, like silver tried in a furnace of earth, purified seven times" (v.6).

Perhaps a good way to show who owns our lips would be to begin each day with David's prayer from another psalm: "Let the words of my mouth and the meditation of my heart be acceptable in Your sight, O Lord, my strength and my Redeemer" (Ps. 19:14). —David McCasland

A careless word may kindle strife,
A cruel word may wreck a life;
A timely word may lessen stress,
A loving word may heal and bless. —*Anon.*

He who guards his mouth preserves his life.
—Proverbs 13:3

March 18
Wednesday

Can't Do Everything

Read
Galatians 6:1-10

Let each one examine his own work, and then he will have rejoicing in himself alone, and not in another.
—Galatians 6:4

The Bible In One Year:
- **Deuteronomy 32–34**
- **Mark 15:26-47**

Four-year-old Eliana was helping her mom pick up some of Eliana's things before bedtime. When Mommy told her to put away the clothes on her bed, Eliana hit her limit. She turned around, put her little hands on her hips, and said, "I can't do everything!"

Do you ever feel that way with the tasks God has called you to do? It's easy to feel overwhelmed with church involvement, witnessing, and raising a family. We might sigh in exasperation and pray, "Lord, I can't do everything!"

Yet God's instructions indicate that His expectations are not overwhelming. For instance, as we deal with others, He gives us this qualifier: "As much as depends on you, live peaceably with all" (Rom. 12:18). God understands our limitations. Or this: "Whatever you do, do it heartily, as to the Lord" (Col. 3:23). He's not asking for perfection that we might impress people, but simply to honor Him with the work we do. And one more: "Let each one examine his own work, and then he will have rejoicing in himself alone, and not in another" (Gal. 6:4). We are not doing our work as a competition with others, but simply to carry our own load.

In wisdom, God has equipped us to do just what He wants us to do—and that's certainly not everything! —Dave Branon

He gives me work that I may seek His rest,
He gives me strength to meet the hardest test;
And as I walk in providential grace,
I find that joy goes with me, at God's pace. —*Gustafson*

When God gives an assignment, it comes with His enablement.

March 19
Thursday

First Things First

Read:
1 Chronicles 28:5-10

Know the God of your father, and serve Him with a loyal heart and with a willing mind.
—1 Chronicles 28:9

The Bible In One Year:
- **Joshua 1–3**
- **Mark 16**

When our granddaughter Sarah was very young, she told us she wanted to be a basketball coach like her daddy when she grew up. But she couldn't be one yet, she said, because first she had to be a player; and a player has to be able to tie her shoelaces, and she couldn't tie hers yet!

First things first, we say. And the first thing in all of life is to know God and enjoy Him.

Acknowledging and knowing God helps us to become what we were meant to be. Here is King David's counsel to his son Solomon: "Know the God of your father, and serve Him with a loyal heart and with a willing mind" (1 Chron. 28:9).

Remember, God can be known. He is a Person, not a logical or theological concept. He thinks, wills, enjoys, feels, loves, and desires as any person does. A. W. Tozer writes, "He is a person and can be known in increasing degrees of intimacy as we prepare our hearts for the wonder of it." Ah, there's the rub: We must "prepare our hearts."

The Lord is not playing hard to know; those who want to know Him can. He will not foist His love on us, but He does wait patiently, for He wants to be known by you. Knowing Him is the first thing in life. —David Roper

He walks with me, and He talks with me,
And He tells me I am His own;
And the joys we share as we tarry there
None other has ever known. —*Miles*

The thought of God staggers the mind but to know Him satisfies the heart.

March 20
Friday

Thoughts On Rain

Read:
Matthew 5:38-48

He makes His sun rise on the evil and on the good, and sends rain on the just and on the unjust. —Matthew 5:45

The Bible In One Year:
- **Joshua 4–6**
- **Luke 1:1-20**

When torrential downpours beat on the heads of my newly planted petunias, I felt bad for them. I wanted to bring them inside to shelter them from the storm. By the time the rain stopped, their little faces were bowed to the ground from the weight of the water. They looked sad and weak. Within a few hours, however, they perked up and turned their heads skyward. By the next day, they were standing straight and strong.

What a transformation! After pounding them on the head, the rain dripped from their leaves, soaked into the soil, and came up through their stalks, giving them the strength to stand straight.

Because I prefer sunshine, I get annoyed when rain spoils my outdoor plans. I sometimes wrongly think of rain as something negative. But anyone who has experienced drought knows that rain is a blessing. It nourishes the earth for the benefit of both the just and the unjust (Matt. 5:45).

Even when the storms of life hit so hard that we nearly break from the force, the "rain" is not an enemy. Our loving God has allowed it to make us stronger. He uses the water that batters us on the outside to build us up on the inside, so we may stand straight and strong. —Julie Ackerman Link

Lord, we know that we don't need to fear the storms of life. Because You are good, we can trust You to use even our hard times to build our faith in You. We lean on You now.

The storms that threaten to destroy us God will use to strengthen us.

March 21
Saturday

MAKE IT COUNT

READ:
1 Peter 4:1-8

Since Christ suffered for us in the flesh, arm yourselves also with the same mind. —1 Peter 4:1

THE BIBLE IN ONE YEAR:
- Joshua 7–9
- Luke 1:21-38

In his battle with cancer, Steve Jobs, co-founder of Apple Inc., said: "Remembering that I'll be dead soon is the most important tool I've ever encountered to help me make the big choices in life. Because almost everything—all external expectations, all pride, all fear of embarrassment or failure—these things just fall away in the face of death, leaving only what is truly important." His suffering influenced the choices he made.

In contrast, the apostle Peter wanted to motivate his readers to use their suffering to make their lives count for eternity. And he wanted Jesus' suffering and death to inspire them to accept the spiritual conflict and persecution that would result from bearing the name of Jesus. Because they loved Jesus, suffering was going to be normative. Jesus' suffering was to serve as motivation to give up sinful passions and to be obedient to the will of God (1 Peter 4:1-2). If their lives were going to count for eternity, they needed to stop indulging in fleeting pleasures and instead exhaust their lives on what pleased God.

Remembering that Jesus suffered and died to forgive our sins is the most important thought we have to inspire us to make godly choices today and to make our lives count for eternity. —Marvin Williams

Jesus, You have suffered and died to forgive our sin; may Your death and resurrection inspire us to never return to where we've been. Help us in our resolve to live for Your will alone.

Jesus' death forgave my past sins and inspires my present obedience.

March 22
Sunday

Going For The Prize

Read:
1 Corinthians 9:24-27

Everyone who competes for the prize . . . [does] it to obtain a perishable crown, but we for an imperishable crown.
—1 Corinthians 9:25

The Bible In One Year:
- Joshua 10–12
- Luke 1:39-56

Every March, the Iditarod Trail Race is held in Alaska. Sled dogs and their drivers, called "mushers," race across a 1,049-mile route from Anchorage to Nome. The competing teams cover this great distance in anywhere from 8 to 15 days. In 2011, a record time was set by musher John Baker who covered the entire route in 8 days, 19 hours, 46 minutes, and 39 seconds. The teamwork between dogs and driver is remarkable, and those who compete are tenacious in their efforts to win. The first-place winner receives a cash prize and a new pickup truck. But after so much perseverance in extreme weather conditions, the accolades and prizes may seem insignificant and transient.

The excitement of a race was a familiar concept to the apostle Paul, but he used competition to illustrate something eternal. He wrote, "Everyone who competes for the prize is temperate in all things. Now they do it to obtain a perishable crown, but we for an imperishable crown" (1 Cor. 9:25).

Sometimes we are tempted to place our emphasis on temporal rewards, which perish with the passing of time. The Scriptures, however, encourage us to focus on something more permanent. We honor God by seeking spiritual impact that will be rewarded in eternity. —Dennis Fisher

Here we labor, here we pray,
Here we wrestle night and day;
There we lay our burdens down,
There we wear the victor's crown. —*Anon.*

Run the race with eternity in view.

March 23
Monday

Hope Is For . . .

Read:
Hebrews 10:19-25

Let us hold fast the confession of our hope without wavering, for He who promised is faithful.
—Hebrews 10:23

The Bible In One Year:
- Joshua 13–15
- Luke 1:57-80

Although I try not to be shocked by the things I see these days, I was caught off-balance by the message on the woman's T-shirt as she walked past me in the mall. The bold letters declared: "Hope Is For Suckers." Certainly, being naïve or gullible can be foolish and dangerous. Disappointment and heartache can be the tragic offspring of unfounded optimism. But not allowing oneself to have hope is a sad and cynical way to view life.

Biblical hope is unique; it's a confident trust in God and what He is doing in the world and in our lives. That's something everyone needs! The writer to the Hebrews clearly stated the importance of hope when he wrote, "Let us hold fast the confession of our hope without wavering, for He who promised is faithful" (Heb. 10:23).

Having biblical hope is not foolish, because it has a strong foundation. We hold fast to the hope we have received in Christ because our God is faithful. He can be trusted with anything and everything we will ever face—both for today and forever. Our hope is grounded in the trustworthy character of the God who loves us with an everlasting love. So, the T-shirt had it wrong. Hope is not for suckers; it's for you and for me! —Bill Crowder

My hope is built on nothing less
Than Jesus' blood and righteousness;
I dare not trust the sweetest frame,
But wholly lean on Jesus' name. —*Mote*

Hope that has its foundation in God will not crumble under the pressures of life.

March 24
Tuesday

O Love That Will Not Let Me Go

Read:
1 John 4:7-21

Beloved, if God so loved us, we also ought to love one another.
—1 John 4:11

The Bible In One Year:
- Joshua 16–18
- Luke 2:1-24

Love is the centerpiece of thriving relationships. Scripture makes it clear that we need to be people who love—love God with all our hearts, love our neighbor as ourselves, and love our enemies. But it's hard to love when we don't feel loved. Neglected children, spouses who feel ignored by their mates, and parents who are alienated from their children all know the heartache of a life that lacks love.

So, for everyone who longs to be loved, welcome to the pleasure of knowing that you are richly loved by God. Think of the profound impact of His love that was poured out for you at the cross. Meditate on the fact that if you've trusted in Him, His love covers your faults and failures and that you are clothed with His spotless righteousness (Rom. 3:22-24). Revel in the fact that nothing can separate you from His love (8:39). Embrace His loving provision of a future secured for you where you will be eternally loved (John 3:16).

When John tells us that we "ought to love one another," he calls us the "beloved" (1 John 4:11; see also 3:1-2). Once you embrace how wonderfully loved you are by God, it will be much easier to be the loving person God calls you to be—even toward those who don't show you love. —Joe Stowell

Were the whole realm of nature mine,
That were a present far too small:
Love so amazing, so divine,
Demands my soul, my life, my all. —*Watts*

Embracing God's love for us is the key to loving others.

March 25
Wednesday

Too Heavy

Read:
Psalm 32:1-6;
Matthew 11:28-30

Come to Me, all you who labor and are heavy laden, and I will give you rest.
—Matthew 11:28

The Bible In One Year:
- **Joshua 19–21**
- **Luke 2:25-52**

As I started up my car in the dark hours of early morning, I noticed a seatbelt light on the dashboard. I checked my door, opening and pulling it shut again. I tugged on my seatbelt to test it. But the sensor light still beamed. Then, in slow realization, I reached over and lifted my purse a few inches above the passenger seat. The light clicked off.

Apparently, a cell phone, three rolls of quarters, a hardcover book, and my lunch stuffed in my very large purse had equaled the weight of a small passenger, thus setting off the sensor!

While I can easily empty out a handbag, other weights are not so easy to shed. Those burdens of life involve a heaviness of spirit.

Whether the burden that weighs us down is one of guilt such as the one that consumed David's thoughts (Ps. 32:1-6), the fear Peter experienced (Matt. 26:20-35), or the doubt Thomas carried (John 20:24-29), Jesus has invited us to bring them all to Him: "Come to Me, all you who labor and are heavy laden, and I will give you rest" (Matt. 11:28).

We are not built to bear burdens alone. When we cast them on the One who wants to bear our burdens (Ps. 68:19; 1 Peter 5:7), He replaces them with forgiveness, healing, and restoration. No burden is too heavy for Him. —Cindy Hess Kasper

Lord, thank You for lovingly carrying our burdens.
In times of trouble, help us to leave those burdens
in Your strong hands and to find our rest in You.
In Jesus' name, amen.

Burden God with what burdens you.

March 26
Thursday

Our Father's World

Read:
Genesis 1:26-28

The earth is the Lord's, and all its fullness, the world and those who dwell therein. —Psalm 24:1

The Bible In One Year:
- **Joshua 22–24**
- **Luke 3**

When Amanda Benavides was a sophomore at Point Loma Nazarene University in San Diego, California, she began to rethink her views on Christian stewardship of the earth. Amanda had grown up thinking that being conscious of the environment had nothing to do with her relationship with Jesus. All this changed when she was challenged to consider the Christian's role in caring for the planet—especially how that relates to reaching the most needy in the world.

Our stewardship of the beautiful world God gave us, and our care for the people in it, express our reverence for God and is grounded in two biblical principles.

First, the earth belongs to God (Ps. 24:1-2). The psalmist praised the Lord for His creation and His ownership of it. The heavens, the earth, and all that are in it are His. He created it, He is sovereign over it (93:1-2), and He cares for it (Matt. 6:26-30). Second, God delegated the responsibility for the well-being of His earth to us (Gen. 1:26-28). This includes appreciation of and care for both nature (Lev. 25:2-5,11; Prov. 12:10) and people (Rom. 15:2).

This is our Father's world. Let's show Him how much we love Him by respecting it and caring for the people who populate it. —Marvin Williams

The natural world that God has made
Must not be used at whim;
We serve as stewards of His earth,
Responsible to Him. —D. DeHaan

To mistreat God's creation is to offend the Creator.

March 27
Friday

Out Of Context

Read:
Luke 4:1-13

Your Word is truth.
—John 17:17

The Bible In One Year:
- **Judges 1–3**
- **Luke 4:1-30**

When a friend started making random despairing statements, people were concerned for him and started giving advice and offering encouragement. As it turned out, he was simply having fun by quoting song lyrics out of context to start a conversation. Friends who tried to help wasted their time by offering help he didn't need and advice he didn't want. The consequences of my friend's misleading statements were not serious, but they could have been. In taking time to respond to his false need, someone could have neglected someone else's truly serious need.

Some people who take words out of context just want to gain attention or win an argument. But others are more sinister. They twist truth to gain power over others. They endanger not only lives but also souls.

When people use words to manipulate others to behave in certain ways—or worse, when they quote the Bible out of context to convince others to do wrong—there's only one defense: We need to know what God truly says in His Word. Jesus was able to resist temptation with the truth (Luke 4). We have the same resource. God has given us His Word and Spirit to guide us and keep us from being deceived or misled. —Julie Ackerman Link

Your words of pure, eternal truth
Shall yet unshaken stay,
When all that man has thought or planned
Like chaff shall pass away. —*Anon.*

**If we hold on to God's truth,
we won't be trapped by Satan's lies.**

March 28
Saturday

FRIENDSHIP

READ:
1 Samuel 23:14-18

A friend loves at all times.
—Proverbs 17:17

THE BIBLE IN ONE YEAR:
- **Judges 4–6**
- **Luke 4:31-44**

Friendship is one of life's greatest gifts. True friends seek a special kind of good for their friends: the highest good, which is that they might know God and love Him with all of their heart, soul, and mind. German pastor and martyr Dietrich Bonhoeffer said, "The aim of friendship is exclusively determined by what God's will is for the other person."

Jonathan, David's friend, is a sterling example of true friendship. David was in exile, hiding in the Desert of Ziph, when he learned that "Saul had come out to seek his life" (1 Sam. 23:15). Jonathan went to Horesh to find David. The significance of this scene lies in Jonathan's intent: He helped David find strength in God or, as the text puts it, he "strengthened his hand [grip] in God" (v.16).

That is the essence of Christian friendship. Beyond common interests, beyond affection, beyond wit and laughter is the ultimate aim of sowing in others the words of eternal life, leaving them with reminders of God's wisdom, refreshing their spirit with words of His love, and strengthening their grip on God.

Pray for your friends and ask God to give you a word "in season" to help them find renewed strength in our God and His Word. —David Roper

Dear Lord, thank You for loving us. May Your love compel us to show love to others. Give us sensitivity to Your Spirit that we might know how to encourage them in their walk with You.

A true friend is a gift from God and one who points us back to Him.

March 29
Palm Sunday

Let It Go

Read:
Mark 11:1-11

Say, "The Lord has need of it," and immediately he will send it here.
—Mark 11:3

The Bible In One Year:
- Judges 7–8
- Luke 5:1-16

Many years ago, when a young friend asked if he could borrow our car, my wife and I were hesitant at first. It was *our* car. We owned it, and we depended on it. But we soon felt convicted to share it with him because we knew that God wanted us to care for others. So we handed the keys over to him, and he traveled to a church 30 miles away to conduct a youth rally. The meeting was used by the Lord to bring teens to Christ.

Jesus instructed His disciples to take another man's donkey. The Son of God told His men to "loose it and bring it" to Him (Mark 11:2). If someone objected, they were to say, "The Lord has need of it," and they would then be permitted to lead it away. That donkey carried Christ into Jerusalem on what we call Palm Sunday.

There's a lesson here for us to consider. We all have things that we hold dear. We may have thought, *I could never part with that.* It may be a new truck, a coat, some other possession, or our precious few free hours during the week. Will we be open to give when someone obviously needs something we have?

If you sense that the Spirit is speaking to you, let your time or possession go, as the owner released his animal to Jesus. He will then be glorified as He deserves! —David Egner

Make me a channel of blessing today,
Make me a channel of blessing, I pray;
My life possessing, my service blessing,
Make me a channel of blessing today. —*Smyth*

God gives us all we need,
so we can give to others in their need.

March 30
Monday

Supernatural Surveillance

Read:
Matthew 6:1-6,16-18

Your Father who sees in secret will reward you openly. —Matthew 6:18

The Bible In One Year:
- **Judges 9–10**
- **Luke 5:17-39**

Not far from my house, authorities have rigged a camera to snap pictures of drivers who race through red lights. The offenders later receive in the mail a ticket along with a "red-light photo," which is visual proof of their traffic violation.

Sometimes I think of God in the same way I think of that camera—He's up there, just waiting to catch me doing the wrong thing. While God does see our sin (Heb. 4:13), He sees and takes interest in our good deeds as well. Due to His supernatural surveillance, God sees the size of our sacrifice when we give money to the church or to those in need (Mark 12:41-44). He hears our private prayers (Matt. 6:6). And when we fast, we can carry on as usual being assured that our "Father . . . sees in secret" (v.18).

Knowing that God sees everything frees us from thinking about the watchful eyes of others. When we do what is right, we need no applause from onlookers; when we sin, we do not need to worry about our reputation once we settle the issue with God and anyone we've harmed. We can rest knowing that "the eyes of the Lord run to and fro throughout the whole earth, to show Himself strong on behalf of those whose heart is loyal to Him" (2 Chron. 16:9). —Jennifer Benson Schuldt

Lord, thank You for Your all-seeing nature. You know everything I think and do. Help me to value Your approval and live according to Your standards, no matter what anyone else may think.

Others see what we do, but God sees why we do it.

March 31
Tuesday

No Fine Print

Read:
Deuteronomy 30:11-20

For this commandment which I command you today is not too mysterious for you, nor is it far off.
—Deuteronomy 30:11

The Bible In One Year:
- **Judges 11–12**
- **Luke 6:1-26**

Writing in the *Wall Street Journal,* Missy Sullivan noted that many user agreements, warranties, and disclaimers that come with products are nearly unreadable. Intentionally set in very small type, they actually discourage people from understanding them. Because of this, many people don't read all the terms of contracts before signing them. A university professor of graphic communication pointed to a 32-page user agreement that came with his new smartphone, and said of the company, "They don't want you to read it."

In contrast, the Lord is always seeking to communicate with His people in clear and compelling ways, with no attempt to confuse or deceive. When Moses spoke to the Israelites just before they entered the Promised Land, he said, "For this commandment which I command you today is not too mysterious for you, nor is it far off. . . . I have set before you life and death, blessing and cursing; therefore choose life, that both you and your descendants may live" (Deut. 30:11,19).

The Lord wants us to understand His plan and purpose clearly, so that we may love, obey, and cling to Him—for He is our "life and the length of [our] days" (v.20). That's plain to see. —David McCasland

Father, we want to learn and experience more of who You are in our relationship with You. Teach us so that we will grow in our understanding of You and Your plan for our lives.

There is no fine print in God's communication with us.

April 1
Wednesday

No Substitute Needed

Read:
Psalm 139:1-12

Where can I go from Your Spirit? Or where can I flee from Your presence?
—Psalm 139:7

The Bible In One Year:
- **Judges 13–15**
- **Luke 6:27-49**

While I was visiting my son in San Diego, we decided to go to Shadow Mountain Church to hear Dr. David Jeremiah preach. Steve and I got up early on Sunday morning and took the hour-long drive to the church. But our anticipation turned to disappointment when we discovered that Dr. Jeremiah was not there that day. "Some other guy"—a substitute—was preaching.

A couple of weeks later, I was scheduled to preach at the church in Grand Rapids where my wife and I attend. As I stood in front of the congregation, I realized that now I was "some other guy" and they might be disappointed because they had come to hear our pastor—not me—speak.

While we find comfort in the familiarity of those we depend on in life, we have to recognize that at times they can be substituted. But the One we need most—the One on whom we depend for life itself—is always present (Ps. 139:7-8). When we desire to enter God's presence in prayer, He is always there: "Evening and morning and at noon I will pray, and cry aloud, and He shall hear my voice" (55:17).

Looking for God? He's always right there. No substitute needed. —Dave Branon

Dear Lord, I am so thankful that You are always present. I never need to make an appointment to speak to You, the God of the universe. No matter where I go or what time it is, I can depend on Your presence.

When you come to the Lord, there is no waiting line—His ears are always open to your cry.

April 2
Thursday

"And It Was Night"

Read:
John 13:21-30

Having received the piece of bread, [Judas] then went out immediately. And it was night. —John 13:30

The Bible In One Year:
- Judges 16–18
- Luke 7:1-30

During a business trip to Philadelphia, I attended an evening service on the Thursday before Easter—a service of Communion and Tenebrae (darkness) held in a small chapel lit by candles. Following the bread and the cup, a passage was read aloud from the gospel of John, one candle was extinguished, and we sang a verse from a hymn about Jesus' journey to the cross. This was repeated 14 times until the chapel was completely dark. In silence we knelt in prayer and then left one by one without speaking.

The darkness of this type of service can remind us of the dark elements surrounding Jesus' death. Think of His last meal with the disciples (John 13:21-30) as He explained that one of them would betray Him. Only Jesus knew it was Judas. "Having received the piece of bread, [Judas] then went out immediately. And it was night" (v.30).

On the darkest evening of Jesus' life, He agonized in prayer in the Garden, faced a wrongful arrest, endured humiliation at the hands of religious leaders, and winced at Peter's denials. Yet He moved faithfully toward the cross where He would die for our sins.

Jesus endured darkness and death to give us light and life. Praise Him for what He went through for us! —David McCasland

See, from His head, His hands, His feet,
Sorrow and love flow mingled down;
Did e'er such love and sorrow meet,
Or thorns compose so rich a crown? —*Watts*

Calvary reveals the vileness of our sin and the vastness of God's love.

April 3
Good Friday

Shout Of Triumph

Read:
John 19:28-37

It is finished!
—John 19:30

The Bible In One Year:
- Judges 19–21
- Luke 7:31-50

Recently I read about Aron Ralston, a hiker who was trapped alone at the bottom of a remote canyon. With scant hope of being found and his strength ebbing away, he had to take drastic measures to save his life. During a moment of excruciating pain, he shouted in agony and in victory, because he had freed himself and now had a chance to escape and live.

Those who witnessed the crucifixion of Jesus saw His hours of agony and heard Him cry out in a loud voice, "It is finished!" as He gave up His spirit (John 19:30). His final words from the cross were not a cry of painful defeat but a shout of triumph, because He had accomplished all that the Father sent Him to do.

When Jesus died, He shared in what all of us must experience. But far beyond that, He did what none of us can do. He paid the price for our sins that we might be forgiven and have eternal life through faith in Him.

"It is finished!" was the Lord's shout of victory because now, through Him, we can escape the power of sin; we can live and be free.

Because of Jesus' sacrifice for us, we call the day of His death *Good* Friday. —David McCasland

I have been to the cross where my Savior died,
And all of my life is made new—
In the person of Him I am crucified.
I have been to the cross. Have you? —*Frazee-Bower*

Jesus died that we might live.

April 4
Saturday

You Can Beat It!

Read:
Matthew 28:1-10

O Death, where is your sting?
—1 Corinthians 15:55

The Bible In One Year:
■ **Ruth 1–4**
■ **Luke 8:1-25**

The radio ad for an upcoming seminar sounded intriguing. The announcer said, "You can beat death—for good! Attend my seminar and I'll show you how." I wondered for a few moments what the speaker would claim could beat death and what his suggestions might be. Perhaps something about diet or exercise or freezing our bodies? After listening a little longer, though, I realized he had said, "You can beat *debt*—for good."

The most wonderful news is that we *can* beat death because Jesus paid our debt! (1 Cor. 15:55-57). Our debt of sin meant separation from God, but Jesus willingly gave up His life and was crucified on a cross to pay what we owed. As Mary Magdalene and another Mary went to the tomb on the third day to anoint His body, an angel told them: "He is not here; for He is risen, as He said" (Matt. 28:6). With great joy they ran to bring His disciples the word. On their way, Jesus met them and said, "Rejoice!" (v.9). Jesus had risen, and His followers had reason for rejoicing.

Jesus has removed the sting of death (1 Cor. 15:55). Now we too have victory by believing in the Son of God's death and resurrection for us. Through Jesus' perfect work, we can beat death—for good! —Anne Cetas

Dear Lord, thank You for sacrificing Your life for our sins so that we might live. We're thankful that because You died and rose again, we can have assurance that one day we'll be with You in a place of no more death.

We owed a debt we couldn't pay;
Jesus paid a debt He didn't owe.

April 5
Easter Sunday

Knee-Deep In Daffodils

Read:
Luke 24:13-34

The Lord is risen indeed! —Luke 24:34

The Bible In One Year:
- **1 Samuel 1–3**
- **Luke 8:26-56**

When the first flowers of spring bloomed in our yard, my 5-year-old son waded into a patch of daffodils. He noticed some debris from plants that had expired months before and remarked, "Mom, when I see something dead, it reminds me of Easter because Jesus died on the cross." I replied, "When I see something alive—like the daffodils—it reminds me that Jesus came back to life!"

One reason we know Jesus rose from the grave is that, according to the gospel of Luke, He approached two travelers headed to Emmaus 3 days after His crucifixion. Jesus walked with them; He ate dinner with them; He even gave them a lesson in Old Testament prophecy (24:15-27). This encounter showed the travelers that Jesus conquered the grave—He had risen from the dead. As a result, the pair returned to Jerusalem and told the disciples, "The Lord is risen indeed!" (v.34).

If Jesus had not come back to life, our faith as Christians would be pointless, and we would still be under the penalty of our sin (1 Cor. 15:17). However, the Bible tells us that Jesus "was raised to life for our justification" (Rom. 4:25 NIV). Today, we can be right with God because Jesus is alive! —Jennifer Benson Schuldt

I serve a risen Savior, He's in the world today;
I know that He is living, whatever men may say.
I see His hand of mercy, I hear His voice of cheer,
And just the time I need Him He's always near. —Ackley

The empty cross and the empty tomb provide a full salvation.

April 6
Monday

Unseen Danger

Read:
James 1:13-25

Each one is tempted when he is drawn away by his own desires and enticed. —James 1:14

The Bible In One Year:
- **1 Samuel 4–6**
- **Luke 9:1-17**

When I was a young child, our family escaped near tragedy. Most of the main appliances in the house, as well as the furnace, were fueled by natural gas, but a small leak in one of the gas lines put our lives at risk. As the gas poured into our little house, our family was overcome by the lethal fumes and we lost consciousness. Had we not been discovered by a neighbor who happened to stop by for a visit, we all could have been killed by this dangerous, unseen enemy.

As followers of Christ, we can also find ourselves surrounded by unseen dangers. The toxic realities of temptation and the weaknesses of our own human frailty can endanger our lives and relationships. Unlike the natural gas in my childhood home, however, these unseen dangers do not come from outside of us—they reside within us. James wrote, "Each one is tempted when he is drawn away by his own desires and enticed" (James 1:14).

Our natural tendency to sin, compounded by blind spots that prevent us from seeing our own weaknesses, can lead to toxic choices that ruin us. It is only by submitting to God as He shows us our hearts in His Word (vv.23-25) that we can live a life that pleases the Master. —Bill Crowder

Spirit of God, descend upon my heart;
Wean it from earth, through all its pulses move;
Stoop to my weakness, mighty as Thou art,
And make me love Thee as I ought to love. —*Croly*

The unseen Spirit of God is the greatest protection against sin's unseen dangers.

April 7
Tuesday

I L-O-V-E . . .

READ:
Romans 6:1-11

Now if we died with Christ, we believe that we shall also live with Him. —Romans 6:8

THE BIBLE IN ONE YEAR:
■ 1 Samuel 7–9
■ Luke 9:18-36

My husband and I were at a public swimming pool when the people around us started staring into the sky. A small plane was emitting smoke in the form of letters. As we watched, the pilot spelled out the letters: "I L-O-V-E." People began speculating: Maybe it was to be a marriage proposal. Perhaps a romantic man is standing nearby on a balcony with his girlfriend and will soon pop the Will-you-marry-me? question. We kept gazing upward: "I L-O-V-E Y-O-U J-E-." I heard young girls guessing: "I bet it will be Jen or maybe Jessica." He kept spelling. No. It was: "J-E-S-U-S." The pilot was declaring love for Jesus for many people to see.

A friend of mine often ends his prayers with "I love You, Lord." He says, "I can't help but say 'I love You' after all He's done for me." In Romans 6:1-11, our Bible text for today, the apostle Paul tells us some of what Jesus has done for us that deserves our love: He was crucified, buried, and raised to life. Because of that, those of us who have put our faith in Jesus now have a new life (v.4), we no longer have to be controlled by sin or fear of death (vv.6,9), and one day we too will be resurrected to live with Him forever (v.8).

No wonder we say, "I love You, Jesus!" —Anne Cetas

Redeemed—how I love to proclaim it!
Redeemed by the blood of the Lamb;
Redeemed through His infinite mercy—
His child, and forever, I am. —*Crosby*

To show His love, Jesus died for us;
to show our love, we live for Him.

April 8
Wednesday

Guard Your Brand

Read:
Colossians 3:1-14

Above all these things put on love, which is the bond of perfection. —Colossians 3:14

The Bible In One Year:
- **1 Samuel 10-12**
- **Luke 9:37-62**

A popular clothing retailer requires that its sales clerks dress like the models in the store windows who advertise its clothes. This practice is referred to as "guarding their brand." The idea behind it is that shoppers will be more likely to purchase clothes because they will want to look like the people they see wearing them.

In a consumer-oriented culture, it's easy to be seduced into thinking that we can "buy" acceptance by wearing the things that beautiful people wear. Retailers would have us believe that looking good will make us desirable.

Sometimes we even convince ourselves that we can win followers for God by making ourselves attractive to the world. But the Bible is clear about what's really important to God. He wants us to look like Jesus in our character. In a sense, Jesus is our "brand," for we are being conformed to His image (Rom. 8:29). We attract others to Christ when we put on His attributes, which include tender mercies, kindness, humility, meekness, longsuffering (Col. 3:12), and, above all, love (v.14).

Instead of polishing and protecting our own image, we need to be guarding and reflecting the image of God, which is being perfected in us through Christ. —Julie Ackerman Link

O to be like Thee! blessed Redeemer,
This is my constant longing and prayer;
Gladly I'll forfeit all of earth's treasures,
Jesus, Thy perfect likeness to wear. —*Chisholm*

One of the Spirit's roles is to form the likeness of Christ in us.

April 9
Thursday

Is Ambition Wrong?

Read:
Colossians 3:22-24

Whatever you do, do it heartily, as to the Lord.
—Colossians 3:23

The Bible In One Year:
■ 1 Samuel 13–14
■ Luke 10:1-24

Is ambition wrong? Is it wrong to be driven, to push to be the best? It can be. The difference between right and wrong ambition is in our goal and motivation—whether it's for God's glory or our own.

In 1 Thessalonians 4:1, Paul tells us that Christians are to live lives "to please God." For some, the drive to please Him is an instant transformation at the time of salvation; for others, the transformation is full of stutter-steps and mis-starts. Whether the change happens instantly or gradually, the Christian is to pursue God's goals, not selfish ones.

So, in the workplace we ask: "How will that job change help me serve others and glorify God?" Ambition oriented toward God is focused outward on Him and others, always asking how He has gifted us and wants to use us.

Paul suggests we work with "sincerity of heart, fearing God" (Col. 3:22). Whatever we're doing—in the board room, on the docks, wherever we're working—we're to serve as if doing it for God (vv.23-24).

We glorify Him most and enjoy Him most when we work with fervor and excellence for His pleasure, not ours. For His service and the service of others, not self-service and personal gain—because He deserves our all. —Randy Kilgore

Lord, help me to apply zest to my work efforts
that I might please You. I offer my actions and words
today as a testimony to bring You glory.
Use me today to point others to You. Amen.

"We grow small trying to be great."
—Eli Stanley Jones, missionary

April 10
Friday

Keep It Simple

Read:
2 Corinthians 1:12-14

We are not writing any other things to you than what you [can] read or understand.
—2 Corinthians 1:13

The Bible In One Year:
- **1 Samuel 15–16**
- **Luke 10:25-42**

James Madison, fourth president of the United States, was instrumental in the drafting of the US constitution. He warned against creating laws "so voluminous that they cannot be read, or so incoherent that they cannot be understood." Based on some of the complicated government forms I've read, that's advice that still needs to be heeded a little more often!

Sometimes when sharing the gospel, we make it more complicated than it needs to be. We can be glad that the Bible presents the good news of salvation in clear, easily understood language. Jesus said to Nicodemus, an educated Pharisee, that "God so loved the world that He gave His only begotten Son, that whoever believes in Him should not perish but have everlasting life" (John 3:16). He later said, "I am the way, the truth, and the life. No one comes to the Father except through Me" (14:6). The apostle Paul said it in straightforward language to the jailor in Philippi who asked how to be saved: "Believe on the Lord Jesus Christ, and you will be saved" (Acts 16:31).

God's precious love story is simple. He sent His Son to rescue us from sin and death. Wonderful news that even children can understand. —Dave Egner

Tell me the story of Jesus,
Write on my heart every word;
Tell me the story most precious,
Sweetest that ever was heard. —*Crosby*

Through faith in Christ, we receive God's pardon and escape sin's penalty.

April 11
Saturday

Making Up For Lost Time

Read:
Joel 2:21-27

I will restore to you the years that the swarming locust has eaten. —Joel 2:25

The Bible In One Year:
- **1 Samuel 17–18**
- **Luke 11:1-28**

None of us can say that we have no regrets. Often we are led down paths of bad choices—some paths longer than others—which can have a lingering effect on the mind, body, and soul.

A friend of mine spent a number of years living a life of alcohol and drug abuse. But God did an amazing work in his life, and he recently celebrated 25 years of being free from substance abuse. He now runs a successful business, has a devoted wife, and his children love Jesus. He has a passion to reach out to others who are in the ditch of life, and he serves as a wise and loving mentor in the rescue operations of their lives.

God never gives up on us! Even if we've made poor choices in the past that have left us with regret, we can choose how we will live now. We can choose to continue destructive living, simply wallow in regret, or we can run to Christ believing that He has ways to "restore . . . the years that the swarming locust has eaten" (Joel 2:25). When we repentantly seek His healing and freeing power, He is merciful.

While some consequences from the past may remain, we can be confident that God has a good and glorious future for those who trust in Him! —Joe Stowell

Lord, it is with humble and grateful hearts that we come to You and lay all that we have been in the past at Your feet. Take us as we are and make something beautiful out of our lives that brings glory to You!

God never gives up on making something beautiful out of our lives.

April 12
Sunday

Honor System

Read:
Luke 16:1-10

He who is faithful in what is least is faithful also in much; and he who is unjust in what is least is unjust also in much. —Luke 16:10

The Bible In One Year:
■ 1 Samuel 19–21
■ Luke 11:29-54

Many homes near ours offer produce and perennials for sale by the road. Sometimes we'll drive up to an unattended stand that operates on the "honor system." As we make our selection, we put our money into a cash box or an old coffee can. Then we go home to enjoy the freshly picked fruits and vegetables.

But the honor system doesn't always work. My friend Jackie has a flower stand in front of her house. One day, as she glanced out her window she saw a well-dressed woman with a big hat loading pots of perennials into the trunk of her car. Jackie smiled as she mentally calculated a $50 profit from her labors in the garden. But when she checked the cash box later, it was empty! The honor system revealed that this woman was not honorable.

Perhaps to her, taking the flowers seemed like a small thing. But being honest in little things indicates how we will respond in the big things (Luke 16:10). Honesty in all areas of our lives is one way we can bring honor to Jesus Christ, our Savior.

The best "honor system" for a follower of Christ is Colossians 3:17, "Whatever you do in word or deed, do all in the name of the Lord Jesus." —Cindy Kasper

Give of your best to the Master;
Give Him first place in your heart;
Give Him first place in your service,
Consecrate every part. —Grose

Honesty means never having to look over your shoulder.

April 13
Monday

Tell The Story

Read:
Psalm 78:1-8

[Tell] to the generation to come the praises of the Lord, and His strength and His wonderful works that He has done.
—Psalm 78:4

The Bible In One Year:
- 1 Samuel 22–24
- Luke 12:1-31

In an interview with *Wired* magazine, filmmaker George Lucas was asked how he wanted to be remembered. He replied: "I'll be remembered as a filmmaker. . . . Hopefully some of the stories I told will still be relevant. . . . If you've raised children, you know you have to explain things to them, and if you don't, they end up learning the hard way. . . . So the old stories have to be reiterated again in a form that's acceptable to each new generation. I don't think I'm ever going to go much beyond the old stories, because I think they still need to be told."

In Psalm 78, the psalmist was aware of the possibility of God's mighty works being forgotten and a generation being lost, so he called God's people to never tire of telling the old story of His redemptive acts to future generations (v.4). The goal of this perpetual rehearsing of their history wasn't just for memorizing historical data; it was to inspire faith, obedience, and hope in the Lord (v.7) and to keep future generations from groping in the darkness of unbelief and rebellion like the generations before them (v.8).

Because of God's mighty power and grace in our lives we desire to be faithful to tell His stories that we might inspire faith and obedience in future generations. —Marvin Williams

I love to tell the story,
For some have never heard
The message of salvation
From God's own holy Word. —*Hankey*

Past stories of grace inspire future stories of faith.

April 14
Tuesday

Well Done, David Schumm

Read:
Isaiah 35:3-10

Be strong, do not fear! Behold, your God will come. —Isaiah 35:4

The Bible In One Year:
- **1 Samuel 25–26**
- **Luke 12:32-59**

At David Schumm's memorial service, we celebrated the optimism, perseverance, and faith of a man with severe cerebral palsy. For all of David's 74 years, the simple tasks of daily life required great effort. Through it all, he kept smiling and helping others by giving more than 23,000 hours as a hospital volunteer, along with encouraging at-risk teens.

David selected Isaiah 35:3-10 to be read at his service: "Strengthen the weak hands, and make firm the feeble knees. Say to those who are fearful-hearted, 'Be strong, do not fear! Behold, your God will come with vengeance, with the recompense of God; He will come and save you. . . . Then the lame shall leap like a deer, and the tongue of the dumb sing. For waters shall burst forth in the wilderness, and streams in the desert" (vv.3-4,6). This promise, given to the people of Israel while in captivity, reminds us of our hope for the time when Christ will return for those who trust and follow Him.

During David's last weeks, he often pointed visitors to a large picture of Jesus near his bed, saying, "He's coming to get me soon." This is the hope Jesus Christ gives to all His children, which calls forth our thanks and praise to Him!
—David McCasland

Marvelous message we bring,
Glorious carol we sing,
Wonderful word of the King:
Jesus is coming again! —*Peterson*

Live as if Christ died yesterday and is coming back today.

April 15
Wednesday

Money Talk

Read:
1 Timothy 6:6-12

Command those who are rich in this present age not to be haughty, nor to trust in uncertain riches but in the living God.
—1 Timothy 6:17

The Bible In One Year:
- **1 Samuel 27–29**
- **Luke 13:1-22**

Marilyn and Steven had been married just a few years, and money was tight. But as she looked at their threadbare bedspread, she wanted to replace it. So she decided she would buy a new one with a credit card—hoping to somehow find the money to pay it off.

Her devotional reading for the day surprised her when it pointed her to Proverbs 22:27, "If you lack the means to pay, your very bed will be snatched from under you" (NIV). Marilyn decided not to go into debt for a new bedspread that day.

Decisions about the way we spend our money are a personal matter between us and the Lord and can be difficult to make. But God hasn't left us without help. He tells us: "Honor the LORD with your possessions" (Prov. 3:9), and "You cannot serve both God and Money" (Matt. 6:24 NIV).

With such truths in mind, we look further in His Word for help to use money wisely. We find this: "Beware of covetousness" (Luke 12:15). Another says, "The borrower is servant to the lender" (Prov. 22:7). And in 1 Timothy we read, be "ready to give, willing to share" (6:18).

Money is a big issue. God, who provides for all our needs, can show us how to use it to bring Him honor. —Dave Branon

Lord, sometimes money and finances are
overwhelming. It's hard to know what decisions
to make, so please lead me and give the wisdom
to use my finances in a way that pleases You.

Never let gold become your god.

April 16
Thursday

Cape Tribulation

Read:
James 1:1-8

My brethren, count it all joy when you fall into various trials, knowing that the testing of your faith produces patience. —James 1:2-3

The Bible In One Year:
■ 1 Samuel 30–31
■ Luke 13:23-35

On June 10, 1770, British navigator James Cook's ship hit a reef off the northeast coast of Australia. He sailed the ship out into deeper water only to hit the reef again, and this time the collision almost sank the ship. This experience moved Cook to write in the ship's log: "The north point [was named] Cape Tribulation because here began all our troubles."

Many of us have experienced a trial that has seemed to trigger a string of other trials. The loss of a job, the death of a loved one, an unwanted divorce, or a decline in health could all be part of the list.

Even though a crisis may seem to be our "Cape Tribulation," God is still sovereign and He most certainly is in control. It is His purpose to use tribulation to build resilience into us. James writes: "My brethren, count it all joy when you fall into various trials, knowing that the testing of your faith produces patience" (James 1:2-3). The word translated "patience" means to have staying power or the ability to endure.

In the midst of your life-changing trial, remember that God is still at work. He wants to use your "Cape Tribulation" experience to build your character. He has promised His grace to see you through (2 Cor. 12:9). —Dennis Fisher

He giveth more grace when the burdens grow greater,
He sendeth more strength when the labors increase;
To added affliction He addeth His mercy,
To multiplied trials, His multiplied peace. —*Flint*

Faith grows best in the winter of trial. —Rutherford

April 17
Friday

All The Comforts Of Home

Read:
John 14:1-6

In My Father's house are many mansions; . . . I go to prepare a place for you. —John 14:2

The Bible In One Year:
- 2 Samuel 1–2
- Luke 14:1-24

Once, during my tenure as a human resource officer for a construction company, we took some jobs in a neighboring state. This meant our workers were faced with a 2-hour commute each way, plus a full workday. To ease the burden, we booked motel rooms for the week, but we also arranged vans and drivers to transport those who decided to commute. Almost every worker took the vans!

One of our grumpiest workers discarded his usual demeanor as he described the thrill and surprise of his wife and four boys on the first night. He hadn't told them he had an option to come home, so he showed up unexpectedly to surprise them. Later his wife called to thank the company owner, telling him their family was "loyal for life" to anyone who understood how important home was to workers.

Anyone who has been deprived of home, even for a short time, will understand the comfort Jesus' disciples drew from His words when He promised that an eternal home awaited them (John 14:2). Then, to make their joy complete, Jesus told them He would prepare and guide them to that home, and, joy of joys, He would be there too (v.3).

Remember the greatest comfort of this life: Jesus promised that one day we will go home to be with Him. —Randy Kilgore

Heavenly Father, we praise You for these words
from Jesus that touch the deepest longing in
our soul—the hope and comfort of home. We
want to be with You. In Jesus' name, amen.

There is no place like home—
especially when home is heaven.

April 18
Saturday

From Bleak To Beautiful

Read:
Job 42:10-17

The Lord blessed the latter days of Job more than his beginning. —Job 42:12

The Bible In One Year:
- 2 Samuel 3–5
- Luke 14:25-35

Spring is the time of year when God reminds us that things are not always as they seem. Over the course of a few short weeks, what appears hopelessly dead comes to life. Bleak woodlands are transformed into colorful landscapes. Trees whose naked arms reached to heaven all winter, as if pleading to be clothed, suddenly are adorned with lacy green gowns. Flowers that faded and fell to the ground in surrender to the cold rise slowly from the earth in defiance of death.

In Scripture, we read about some apparently hopeless situations. One example is that of a wealthy man named Job whom God described as having integrity (Job 2:3). Disaster struck and Job lost everything important to him. In misery, he said, "My days are . . . spent without hope" (7:6). What appeared to Job and his friends as evidence that God had turned against him was just the opposite. God was so confident of Job's integrity that He trusted him in this battle with Satan. Later, Job's hope and life were renewed.

The faithful arrival of spring every year comforts me when I'm in a situation that seems hopeless. With God, there is no such thing. No matter how bleak the landscape of life may look, God can transform it into a glorious garden of color and fragrance. —Julie Ackerman Link

Dear God, we pray for faith anew,
For greater trust in all we do,
For hope that never knows defeat,
For victory at Thy mercy seat. —*Brandt*

With God, there is hope even in the most hopeless situation.

April 19
Sunday

Strengthened Through Suffering

Read:
1 Peter 5:1-11

May the God of all grace, . . . after you have suffered a while, . . . strengthen, and settle you. —1 Peter 5:10

The Bible In One Year:
■ 2 Samuel 6–8
■ Luke 15:1-10

Church services often end with a benediction. A common one is taken from Peter's concluding remarks in his first epistle: "May the God of all grace, who called us to His eternal glory by Christ Jesus, after you have suffered a while, perfect, establish, strengthen, and settle you" (1 Peter 5:10). Sometimes omitted in the benediction is the phrase "after you have suffered a while." Why? Perhaps because it is not pleasant to speak of suffering.

It should not surprise us, however, when suffering comes our way. The apostle Paul, who knew well what it was to suffer, wrote: "All who desire to live godly in Christ Jesus will suffer persecution" (2 Tim. 3:12).

If we live a life of submission to God (1 Peter 5:6) and resisting the devil (v.9), we can expect to be maligned, misunderstood, and even taken advantage of. But the apostle Peter says that there is a purpose for such suffering. It is to "restore you and make you strong, firm, and steadfast" (v.10 NIV).

God's path for our Christian growth often leads us through difficulties, but they fortify us to withstand life's future storms. May God help us to be faithful as we seek to boldly live a life that honors Him. —C. P. Hia

Forbid it, Lord, that I should be
Afraid of persecution's frown;
For Thou hast promised faithful ones
That they shall wear the victor's crown. —Bosch

When God would make us strong
He schools us through hardships.

April 20
Monday

WONDERFULLY MADE

READ:
Psalm 139:13-18

Marvelous are Your works, and that my soul knows very well.
—Psalm 139:14

THE BIBLE IN ONE YEAR:
■ 2 Samuel 9–11
■ Luke 15:11-32

While getting an eye exam recently, my doctor hauled out a piece of equipment that I hadn't seen before. I asked him what the device was, and he responded, "I'm using it to take a picture of the inside of the back of your eye."

I was impressed that someone had invented a camera that could do that. But I was even more impressed by what my doctor could learn from that picture. He said, "We can gather a lot of details about your current general health simply by looking at the back of your eye."

My doctor's comment amazed me. It is remarkable that a person's overall health can be measured by the health of the eye. What care the Lord has taken to place these details in the bodies He has created! It immediately brings to my mind the words of David, the psalmist, who reveled in God's creativity: "I will praise You, for I am fearfully and wonderfully made; marvelous are Your works, and that my soul knows very well" (Ps. 139:14).

The enormous complexities of our bodies reflect the genius and wisdom of our great Creator. The wonder of His design is more than breathtaking—it gives us countless reasons to worship Him! —Bill Crowder

Lord, we are in awe of You! Thank You that You
created us with such complexity and care
and that You know us with such intimacy.
We love You and trust You with our lives.

All life is created by God and bears His autograph.

April 21
Tuesday

One By One

Read:
Acts 8:26-35

Philip . . . preached Jesus to him.
—Acts 8:35

The Bible In One Year:
■ 2 Samuel 12–13
■ Luke 16

Edward Payson was a famous preacher in a bygone era. One stormy Sunday, he had only one person in his audience. Some months later, his lone attendee called on him: "I was led to the Savior through that service," he said. "For whenever you talked about sin and salvation, I glanced around to see to whom you referred, but since there was no one there but me, I had no alternative but to lay every word to my own heart and conscience!"

God saves us one by one. If you have access to one, that is your mission field. "Every soul with Christ is a missionary; every soul without Christ is a mission field," the slogan goes. One person cannot reach the entire world, but we can love our neighbor. "Who is my neighbor?" we ask. The next person we meet along the way.

The Spirit brought Philip to the Ethiopian eunuch who was reading the Scriptures and needed someone to explain them to him (Acts 8:26-35). The Spirit gave Philip the right words to say, and the eunuch confessed his faith in Christ (v.37).

Ask God to bring you to the one He has prepared. He'll get you to the right place at the right time to speak to that individual. He will speak through your lips, work through your hands, and fulfill in you the great purpose of His will. —David Roper

Father, we've been called to witness—
Called to speak of Your dear Son;
Holy Spirit, grant discernment;
Lead us to some seeking one. —D. DeHaan

You are a success in God's kingdom if you are faithful where He has placed you.

April 22
Wednesday

Dust Art

Read:
Genesis 2:1-7

The Lord God formed man of the dust of the ground, and breathed into his nostrils the breath of life; and man became a living being. —Genesis 2:7

The Bible In One Year:
- **2 Samuel 14–15**
- **Luke 17:1-19**

When God chose dust as His artistic medium to create Adam (Gen. 2:7), He didn't have to worry about running out of material. According to Hannah Holmes, author of *The Secret Life of Dust,* "Between 1 and 3 billion tons of desert dust fly up into the sky annually. One billion tons would fill 14 million boxcars in a train that would wrap six times around the Earth's equator."

No one has to buy dust, for we all have more than we want. I ignore it as long as I can in my house. My reasoning is this: If I don't disturb it, it's not as noticeable. But eventually it accumulates to the point that I can no longer pretend it's not there. So I haul out my cleaning supplies and start removing it from wherever it has found a resting place.

As I remove the dust, I see myself reflected in the smooth surface. Then I see another thing: I see that God took something worthless, dust, and made it into something priceless—you and me and every other person (Gen. 2:7).

The fact that God used dust to create humans makes me think twice about labeling someone or something worthless. Perhaps the very thing that I want to get rid of—a person or problem that annoys me—is the artistic medium God has given to display His glory. —Julie Ackerman Link

Lord, too often I want to quickly ignore
or dismiss difficult people and circumstances.
Help me to be open to learn
from You through them and to see Your glory.

Being all fashioned of the self-same dust, let us be merciful as well as just. —Longfellow

April 23
Thursday

Now I See

Read:
John 14:15-27

The Helper, the Holy Spirit, whom the Father will send in My name, He will teach you all things, and bring to your remembrance all things that I said to you. —John 14:26

The Bible In One Year:
- 2 Samuel 16–18
- Luke 17:20-37

Deborah Kendrick loves to attend Broadway musicals even though she is blind and always struggles to understand the setting and the movements of the characters onstage. Recently, however, she attended a play that used D-Scriptive, a new technology that conveys the visual elements of the stage production through a small FM receiver. A recorded narration, keyed to the show's light and sound boards, describes the set and the action as it unfolds onstage. Writing in *The Columbus Dispatch,* Deborah said, "If you ask me if I saw a show last week in New York, my answer is yes . . . I genuinely, unequivocally mean that I *saw* the show."

Her experience struck me as a vivid illustration of the Holy Spirit's role in our understanding of God's Word. Just before Jesus went to the cross, He told His followers that "the Helper, the Holy Spirit, whom the Father will send in My name, He will teach you all things, and bring to your remembrance all things that I said to you" (John 14:26).

As we open the Bible to read or study, the Spirit of Truth is with us to guide us into all truth (16:13). On our own we are blind, but through the guidance of God's Holy Spirit we can see. —David McCasland

Break Thou the bread of life, dear Lord, to me,
As Thou didst break the loaves beside the sea.
Beyond the sacred page I seek Thee, Lord;
My spirit pants for Thee, O Living Word. —*Lathbury*

The Father gave the Spirit to teach us from the Word.

April 24
Friday

FAITHFUL TO THE FINISH

READ:
Hebrews 12:1-4

Let us run with endurance the race that is set before us. —Hebrews 12:1

THE BIBLE IN ONE YEAR:
■ 2 Samuel 19–20
■ Luke 18:1-23

After running 32 kilometers (20 miles) of the Salomon Kielder Marathon in Great Britain, a runner dropped out and rode a bus to a wooded area near the finish line. Then, he re-entered the race and claimed third prize. When officials questioned him, he stated that he stopped running because he was tired.

Many of us can relate to the exhaustion of a worn-out athlete as we run the race of the Christian faith. The book of Hebrews encourages us to "run with endurance the race that is set before us" (12:1). Running with endurance requires that we lay aside the sin that stands in our way and shed the weights that hold us back. We may even have to press on through persecution (2 Tim. 3:12).

To prevent weariness and discouragement in our souls (Heb. 12:3), the Bible urges us to focus on Christ. When we pay more attention to Him than to our struggles, we will notice Him running alongside us—supporting us when we stumble (2 Cor. 12:9) and encouraging us with His example (1 Peter 2:21-24). Keeping our eyes on "the author and finisher of our faith" (Heb. 12:2) will help us stay close to the source of our strength and remain faithful to the finish. —Jennifer Benson Schuldt

Turn your eyes upon Jesus,
Look full in His wonderful face;
And the things of earth will grow strangely dim
In the light of His glory and grace. —*Lemmel*

We can finish strong when we focus on Christ.

April 25
Saturday

TOUGH TO LOVE

READ:
Acts 13:13-23

Now for a time of about forty years [God] put up with their ways in the wilderness.
—Acts 13:18

THE BIBLE IN ONE YEAR:
■ 2 Samuel 21–22
■ Luke 18:24-43

Years ago I was a camp counselor for some rebellious boys. I found it challenging to deal with their behavior. They would mistreat the animals at the petting zoo and occasionally fight among themselves. So I adopted a calm and firm approach to leading them. And although they often exasperated me, I always made sure their physical needs were taken care of.

Even though I had a kind and loving exterior, I often felt on the inside that I was just "putting up with them." That caused me to prayerfully reflect on how a loving heavenly Father provides for His rebellious children. In telling the story of the Israelites during the exodus, Paul said, "For a time of about forty years [God] put up with their ways in the wilderness" (Acts 13:18). In Greek "put up with" most likely means to patiently provide for people's needs despite an ungrateful response.

Some people may not react favorably to our efforts to show care and concern. When this happens, it may help to remember that God is patient with us. And He has given us His Spirit to help us respond with love to those who are hard to love or who are ungrateful (Gal. 5:22-23).

Give us Your patience, Lord, for anyone in our lives who is difficult to love. —Dennis Fisher

I want the love that sweetly bears
Whate'er my Father's hand may choose to send;
I want the love that patiently endures
The wrongs that come from enemy or friend. —Anon.

Be as patient with others as God has been with you.

April 26
Sunday

THE BEST SEASON YET

READ:
Ephesians 5:15-21

See then that you walk circumspectly, . . . redeeming the time, because the days are evil.
—Ephesians 5:15-16

THE BIBLE IN ONE YEAR:
- 2 Samuel 23–24
- Luke 19:1-27

Life is a lot like the weather . . . it's seasonal. It has a way of pushing us into the next season whether we like it or not. And when pushed into the next season, we are often uncertain and even fearful of what it might hold for us.

This is especially true of later seasons of life, when we are haunted by thoughts such as: *Will I be left all alone? Will my health hold up? Will my money last? Will my mind stay fresh?* As with every season of life, we have to make a choice—to waste the season in fearful thoughts or, as Paul says, make "the best use of the time, because the days are evil" (Eph. 5:16 ESV).

Regardless of your season, you can count on God's faithfulness. He says, " 'I will never leave you nor forsake you.' So we may boldly say: 'The LORD is my helper; I will not fear' " (Heb. 13:5-6).

Because you have God's presence and provision, you can make the most of your time in *every* season by following Jesus closely, spending time in His Word and prayer, loving and forgiving more freely than ever before, and serving others with joy and generosity.

God has blessed us with our present season—make the most of it! —Joe Stowell

Lord, give me the grace to accept life right where it has put me, and help me to overcome the fear that would waste my days. Give me the wisdom and desire to make every day count for You.

Life matters—make the most of it!

April 27
Monday

Calling You

Read:
1 Samuel 3:1-10

The Lord called yet again, "Samuel!" —1 Samuel 3:6

The Bible In One Year:
- **1 Kings 1–2**
- **Luke 19:28-48**

A couple of co-workers and I had just gone through airport security and were walking to our gate when I heard my name: "Paging Anne Cetas. Paging Anne Cetas." It's not a common name, so we knew it had to be mine. I assumed I had absent-mindedly left something at the check-in point. I checked with an airline agent, who told me to pick up a red phone, give my name, and ask why I was being paged. I searched for a phone and called, but the operator said, "No, we didn't page you." I said, "It was definitely my name." He replied twice, "No, we did *not* page you." I never did find out why I had been called that day.

A young boy named Samuel heard his name being "paged" long ago (1 Sam. 3:4). The Scriptures say that he "did not yet know the Lord, nor was the word of the Lord yet revealed to him" (v.7), so the temple priest Eli had to help him understand who was calling him (vv.8-9). God then revealed His plan for Samuel's life.

The Lord has a plan for us as well, and He calls to our hearts: "Come to Me, all you who labor and are heavy laden, and I will give you rest" (Matt. 11:28). That's His call to us to receive the gift of His salvation, rest, and peace.

The Savior is calling us to come to Him. —Anne Cetas

Jesus calls me—I must follow,
Follow Him today;
When His tender voice is pleading,
How can I delay? —*Brown*

Christ calls the restless ones to find their rest in Him.

April 28
Tuesday

TERRIFYING MOMENTS

READ:
Psalm 23

Yea, though I walk through the valley of the shadow of death, I will fear no evil; for You are with me; Your rod and Your staff, they comfort me. —Psalm 23:4

THE BIBLE IN ONE YEAR:
- 1 Kings 3–5
- Luke 20:1-26

When our first child was born, my wife, Marlene, was in labor for more than 30 hours, creating tremendous stress for both her and thc baby. The doctor, a fill-in for her regular physician, was unfamiliar with her and her pregnancy. As a result, he waited too long to make the decision to perform an emergency Caesarean section, and the resulting trauma put our infant son in the neo-natal intensive care unit. There was nothing they could do to help our baby to overcome his trauma-induced condition.

By God's grace, Matt recovered—but I cannot remember any moment in my life as terrifying as when I stood by his crib in intensive care. Yet I knew the Lord was near as I talked with Him through prayer.

In the terrifying moments of life (and all the other moments as well) nothing can bring comfort to the hurting heart like the reality of God's presence and care. The psalmist David wrote, "Yea, though I walk through the valley of the shadow of death, I will fear no evil; for You are with me; Your rod and Your staff, they comfort me" (Ps. 23:4).

When fear is overwhelming, the Lord is there. His comforting presence will carry us through our deepest trials.
—Bill Crowder

When peace, like a river, attendeth my way,
When sorrows like sea billows roll—
Whatever my lot, Thou has taught me to say,
"It is well, it is well with my soul." —*Spafford*

Peace is the presence of God.

April 29
Wednesday

Overcoming Bad News

Read:
Psalm 4

Lord, lift up the light of Your countenance upon us. —Psalm 4:6

The Bible In One Year:
- 1 Kings 6–7
- Luke 20:27-47

There are many who say, 'Who will show us any good?' " (Ps. 4:6). These words of David seem to describe the pessimistic outlook we so easily develop in our world today. The front page of newspapers and the top stories on the Internet or television seem to focus on crime, accidents, politics, the economy, and prominent people behaving badly. Our conversations at work and home begin to dwell on difficulties, and it's enough to discourage anyone. Where can we turn for better news?

In the midst of his troubles, David turned to the Lord, who relieved his distress (v.1) and heard his prayer (v.3). Instead of hoping for temporary good from altered circumstances, he found unceasing encouragement in God. "Lord, lift up the light of Your countenance upon us" (v.6). The result was a gladness of heart that surpassed any earthly prosperity or success (v.7).

Throughout David's life, before and after he became king of Israel, he was never without opposition. But at the end of the day, he could say, "I will both lie down in peace, and sleep; for You alone, O Lord, make me dwell in safety" (v.8).

Pondering the truths in Psalm 4 about God's care for us is a good way to begin and end every day. —David McCasland

In His care confiding
I will sweetly sleep,
For the Lord my Savior
Will in safety keep. —*Psalter*

God is a safe dwelling place in life's storms.

April 30
Thursday

Fantastic Offers

Read:
1 Peter 1:3-9

[God's] abundant mercy has begotten us again to a living hope through the resurrection of Jesus. —1 Peter 1:3

The Bible In One Year:
- 1 Kings 8–9
- Luke 21:1-19

I am amazed at the unbelievable offers that flood my e-mail box every day. Recently, I added up the offers of free money that came to me in a week, and my "take" totaled $26 million. But each of those offers was a fraud. Every one—from a $1 million prize to a $7 million offer—was nothing but a lie sent by unscrupulous people to squeeze money from me.

We're all vulnerable to fantastic offers—to scams that in reality pay off with nothing but trouble. We are offered false hope that ends in dashed dreams.

There is one offer, however, that is genuine, though fantastic beyond belief. It's the offer God makes to us—salvation through faith in Jesus' finished work on the cross: "Believe on the Lord Jesus Christ, and you will be saved" (Acts 16:31). It is an offer that cost Him greatly—and we get the benefits. The book of Romans tells us, "He was delivered over to death for our sins and was raised to life for our justification" (4:25 NIV).

By saying yes to salvation, we can have hope (Titus 1:2), peace (Rom. 5:1), forgiveness (Eph. 1:7), incomparable riches (2:7), and redemption (4:30). This is the real deal. Jesus' death and resurrection guarantees it. —Dave Branon

Amazing love! How can it be
That Thou, my God, shouldst die for me?
Amazing love! How can it be
That Thou, my God, shouldst die for me? —*Wesley*

Our salvation was infinitely costly to God, but it is absolutely free to us.

May 1
Friday

All That Is Precious

Read:
1 Peter 2:1-10

Coming to Him as to a living stone, rejected indeed by men, but chosen by God and precious. —1 Peter 2:4

The Bible In One Year:
- **1 Kings 10–11**
- **Luke 21:20-38**

Throughout my life, I've accumulated a lot of stuff. I have boxes of things that at one time were important but over time have lost their intrigue. And, as an unrepentant collector, I've realized that the thrill is in searching for and acquiring a new piece to add to the collection. Then my attention turns toward the hunt for the next item.

While we pile up many things that are important to us, very little of it is really precious. In fact, over time I have learned that the most precious things in life are not material items at all. Rather, it's the people who have loved me and built into my life who are precious. When I find my heart saying, "I don't know what I'd do without them," I know that they are indeed precious to me.

So when Peter refers to Jesus as "a chief cornerstone, elect, precious" (1 Peter 2:6), it should resonate in our hearts that He is truly precious—our prized possession above everything and everyone else. Where would we be today without the constant unfailing companionship of His faithful presence, wise and perfect guidance, merciful patience, comfort, and transforming reproof? What would we do without Him? I can't even imagine! —Joe Stowell

Lord, help us not to focus on fleeting treasures but on You, our most precious treasure. Teach us the joy of reveling in You and Your loving presence and provision in our lives.

**Of all that is precious,
Jesus tops the list.**

May 2
Saturday

A Plea For Prayer

Read:
2 Thessalonians 3:1-5

Brethren, pray for us.
—2 Thessalonians 3:1

The Bible In One Year:
■ **1 Kings 12–13**
■ **Luke 22:1-20**

A missionary recently visited the Bible study I was attending. She described what it had been like to pack up her household, part with friends, and relocate to a distant country. When she and her family arrived, they were greeted with a flourishing drug-trade and hazardous roadways. The language barrier brought on bouts of loneliness. They contracted four different stomach viruses. And her oldest daughter narrowly escaped death after falling through a railing on an unsafe stairwell. They needed prayer.

The apostle Paul experienced danger and hardship as a missionary. He was imprisoned, shipwrecked, and beaten. It's no surprise that his letters contained pleas for prayer. He asked the believers in Thessalonica to pray for success in spreading the gospel—that God's Word would "run swiftly and be glorified" (2 Thess. 3:1) and that God would deliver him from "unreasonable and wicked men" (v.2). Paul knew he would need to "open [his] mouth boldly" and declare the gospel (Eph. 6:19), which was yet another prayer request.

Do you know people who need supernatural help as they spread the good news of Christ? Remember Paul's appeal, "Brethren, pray for us" (2 Thess. 3:1), and intercede for them before the throne of our powerful God. —Jennifer Benson Schuldt

Commit to pray and intercede—
The battle's strong and great's the need;
And this one truth can't be ignored:
Our only help comes from the Lord. —*Sper*

Intercede for others in prayer;
God's throne is always accessible.

May 3
Sunday

MOMMA'S RULES

READ:
Ephesians 4:17-32

Put off, concerning your former conduct, the old man which grows corrupt.
—Ephesians 4:22

THE BIBLE IN ONE YEAR:
■ 1 Kings 14–15
■ Luke 22:21-46

I met a delightful woman named "Momma Charlie," who has raised a dozen or so foster kids. These youngsters were assigned to her by the courts, and she gave them a home with stability, guidance, and love. She told me that every time a new child arrived, the first order of business was to explain "Momma's Rules." These included behavioral standards, plus chores that would provide much-needed help in the busy household while teaching accountability to kids with little previous training.

Some of the children may have balked at "Momma's Rules," thinking they were robbing them of fun or pleasure—yet nothing would be further from the truth. Those standards allowed for an orderly household where both Momma and the children could find life enjoyable and peaceful.

Similarly, some look at the standards God set forth in the Bible as obstacles that prevent us from enjoying life. However, the boundaries God places actually protect us from our worst inclinations and foster healthy responses to Him.

In Ephesians 4, for example, Paul provides some guidance for how we are to live. As we live by these and other loving instructions from God, we find protection and the opportunity for true, lasting joy. —Bill Crowder

Father, thank You for the boundaries of life that protect us from sin and from ourselves. Give us the wisdom and grace to respond gratefully to Your Word in areas of danger and temptation.

God's Word is the compass that keeps us on course.

May 4
Monday

Songs Born Out Of Struggle

Read:
Psalm 31:9-20

Have mercy on me, O Lord . . . ; my eye wastes away with grief, yes, my soul and my body! —Psalm 31:9

The Bible In One Year:
- **1 Kings 16–18**
- **Luke 22:47-71**

In a documentary film about three legendary guitarists, Jack White described the first essential for writing a song: "If you don't have a struggle already inside of you or around you, you have to make one up."

The songs that mean the most to us give expression to our deepest feelings. Many of the Psalms, often called "the Bible's songbook," were born out of struggle. They capture our disappointments and fears, yet they always point us toward the faithful love of God.

In Psalm 31, David wrote: "Have mercy on me, O Lord, for I am in trouble; my eye wastes away with grief, yes, my soul and my body!" (v.9). He speaks of a trap set for him (v.4), his own sin (v.10), abandonment by friends (vv.11-12), and plots against his life (v.13).

Yet, David's hope was not in his own strength, but in God. "I trust in You, O Lord; I say, 'You are my God.' My times are in Your hand; deliver me from the hand of my enemies, and from those who persecute me" (vv.14-15).

The Psalms invite us to pour out our hearts to God, because He has stored up His goodness for those who trust in Him (v.19). —David McCasland

God gives to His servants this promise:
You'll not have to face life alone;
For when you grow weak in your struggle,
His strength will prevail—not your own. —*Hess*

When in your deepest need,
find God's comfort in the Psalms.

May 5
Tuesday

Digesting The Word

Read:
Jeremiah 15:15-21

Your Word was to me the joy and rejoicing of my heart. —Jeremiah 15:16

The Bible In One Year:
- 1 Kings 19–20
- Luke 23:1-25

King James is famous for the Bible translation that bears his name. Around the same time as the printing of the Bible, he also made revisions to *The Book of Common Prayer.* Still used today, this guide to intercession and worship contains a marvelous prayer for internalizing the Bible: "Blessed Lord, who hast caused all holy Scriptures to be written for our learning; grant that we may . . . hear them, read, mark, learn, and inwardly digest them, that by patience, and comfort of [Your] holy Word, we may embrace and ever hold fast the blessed hope of everlasting life."

Many centuries earlier, Jeremiah the prophet expressed a similar way of letting the Scriptures nourish our hearts: "Your words were found, and I ate them; and Your Word was to me the joy and rejoicing of my heart: for I am called by Your name, O Lord God of hosts" (Jer. 15:16). We internalize the Word as we "read, mark, learn, and inwardly digest" a passage of Scripture through prayerful meditation.

Ask the Lord to help you apply the Bible to your heart today. Take time to ponder the meat and milk of the Word (Heb. 5:12). As you quiet your heart, God will teach you about Himself through His Book. —Dennis Fisher

Lord, I meditate on Your precepts and contemplate
Your ways. I delight myself in Your statutes; I
will not forget Your Word. Open my eyes that
I may see wondrous things from Your law.

Some books are to be tasted, others to be swallowed, and some few to be chewed and digested. —Bacon

May 6
Wednesday

Always Preparing

Read:
2 Timothy 2:19-26

If anyone cleanses himself from [dishonor], he will be a vessel for honor, . . . prepared for every good work.
—2 Timothy 2:21

The Bible In One Year:
- 1 Kings 21–22
- Luke 23:26-56

While my son was home for an extended visit, he knocked on my office door one morning and asked me what I was doing. "I'm preparing for Sunday school," I told him. Then, thinking about all the time I spend in my office, I said, "It seems like I'm always preparing for something."

I'm grateful for the opportunities God gives me to reach out to others. There's some stress, though, when you're always getting something ready for somebody. It's hard to balance priorities with the pressure to prepare a lesson, a message, or a document continually on your mind.

This idea of constant preparation intrigued me, so I checked the Bible to see if it talks about the subject. I found that we are called to always be preparing. A heart dedicated to God must be prepared to serve Him (1 Sam. 7:3). We are to be ready to do good works (2 Tim. 2:21) and to defend scriptural truth (1 Peter 3:15). And Paul reminds us that even our giving takes planning (2 Cor. 9:5).

That's just a start. Living a life that pleases the Lord takes mental, spiritual, and physical preparation. But we don't need to stress, because He will enable us with His power. Let's ask God to guide us as we prepare to serve, honor, and tell others about Him. —Dave Branon

Savior, like a shepherd lead us,
Much we need Thy tender care;
In Thy pleasant pastures feed us,
For our use Thy folds prepare. —*Thrupp*

The best preparation for tomorrow is the right use of today.

May 7
Thursday

We Can Trust Him

Read:
Matthew 10:32-38

Bless those who curse you, do good to those who hate you, and pray for those who . . . persecute you.
—Matthew 5:44

The Bible In One Year:
- 2 Kings 1–3
- Luke 24:1-35

I know very little about persecution. My physical well-being has never been threatened because of what I believe or what I say. What little I "know" about the subject comes from what I hear and read. But that is not true for many of our brothers and sisters around the world. Some of them live in danger every day simply because they love Jesus and want others to know Him too.

There is another form of persecution that may not be life-threatening, but it is heartbreaking. It's the persecution that comes from non-Christian family members. When loved ones ridicule our faith and mock us for what we believe and how we express our love for God, we feel rejected and unloved.

Paul warned believers that following Jesus would result in persecution: "All who desire to live godly in Christ Jesus will suffer persecution" (2 Tim. 3:12), and we know that sometimes rejection will come from those we love (Matt. 10:34-36). But when people we love reject the God we love, the rejection feels personal.

Jesus told us to pray for those who persecute us (Matt. 5:44), and that includes more than strangers who hate us. God is able to give us grace to persevere through persecution even when it comes from those we love. —Julie Ackerman Link

Lord, give us grace to pray for those
Who seek our harm and not our good;
And teach us how to show them love
In ways that will be understood. —Sper

People may mock our message but they can't stop our prayers.

May 8
Friday

Golden Eagle

Read:
Psalm 145:1-7

I will meditate . . . on Your wondrous works. —Psalm 145:5

The Bible In One Year:
- **2 Kings 4–6**
- **Luke 24:36-53**

My son Mark and I were leaving the Clyde Peterson Ranch in Wyoming to head back to Michigan. In the distance we spotted a huge bird sitting in a solitary tree overlooking a steep canyon. As we approached, the golden eagle leaped from the tree and soared out over the canyon, the golden streaks in its feathers shimmering in the morning sun. Its immense size and beauty filled us with wonder. We felt privileged to witness this magnificent demonstration of God's awesome creativity.

Creation displays God's "wondrous works" (Ps. 145:5). And when we stop to meditate on those works, we can't help but be awed as our minds and spirits are moved to reflect on the character of the God who created them.

That golden eagle told my son and me a story of the creative genius of our mighty God. So does the flitting songbird, the doe with her playful fawn, the pounding surf, and delicate little flowers such as bachelor's-button and spring beauty. In the most unexpected moments and out-of-the-way places the Lord shines His glory in this world in order to reveal Himself to us. Those serendipitous moments are opportunities to "meditate . . . on [His] wondrous works" (v.5). —Dave Egner

This is my Father's world,
I rest me in the thought
Of rocks and trees, of skies and seas—
His hand the wonders wrought. —*Babcock*

Always be on the lookout for wonder. —E. B. White

May 9
Saturday

"Don't Worry, Dad!"

Read:
Exodus 14:19-25

The glory of the Lord shall be your rear guard. —Isaiah 58:8

The Bible In One Year:
- **2 Kings 7–9**
- **John 1:1-28**

Last summer, my husband and I hosted a concert and fundraiser for childhood cancer research. We planned to have the event in our backyard, but weather forecasts were dismal. A few hours before the event, we began calling our 100+ guests to inform them of a change in venue. As our friends and family began feverishly toting food, decorations, and equipment from our house to our church gym, our daughter Rosie took a moment to give her dad a hug and remind him on behalf of the kids and grandkids that they were there for him: "Don't worry, Dad! We've got your back."

Hearing that expression is comforting because it reminds us that we're not on our own. Someone is saying, "I'm here. I'll take care of whatever you might miss. I'll be a second set of eyes and hands for you."

As the Israelites were escaping a life of slavery, Pharaoh sent his army of chariots and horsemen to give chase (Ex. 14:17). But "the Angel of God . . . and the pillar of cloud went from before them and stood behind them" (v.19). In this way, God hid and protected them throughout the night. The next day, He parted the Red Sea so they could safely cross over.

God tells us "Don't worry" as well. "If God is for us, who can be against us?" (Rom. 8:31). —Cindy Hess Kasper

God's hand that holds the ocean's depths
Can hold my small affairs;
His hand that guides the universe
Can carry all my cares. —Anon.

Our work is to cast care; God's work is to take care!

May 10
Sunday

Seasons Of Life

Read:
Luke 2:6-7,25-35

To everything there is a season, a time for every purpose under heaven.
—Ecclesiastes 3:1

The Bible In One Year:
- **2 Kings 10–12**
- **John 1:29-51**

When I was a pastor, I served many women who were moms. I called on them in the hospital and rejoiced with them for their precious babies who had come into the world. I counseled with anxious mothers and tried to assure them that God was watching over their rebellious teenagers. I stood with mothers at the bedside of injured or ill children and felt their pain. And I cried with them in their grief when their son or daughter died.

Mary, the mother of Jesus, also experienced times of joy and sorrow. What joy she must have felt when the Christ-child was born! (Luke 2:7). What excitement when the shepherds and later the wise men came to worship Him (vv.8-20; Matt. 2:1-12). What uneasiness when Simeon prophesied that a sword would pierce her soul (Luke 2:35). And what heart-wrenching grief as Mary watched her Son dying on the cross! (John 19:25-30). But her seasons of being a mother didn't end with that terrible scene. She rejoiced that He rose from the grave.

Mothers, and all of us for that matter, experience many great joys and intense sorrows. But when we submit our lives to the Lord, every season of life can serve His eternal purposes. —Herb Vander Lugt

Thank You, Lord, for motherhood
With all its vale of tears,
For happy moments never dimmed
Through all the many years. —*Strecker*

Being a mom is a sacred partnership with God.

May 11
Monday

Yesterday, Today, And Tomorrow

Read:
Joshua 4:1-6,20-24

That all the peoples of the earth may know the hand of the Lord, that it is mighty. —Joshua 4:24

The Bible In One Year:
■ 2 Kings 13–14
■ John 2

Recently I realized that all of the photos and mementos in my office represent the past. I considered removing them, but wondered if those reminders of people, places, and events might serve some purpose beyond nostalgia. To avoid being mired in the "yesterdays" of life, I needed to discover the value of those items for today and tomorrow.

When God's people crossed the Jordan River into the Promised Land, He told their leader, Joshua, to choose 12 men, have each one take a stone from the middle of the river, and carry it to their campsite that night (Josh. 4:1-5). Joshua set up the stones as a memorial so that when future generations asked, "What do these stones mean to you?" they could tell them about God's faithfulness in holding back the water while they crossed (vv.6-7).

As followers of Christ, it's good for us to have tangible evidence of God's help in the past. Those mementos remind us that His faithfulness continues today, and we can follow Him confidently into the future. Our "stones" may also help others know that God's hand is mighty, as they encourage us to fear the Lord our God forever (v.24).

The memories of what God has done for us can become building blocks for today and tomorrow. —David McCasland

Thinking It Over

How has God shown Himself to be faithful to you and your family? What would help you to remember? Is there someone you can talk to about it today?

Precious memories of yesterday can strengthen our faith today and tomorrow.

May 12
Tuesday

Waiting To Cheer

Read:
Ephesians 3:14-21

. . . to know the love of Christ which passes knowledge; that you may be filled with all the fullness of God.
—Ephesians 3:19

The Bible In One Year:
- **2 Kings 15–16**
- **John 3:1-18**

In his very first Little League baseball game, a young player on the team I was coaching got hit in the face with a ball. He was not hurt but was understandably shaken. For the rest of the season, he was afraid of the ball. Game after game, he bravely tried, but he just couldn't seem to hit the ball.

In our final game, we were hopelessly behind, with nothing to cheer about. Then that young man stepped up to take his turn. Thwack! To everyone's surprise, he hit the ball sharply! His teammates went wild; his parents and his teammates' parents cheered loudly. Even though we were still losing the game, I was jumping up and down! We all loved this kid and cheered him on.

I imagine that the Lord cheers us on in our lives as well. He loves us deeply and desires that we "may be able to comprehend . . . what is the width and length and depth and height—to know the love of Christ which passes knowledge" (Eph. 3:18-19).

Some think of the Lord as unloving and waiting for us to slip up so He can punish us. So we have the privilege of telling them of His deep love for them. Imagine their joy when they hear about the God who loves them so much that He sent His only Son to die on the cross for their sin and who wants to cheer them on! —Randy Kilgore

Help us, heavenly Father, to see the many
ways You love and encourage us; then help
us to love and encourage those around
us so that they can see You in us.

The nail-pierced hands of Jesus reveal the love-filled heart of God.

May 13
Wednesday

Tulip Day

Read:
Matthew 6:25-34

**Consider the lilies of the field . . . ; and yet I say to you that even Solomon in all his glory was not arrayed like one of these.
—Matthew 6:28-29**

The Bible In One Year:
- 2 Kings 17–18
- John 3:19-36

Several countries around the world celebrate Tulip Day to welcome the spring. When I think of tulips, I often think of the Netherlands, but commercial cultivation of the flower began in the Middle East. Today these colorful flowers span the globe. An estimated 109 species of tulips now grace parks, thoroughfares, and home gardens all around the world.

Last fall I planted some tulip bulbs. Several months later, they bloomed with vivid colors, announcing the coming of spring. They reminded me that summer was on the way and with it will come even more flowers to delight the eye.

Flowers are wonderful reminders to me of the grace of God in our lives. Our Lord used lilies of the field to remind us of the provision of our heavenly Father. In His great Sermon on the Mount, Jesus said, "Consider the lilies of the field . . . ; and yet I say to you that even Solomon in all his glory was not arrayed like one of these. . . . Will He not much more clothe you, O you of little faith?" (Matt. 6:28-30).

Tulips alert us to the end of winter and the beginning of spring. But like the lilies of the field, they can also remind us of the One upon whom we can depend to provide food, clothing, and shelter. —Dennis Fisher

In trees and flowers of the field,
In creatures large and small,
We trace the watchful care of Him
Who planned and made them all. —*King*

**If Jesus is concerned about flowers and birds,
He certainly cares about you and me.**

May 14
Thursday

BECOMING

READ:
Luke 2:41-52

Jesus increased in wisdom and stature, and in favor with God and men. —Luke 2:52

THE BIBLE IN ONE YEAR:
- 2 Kings 19–21
- John 4:1-30

I grew up in a small town. No famous people. No busy streets. Not much to do. Yet I've always been thankful for my quiet, uncomplicated upbringing.

One evening when my husband and I were attending a business dinner, a new acquaintance asked me where I was from. When I told her, she said, "Aren't you embarrassed to admit it?" Unsure whether or not she was joking, I simply said, "No."

Although my town was sometimes belittled for its lack of sophistication, it was not lacking in things that matter. My family was part of a church community in which parents brought up children "in the training and admonition of the Lord" (Eph. 6:4).

Jesus also grew up in a small town: Nazareth. A man named Nathanael asked, "Can anything good come out of Nazareth?" (John 1:46). Jesus proved that the answer is yes. Even though He grew up in an insignificant place, He was the most significant person in all of history.

Experience taught me and Scripture confirms that what matters is not *where* you grow up but *how* you grow up. Sometimes we feel insignificant compared to sophisticated people from prominent places. But we are significant to God, and He can make us strong in spirit and filled with His wisdom. —Julie Ackerman Link

O teach me what it cost You, Lord,
To make a sinner whole;
And help me understand anew
The value of one soul! —Anon.

What we become is more important than where we're from.

May 15
Friday

No Loose Laces

Read:
Joshua 7:1-12

The children of Israel committed a trespass regarding the accursed things, for Achan . . . took of the accursed things. —Joshua 7:1

The Bible in One Year:
- **2 Kings 22–23**
- **John 4:31-54**

One person's actions can affect an entire group. This truth became clear to journalist Sebastian Junger as he followed a platoon of soldiers. Junger watched a soldier accost another soldier whose bootlaces were trailing on the ground. He didn't confront him out of concern for his fashion. He confronted him because his loose laces put the entire platoon at risk—he couldn't be counted on not to trip and fall at a crucial moment. Junger realized that what happens to one happens to everyone.

Achan's "bootlaces were loose," and we learn from his story that sin is never private. After the great victory at Jericho, God gave Joshua specific instructions on how to deal with the city and its loot (Josh. 6:18). The people were to "abstain from the accursed things" and to put all the silver and gold "into the treasury of the Lord" (vv.18-19). But they disobeyed his command to them (7:1). The interesting thing is, not all of Israel sinned; only one person did—Achan. But because of his actions, everyone was affected and God was dishonored.

As followers of Jesus, we belong to one another and our individual actions can impact the entire body and God's name. Let's "tie up our laces" so that we may individually and together give God the honor He deserves. —Marvin Williams

Lord, we know our sin is never private, though we may try to hide it. Help us to remember that we belong to You and to one another and that what we do individually grieves You and impacts fellow Christians.

Private sins will inevitably have public impact.

May 16
Saturday

I'M SORRY, MAN

READ:
Matthew 5:21-26

Be reconciled to your brother.
—Matthew 5:24

THE BIBLE IN ONE YEAR:
■ 2 Kings 24–25
■ John 5:1-24

When my son-in-law Ewing and I attended a sporting event, we enjoyed watching both the game and the people around us.

One of those people showed both the bad and good side of humanity. This man had apparently lost track of his seat. As he was looking for it, he stood squarely between us and the field. A man sitting in front of us also had his view blocked, so he told the guy, "Could you move? We can't see."

The lost man responded sarcastically, "Too bad." A second request got a similar but more heated response. Finally the man moved on. Later came a surprise. He returned and told the man he had blocked, "Hey, I'm sorry, man. I was upset that I couldn't find my seat." They shook hands and the incident ended well.

That interaction made me think. As we go through life striving to find our way, situations may frustrate us and cause us to respond to others in an un-Christlike way. If so, we must ask God to give us the courage to apologize to those we have offended. Our worship, according to Jesus, depends on it (Matt. 5:23-24).

We honor God when we make reconciliation with others a priority. After we have been reconciled, we can then fully enjoy communion with our heavenly Father. —Dave Branon

It's not easy, Lord, to swallow our pride and ask
others to forgive us. But You want us to seek
reconciliation before worship can take place.
Help us to seek forgiveness when necessary.

Confession of sin is the soil in which forgiveness flourishes.

May 17
Sunday

God's Strong Arm

Read:
Exodus 6:1-8

I will redeem you with an outstretched arm.
—Exodus 6:6

The Bible In One Year:
- 1 Chronicles 1–3
- John 5:25-47

My friend Joann had a strong desire to become a concert pianist and to travel and perform as either a soloist or as a piano accompanist. While majoring in piano performance in college, she developed tendinitis in her right arm, and it became too weak to perform the solo recital that was required. She graduated with a degree in music history and literature instead.

She knew Jesus as her Savior, but she had been rebelling against Him for several years. Then through further difficult circumstances, she sensed the Lord reaching out to her, and she turned back to Him. Eventually her arm grew stronger, and her dream of traveling and performing came about. She says, "Now I could play to God's glory instead of my own. His outstretched arm restored my spiritual life and the strength in my arm to enable me to serve Him with the gift He gave me."

The Lord promised Moses that His outstretched arm would rescue the Israelites from bondage in Egypt (Ex. 6:6). He kept that promise even though His often-rebellious people doubted (14:30-31). God's mighty arm is outstretched for us as well. No matter the outcome of our situation, He can be trusted to bring about His will for each of His children. We can depend on God's strong arm. —Anne Cetas

What a fellowship, what a joy divine,
Leaning on the everlasting arms;
O how bright the path grows from day to day,
Leaning on the everlasting arms. —*Hoffman*

With God's strength behind you and His arms beneath you, you can face whatever lies ahead of you.

May 18
Monday

A Sure Salvation

Read:
Romans 10:8-15

If you confess with your mouth the Lord Jesus and believe in your heart that God has raised Him from the dead, you will be saved. —Romans 10:9

The Bible In One Year:
■ 1 Chronicles 4–6
■ John 6:1-21

A story is told that Queen Victoria of the UK was deeply moved during a church service. Afterward, she asked her chaplain, "Can one be absolutely sure in this life of eternal safety?" He did not have an answer. But an evangelist named John Townsend heard about the Queen's question, and after much prayer he sent her a note: "With trembling hands, but heartfelt love, and because I know that we can be absolutely sure now of our eternal life in the Home that Jesus went to prepare, may I ask your Most Gracious Majesty to read the following passages of Scripture: John 3:16; Romans 10:9-10?"

Two weeks later, the evangelist received this letter: ". . . I have carefully and prayerfully read the portions of Scripture referred to. I believe in the finished work of Christ for me, and trust by God's grace to meet you in that Home of which He said, 'I go to prepare a place for you.' —Victoria Guelph"

Townsend was confident that in this life we can have assurance of eternal safety (v.9), and he had a concern for others as well. Consider what John 3:16 and Romans 10:9-10 mean for your eternal destiny. God desires to give you the confidence that your sin is forgiven and that after death you'll be with Him forever. —Brent Hackett, RBC Canada Director

Blessed assurance, Jesus is mine!
Oh, what a foretaste of glory divine!
Heir of salvation, purchase of God,
Born of His Spirit, washed in His blood. —*Crosby*

Lives rooted in God's unchanging grace can never be uprooted.

May 19
Tuesday

To Be Continued

Read:
Acts 1:1-11

You shall be witnesses to Me in Jerusalem, and in all Judea and Samaria, and to the end of the earth.
—Acts 1:8

The Bible In One Year:
■ 1 Chronicles 7–9
■ John 6:22-44

The fifth book of the New Testament, the Acts of the Apostles, records the beginnings of the Christian church under the leadership of the people Jesus had appointed. Some scholars have suggested that this book could also be called the Acts of the Holy Spirit, because the Spirit's power supplied courage for the apostles in the face of every hardship.

Just before Jesus was taken up into heaven, He told the ones He had chosen: "You shall receive power when the Holy Spirit has come upon you; and you shall be witnesses to Me in Jerusalem, and in all Judea and Samaria, and to the end of the earth" (Acts 1:8). With those words, one chapter in the story of God's work on earth ended, and a new one began. We are a part of that ongoing story.

The book of Acts describes the faithful witness of Peter, John, Barnabas, Paul, Dorcas, Lydia, and many others during the early days of the church. These ordinary people depended on God to give them strength as they spread His Word and demonstrated His love.

That story continues through us. As we trust God and obey His direction to make Jesus known, He writes through us new pages in His story of redemption. —David McCasland

Gracious Spirit, use my words to help and heal.
Use my actions, bold and meek, to speak for You.
May You be pleased to reveal
Your life to others through mine.

People know true faith stories when they see them.

May 20
Wednesday

True Hospitality

Read:
Revelation 22:16-21

Let him who thirsts come. Whoever desires, let him take the water of life freely.
—Revelation 22:17

The Bible In One Year:
- **1 Chronicles 10–12**
- **John 6:45-71**

In 1987, our family moved to California to take up the pastorate of a church in the Long Beach area. The day we flew into town, my secretary picked us up at the airport to take us to our house. As we pulled into traffic, the very first thing I saw was a bumper sticker that read: "Welcome To California . . . Now Go Home!" It was not exactly a warm and cheery welcome to sunny southern California!

I wonder if there might be occasions in our lives when we send similar signals to people around us. Whether we are at church, in the neighborhood, or at social gatherings, are there times when we fail to make others feel welcome in our world?

In Romans 12:13, Paul instructed his readers to be "given to hospitality." The book of Hebrews goes even further, saying, "Do not forget to entertain strangers, for by so doing some have unwittingly entertained angels" (13:2). By showing gracious kindness to those who come our way, we echo the Savior's invitation for salvation, which declares, "Let him who hears say, 'Come!' And let him who thirsts come. Whoever desires, let him take the water of life freely" (Rev. 22:17).

To show someone loving hospitality just might be the first step in showing that person the way to heaven. —Bill Crowder

Give as 'twas given to you in your need;
Love as the Master loved you;
Be to the helpless a helper indeed;
Unto your mission be true. —*Wilson*

Live so that when people get to know you, they will want to get to know Christ.

May 21
Thursday

Not Abandoned

Read:
Isaiah 49:13-16

I will not forget you. See, I have inscribed you on the palms of My hands.
—Isaiah 49:15-16

The Bible In One Year:
- 1 Chronicles 13–15
- John 7:1-27

Years ago, while my husband and I were visiting the Smithsonian Air and Space Museum in Washington, DC, we noticed a baby stroller by itself with no one nearby. We assumed that the parents had left it there because it was too bulky and were now carrying their child. But as we approached, we saw a sleeping baby inside. Where was a parent . . . a sibling . . . a babysitter? We hung around for quite some time before hailing a museum official. No one had shown up to claim that precious child! The last we saw of him, he was being wheeled away to a safe place.

That experience made me think about what it's like to be abandoned. It's an overwhelming feeling that no one cares anything about you. It's a real and excruciatingly painful feeling. But even though people may abandon us, God's love and presence is assured. The Lord promises that He will never leave us (Deut. 31:8). He will be with us wherever we go, "always, even to the end of the age" (Matt. 28:20).

The Lord will never falter in His commitment to His children. Even if we have been abandoned by others, we can find confidence in His promise that nothing will ever "separate us from [His] love" (Rom. 8:35-39). —Cindy Hess Kasper

Father, thank You for Your never-failing presence
in every aspect of our lives. We count on Your
promise never to abandon us. Please teach us
to rest in that truth. In Jesus' name, amen.

Confidence in God's presence is our comfort.

May 22
Friday

A Missed Lunch

Read:
John 4:27-38

Jesus said to them, "My food is to do the will of Him who sent Me, and to finish His work."
—John 4:34

The Bible In One Year:
■ 1 Chronicles 16–18
■ John 7:28-53

For me, food is more than a necessity—it's a wonderfully enjoyable part of life! I enjoy sitting down to a well-prepared meal, especially when I'm feeling hungry. I imagine that the disciples were hungry for lunch when they returned to the well where Jesus was interacting with the Samaritan woman. They urged Him, "Rabbi, eat" (John 4:31). His response? "I have food to eat of which you do not know" (v.32), which made them wonder if someone had already brought Him something to eat (v.33).

I wonder if the disciples were so consumed with thinking about food that they couldn't see past their picnic. They didn't understand the significance of what was going on at the well. The most important thing to Jesus was "to do the will of Him who sent Me, and to finish His work" (v.34). He was focused on the spiritual needs of this woman who desperately needed what only He could give.

It's easy to become preoccupied with needs of the moment. But Jesus invites us to get beyond our own interests—our own little "lunch"—to open our eyes to the souls who are searching for answers to their deepest needs.

So, join Jesus at the well, and let Him use you to tell others about the spiritual food only He can give. —Joe Stowell

Dear Lord, may my eyes be fixed not just on the things
I am interested in, but lift my eyes to see the
needy souls around me. Give me passion for the lost
and the joy of seeing others satisfied in You.

Be hungry to satisfy the needs of others around you.

May 23
Saturday

Star Shepherd

Read:
Ezekiel 34:11-16

Why do you say, . . . "My way is hidden from the Lord"? —Isaiah 40:27

The Bible In One Year:
■ 1 Chronicles 19–21
■ John 8:1-27

In the spring, shepherds in Idaho move their flocks from the lowlands into the mountains. Thousands of sheep move up the passes into the high country to summer pasture.

My wife and I came across a flock on Shaw Mountain last week. It was bedded down in a meadow by a quiet stream—a picturesque scene that evoked memories of Psalm 23.

But where was the shepherd? The sheep appeared to be alone—until a few broke away from the flock and began to wander toward a distant gully. Then we heard a shrill whistle from above. Looking up, we saw the shepherd sitting high on a hill above the sheep, keeping watch over his flock. A mountain dog and two Border collies stood at his side. The dogs, responding to the shepherd's signal, bounded down the hill and herded the drifting sheep back to the flock where they belonged.

In the same way, the Good Shepherd is watching over you. Even though you cannot see Him, He can see you! He knows you by name and knows all about you. You are the sheep of His pasture (Ezek. 34:31). God promises that He will "seek out" His sheep, "feed them in good pasture," and "bind up the broken" (vv.12,14,16).

You can trust in God's watchful care. —David Roper

I trust in God, I know He cares for me
On mountain bleak or on the stormy sea;
Though billows roll, He keeps my soul,
My heavenly Father watches over me. —*Martin*

The Lamb who died to save us is the Shepherd who lives to care for us.

May 24
Sunday

Heavenly Country

Read:
Hebrews 11:8-16

Our citizenship is in heaven. —Philippians 3:20

The Bible In One Year:
■ 1 Chronicles 22–24
■ John 8:28-59

During high school, my closest friend and I took a pair of horses out for an afternoon ride. We slowly roamed through fields of wildflowers and wooded groves. But when we nosed the horses in the direction of the barn, they took off toward home like twin rockets. Our equine friends knew that it was time for dinner and a good brushing, and they could hardly wait.

As Christians, our true home is heaven (Phil. 3:20). Yet sometimes our desires tether us to the here and now. We enjoy God's good gifts—marriage, children, grandchildren, travel, careers, friends. At the same time, the Bible challenges us to focus on "things above" (Col. 3:1-2). Things above may include the unseen benefits of heaven: God's enduring presence (Rev. 22:3-5), unending rest (Heb. 4:9), and an everlasting inheritance (1 Peter 1:4).

Recently I read, "Believers desire the heavenly inheritance; and the stronger the faith is, the more fervent [the desire]." Several Old Testament believers mentioned in Hebrews 11 had strong faith in God that enabled them to embrace His promises before receiving them (v.13). One such promise was heaven. If we too put our faith in God, He will give us a desire for that "heavenly country" (v.16) and will loosen our grip on this world. —Jennifer Benson Schuldt

When we all get to heaven,
What a day of rejoicing that will be!
When we all see Jesus,
We'll sing and shout the victory. —*Hewitt*

For the Christian, heaven is spelled H-O-M-E.

May 25
Monday

TRUE SACRIFICE

READ:
Romans 5:1-11

Greater love has no one than this, than to lay down one's life for his friends.
—John 15:13

THE BIBLE IN ONE YEAR:
- 1 Chronicles 25–27
- John 9:1-23

Eric was one of the good guys. As a police officer, he saw his work as service to his community and was fully committed to serving at all costs. Evidence of this desire was seen on the door of Eric's locker at the police station, where he posted John 15:13.

In that verse, our Lord said, "Greater love has no one than this, than to lay down one's life for his friends." Those words, however, were not merely noble ideals. They expressed Eric's commitment to his duty as a police officer—a commitment that demanded the ultimate price when he was killed in the line of duty. It was a real-life display of the heart of true sacrifice.

Jesus Christ lived out the powerful words of John 15:13 within hours of stating them. The upper room event where Jesus spoke of such sacrifice was followed by communion with the Father at Gethsemane, a series of illegal trials, and then crucifixion before a mocking crowd.

As the Son of God, Jesus could have avoided the suffering, torture, and cruelty. He was utterly without sin and did not deserve to die. But love, the fuel that drives true sacrifice, drove Him to the cross. As a result, we can be forgiven if we will accept His sacrifice and resurrection by faith. Have you trusted the One who laid down His life for you? —Bill Crowder

'Twas not a martyr's death He died,
The Christ of Calvary;
It was a willing sacrifice
He made for you—for me. —Adams

Only Jesus, the perfect sacrifice, can declare guilty people perfect.

May 26
Tuesday

A Debtor

Read:
2 Corinthians 5:12-17

The love of Christ compels us.
—2 Corinthians 5:14

The Bible In One Year:
■ 1 Chronicles 28–29
■ John 9:24-41

As a young man, Robert Robinson (1735–1790) enjoyed getting into trouble with his friends, so the stories go. At age 17, though, he heard a sermon by George Whitefield from Matthew 3:7, and realized his need for salvation in Christ. The Lord changed Robinson's life, and he became a preacher. He also wrote several hymns, including his best-known "Come, Thou Fount of Every Blessing."

Lately I've been pondering God's amazing grace toward us and the last stanza of that hymn: "O to grace how great a debtor daily I'm constrained to be!" The hymn brings to mind the apostle Paul's words: "The love of Christ compels [or constrains] us . . . that those who live should live no longer for themselves, but for Him who died for them and rose again" (2 Cor. 5:14-15).

We can't earn God's love and grace. But because He has lavished it on us, how can we help but love Him in return by living for Him! I'm not exactly sure what that looks like, but it must include drawing near to Him, listening to His Word, serving Him, and obeying Him out of gratitude and love.

As debtors, we are called to live each day for Jesus who gave Himself for us. —Anne Cetas

Come, Thou Fount of every blessing,
Tune my heart to sing Thy grace;
Streams of mercy, never ceasing,
Call for songs of loudest praise. —*Robinson*

Those who know God's grace show God's grace.

May 27
Wednesday

Navigating The Storm

Read:
Psalm 107:23-32

He commands and raises the stormy wind, . . . and He brings them out of their distresses.
—Psalm 107:25,28

The Bible In One Year:
- **2 Chronicles 1–3**
- **John 10:1-23**

The
Axun
modern Eth
stormy winds
could be harness
navigation. Rather
high winds and rai
how to navigate their w
storm.

Psalm 107 provides a v
word picture of how God allows
to come our way, and then prov
help for us to navigate through then
"He commands and raises the stormy wind, . . . and He brings them out of their distresses" (Ps. 107:25,28).

Trusting God for guidance in troubled times is a biblical theme. Hebrews 11 lists many who used their problems as an opportunity to exercise faith and to experience God's grace, provision, and deliverance: "Who through faith subdued kingdoms, worked righteousness, obtained promises, stopped the mouths of lions, quenched the violence of fire, escaped the edge of the sword, [and] out of weakness were made strong" (vv.33-34).

Stormy circumstances are inevitable. Although our first reaction may be to run from the problem, we can instead ask God to teach us how to trust Him to navigate us through the storm. —Dennis Fisher

When life feels like a storm-tossed sea
With crashing waves of pain and grief,
Turn to the Lord and trust in Him,
He'll give you peace and bring relief. —*Sper*

Better to go through the storm with Christ than to have smooth sailing without Him.

May 29
Friday

Peace, Be Still

Read:
Mark 4:35-41

He arose and rebuked the wind, and said to the sea, "Peace, be still!" —Mark 4:39

The Bible In One Year:
- 2 Chronicles 7–9
- John 11:1-29

My friend Elouise has a wonderful way of putting life into clever perspectives. Once when I asked her, "How are you today?" I expected the usual "fine" response. Instead, she said, "I've got to wake Him up!" When I asked what she meant, she kiddingly exclaimed, "Don't you know your Bible?!" Then she explained: "When the disciples faced trouble, they ran to wake up Jesus. I'm going to run to Him too!"

What do we do when we are stuck in a troubling situation with nowhere to run? Maybe, like the disciples who were stuck in a life-threatening storm, we run to Jesus (Mark 4:35-41). Sometimes, however, we may try to bail ourselves out of trouble by seeking revenge, slandering the one who has caused our problem, or just cowering fearfully in the corner as we sink into despair.

We need to learn from the disciples who fled to Jesus as their only hope. He may not bail us out immediately, but remembering that He is in our boat makes a difference! Thankfully, He is always with us in the storms of life, saying things like "Peace, be still!" (v.39). So, look for Him in your storm and let Him fill you with the peace that comes from knowing He is near. —Joe Stowell

Lord, teach us to run to You in the midst of trouble.
Forgive us for trying to bail ourselves out, and lead
us to the peace of trusting Your wisdom and ultimate
deliverance. Thank You that You will help us!

Make Jesus your first option when the storms of life threaten you.

May 30
Saturday

The Tragic Flaw

Read:
2 Chronicles 26:3-15

His fame spread far and wide, for he was marvelously helped till he became strong.
—2 Chronicles 26:15

The Bible In One Year:
- 2 Chronicles 10–12
- John 11:30-57

In literature, a tragic flaw is a character trait that causes the downfall of a story's hero. That was true of Uzziah, who was crowned king of Judah at age 16. For many years, he sought the Lord; and while he did, God gave him great success (2 Chron. 26:4-5). But things changed when "his fame spread far and wide, for he was marvelously helped till he became strong. But when he was strong his heart was lifted up, to his destruction" (vv.15-16).

Uzziah entered the temple of the Lord to burn incense on the altar (v.16), openly defying God's decree. Perhaps pride convinced him that God's rules applied to everyone except him. When Uzziah raged against the priests who told him this was not right, the Lord struck him with leprosy (vv.18-20).

In literature and in life, how often we see a person of good reputation fall from honor into disgrace and suffering. "King Uzziah was a leper until the day of his death. He dwelt in an isolated house, . . . cut off from the house of the Lord" (v.21).

The only way we can prevent the nectar of praise from becoming the poison of pride is by following the Lord with a humble heart. —David McCasland

Humility's a slippery prize
That seldom can be won;
We're only humble in God's eyes
When serving like His Son. —*Gustafson*

The crucible for silver and the furnace for gold, but man is tested by the praise he receives. —Proverbs 27:21 NIV

May 31
Sunday

Fickle Followers

Read:
John 12:12-19; 19:14-16

Behold, your King is coming, sitting on a donkey's colt.
—John 12:15

The Bible In One Year:
- 2 Chronicles 13–14
- John 12:1-26

How quickly public opinion can change! When Jesus entered Jerusalem for the Passover feast, He was welcomed by crowds cheering to have Him made king (John 12:13). But by the end of the week, the crowds were demanding that He be crucified (19:15).

I recognize myself in those fickle crowds. I love cheering for a team that's winning, but my interest wanes when they start losing. I love being part of a movement that is new and exciting, but when the energy moves to a new part of town, I'm ready to move on. I love following Jesus when He is doing the impossible, but I slink away when He expects me to do something difficult. It's exciting to follow Jesus when I can do it as part of the "in" crowd. It's easy to trust Him when He outsmarts the smart people and outmaneuvers the people in power (see Matt. 12:10; 22:15-46). But when He begins to talk about suffering and sacrifice and death, I hesitate.

I like to think that I would have followed Jesus all the way to the cross—but I have my doubts. After all, if I don't speak up for Him in places where it's safe, what makes me think I would do so in a crowd of His opponents?

How thankful I am that Jesus died for fickle followers so that we can become devoted followers. —Julie Ackerman Link

For Further Thought

Read these Bible verses and ponder Jesus' love for you (Rom. 5:8; Rom. 8:37-39; Heb. 13:5-6,8; 1 John 3:1). Allow your devotion to Him to grow.

Christ deserves full-time followers.

June 1
Monday

I'M BORED

READ:
John 10:7-14

I have come that they may have life, and that they may have it more abundantly.
—John 10:10

THE BIBLE IN ONE YEAR:
■ 2 Chronicles 15–16
■ John 12:27-50

When our kids were teens, we repeatedly had the following discussion after their church youth group meeting: I asked, "How was youth group tonight?" And they responded, "It was boring." After several weeks of this, I decided to find out for myself. I slipped into the gym where their meeting was held, and I watched. I saw them participating, laughing, listening—having a great time. That night on the way home I asked about their evening and, once again, they said, "It was boring." I responded, "I was there. I watched. You had a great time!" They responded, "Maybe it wasn't as bad as usual."

I recognized that behind their reluctance to admit they were enjoying youth group were things such as peer pressure and a fear of not appearing "cool." But then I wondered, *Am I similarly afraid to get too excited about spiritual things?*

Indeed, there is nothing in this universe more worthy of our enthusiasm than who Christ is and what He did for us. Jesus said, "I have come that they may have life, and that they may have it more abundantly" (John 10:10). That's the opposite of boring! At any age, we have a gift from the Savior that is worth celebrating. Our salvation is something to get excited about! —Bill Crowder

Father, please fill my heart with the joy of Christ.
I desire that the abundant life I have found
in Him might contagiously reach
out to others around me.

If you know Christ, you always have a reason to celebrate.

June 2
Tuesday

Show And Tell

Read:
John 13:5-17

I have given you an example, that you should do as I have done to you.
—John 13:15

The Bible In One Year:
■ 2 Chronicles 17–18
■ John 13:1-20

If you take a course on writing or attend a writer's conference, you'll likely hear the phrase, "Show, don't tell." In other words, "show" your readers what is happening, don't just tell them. Don't tell readers what you did; describe doing it.

One of the reasons we tend to tell rather than show is that it's easier and faster. Showing how to do something requires time and effort. In teaching, it's easier to tell students what's wrong with what they did than to show them how to do it right. The latter, however, is more effective.

For thousands of years, the Jewish people had only the law telling them what to do and what not to do. But then came Jesus Christ, who showed them how to live the life God had been telling them about all along. Jesus didn't just say, "Be humble"; He "humbled Himself" (Phil. 2:8). He didn't just say, "Forgive others"; He forgave us (Col. 3:13). He didn't just say, "Love God and your neighbors"; He demonstrated love by His actions (John 15:12).

Christ's perfect example of love shows how great God's love is for us and how we are to show His love to others.
—Julie Ackerman Link

Bless the Lord for love victorious,
Love that conquered on the tree;
For His grace so great and glorious
Flowing out from Calvary. —Peterson

Love is God's will in action.

June 3
Wednesday

Wise Words

Read:
Ecclesiastes 12:6-14

The words of the wise are like goads, and the words of scholars are like well-driven nails, given by one Shepherd. —Ecclesiastes 12:11

The Bible In One Year:
- 2 Chronicles 19–20
- John 13:21-38

Now in my sixties, I reflect back on wise spiritual leaders who had a positive impact on my life. In Bible school, God used my Old Testament professor to make the Word come alive. My Greek teacher relentlessly employed high standards to goad my study of the New Testament. And the senior pastor in my first pastoral ministry shepherded me in building vital ministries to help others grow spiritually. Each of these teachers encouraged me in different ways.

King Solomon wisely observed some ways that spiritual leaders can help us grow: "The words of the wise are like goads, and the words of scholars are like well-driven nails, given by one Shepherd" (Eccl. 12:11). Some teachers prod us; others build solid spiritual structures into our lives. Still others, as caring shepherds, are there with a listening ear when we hurt.

The Good Shepherd has given leaders a variety of gifts: exhorting, developing, and shepherding. Whether we're a leader or a learner, though, He desires that we maintain humble hearts and a love for others. What a privilege to be led and used by our Shepherd to encourage others in their walk with Him. —Dennis Fisher

Give us the wisdom we need, Lord, to encourage
others in their spiritual walk. We know we need Your
Spirit's power to do that. Use the gifts You have
given us to help others along on their journey.

May our words reflect the heart of God and His wisdom.

June 4
Thursday

Pressing On

Read:
Philippians 1:12-18; 3:8-11

That I may know Him and the power of His resurrection, and the fellowship of His sufferings.
—Philippians 3:10

The Bible In One Year:
■ 2 Chronicles 21–22
■ John 14

At a Christian men's conference, I talked with a longtime friend who has encouraged and mentored me for many years. With him were two young men from China, new in their faith and deeply grateful for this man's faithful friendship and spiritual help. My friend Clyde, nearing 80 years of age, glowed with enthusiasm as he said, "I've never been more excited about knowing and loving Christ than I am today."

Paul's letter to the Philippians reveals a heart and purpose that never diminished with time: "That I may know Him and the power of His resurrection, and the fellowship of His sufferings, being conformed to His death" (Phil. 3:10). From the root of Paul's relationship with Jesus came the fruit of his undiminished fervor that others be guided to faith in Him. He rejoiced to share the gospel and was encouraged that others became bolder because of him (1:12-14).

If our goal is merely service for the Lord, we may burn out somewhere along the line. But if our purpose, like Paul's and Clyde's and many others, is to know Christ and love Him, we'll find that He will give us the strength to make Him known to others. Let us joyfully press on in the strength God gives! —David McCasland

Father God, I want to know You in all Your fullness and
to love You completely. I believe that relationship
with You is the basis for my service for You.
Help me not to serve out of my own strength.

Learn from Christ then make Him known.

June 5
Friday

More Than Information

Read:
John 15:1-13

Abide in Me, and I in you.
—John 15:4

The Bible In One Year:
■ 2 Chronicles 23–24
■ John 15

How is behavior altered? In his book *The Social Animal,* David Brooks notes that some experts have said people just need to be taught the long-term risks of bad behavior. For example, he writes: "Smoking can lead to cancer. Adultery destroys families, and lying destroys trust. The assumption was that once you reminded people of the foolishness of their behavior, they would be motivated to stop. Both reason and will are obviously important in making moral decisions and exercising self-control. But neither of these character models has proven very effective." In other words, information alone is not powerful enough to transform behavior.

As Jesus' followers, we want to grow and change spiritually. More than two millennia ago, Jesus told His disciples how that can happen. He said, "Abide in Me, and I in you. As a branch cannot bear fruit of itself, unless it abides in the vine, neither can you, unless you abide in Me" (John 15:4). Jesus is the Vine and we, His followers, are the branches. If we're honest, we know we're utterly helpless and spiritually ineffective apart from Him.

Jesus transforms us spiritually and reproduces His life in us—as we abide in Him. —Marvin Williams

Lord, take my life and make it wholly Thine;
Fill my poor heart with Thy great love divine.
Take all my will, my passion, self, and pride;
I now surrender, Lord—in me abide. —*Orr*

A change in behavior begins with Jesus changing our heart.

June 6
Saturday

Leading From The Front

Read:
Psalm 23

He leads me beside the still waters. He restores my soul; He leads me in the paths of righteousness for His name's sake.
—Psalm 23:2-3

The Bible In One Year:
■ 2 Chronicles 25–27
■ John 16

Stephen Ambrose's book *Band of Brothers* follows the US Army's Easy Company from training in Georgia through the Normandy Invasion of D-Day (June 6, 1944) and ultimately to the end of World War II in Europe. For the bulk of that time, Easy Company was led by Richard Winters. Winters was an especially good officer because he led from the front. The most commonly heard words from Winters in combat were, "Follow me!" Other officers may have sought the safety of the rear areas, but if Winters' men were going into combat, he was going to lead them.

Jesus is the one true Leader of His children. He knows what we need and where we are most vulnerable. His leading is part of what makes Psalm 23 the most beloved song in the Bible's hymnal. In verse 2, David says that the Shepherd "leads me beside the still waters," and in verse 3 he adds, "He leads me in the paths of righteousness for His name's sake." These twin ideas reveal why His care is so complete. Whether it is times of refreshing and strengthening ("still waters") or seasons of doing what pleases Him ("paths of righteousness"), we can follow Him.

As the old song says, "My Lord knows the way through the wilderness; all I have to do is follow." —Bill Crowder

My Lord knows the way through the wilderness;
All I have to do is follow.
Strength for today is mine always
And all that I need for tomorrow. —*Cox*

Jesus knows the way—follow Him!

June 7
Sunday

Guarding Hearts

Read:
2 Timothy 2:10-18

Be diligent to present yourself approved to God, a worker who does not need to be ashamed, rightly dividing the Word of truth. —2 Timothy 2:15

The Bible In One Year:
- 2 Chronicles 28–29
- John 17

For years I taught adult Bible-study classes in a local church and took great pains to consider Scripture carefully before answering questions during the lessons. Later, during a lecture in my first semester of seminary at age 40, I learned that I'd given a woman who had attended one of my classes a terrible answer to her heartfelt question. I was certain my response had been causing her distress over the 2 years since I had seen her, and I was eager to correct myself for her sake.

Racing home, I called her and instantly burst into an apology. A long pause was followed by her saying in a puzzled tone: "I'm sorry, but I'm having trouble placing you right now." I was neither as memorable nor as damaging as I had believed! It was then I realized God is at work guarding His truth even as we grow in our understanding of His Word. I'm thankful He protected this woman's heart.

We are human and will make mistakes sometimes as we share God's Word with others. But we have an obligation to diligently seek His truth and exercise care when we talk about it (2 Tim. 2:15). Then we may boldly proclaim Him, praying that His Spirit will guard not only our hearts but also the hearts of those we seek to serve. God and His Word are deserving of the greatest care. —Randy Kilgore

The words I spoke but yesterday
Are changed as I read Your Word;
I see more clearly Your perfect way,
And my heart is deeply stirred. —Kilgore

Let God's Word fill your memory, rule your heart, and guide your words.

June 8
Monday

WHERE DID I COME FROM?

READ:
Acts 17:22-31

[God] has made from one blood every nation of men to dwell on all the face of the earth.
—Acts 17:26

THE BIBLE IN ONE YEAR:
■ 2 Chronicles 30–31
■ John 18:1-18

My 7-year-old African-American friend Tobias asked me a thought-provoking question the other day: "Since Adam and Eve were white, where did black people come from?" When I told him we don't know what "color" they were and asked him why he thought they were white, he said that's what he always saw in Bible-story books at church and in the library. My heart sank. I wondered if that might make him think he was inferior or possibly not even created by the Lord.

All people have their roots in the Creator God, and therefore all are equal. That's what the apostle Paul told the Athenians: "[God] has made from one blood every nation of men to dwell on all the face of the earth" (Acts 17:26). We are all "from one blood." Darrell Bock, in his commentary on the book of Acts, says, "This affirmation would be hard for the Athenians, who prided themselves in being a superior people, calling others barbarians." However, because we all descended from our first parents, Adam and Eve, no race nor ethnicity is superior or inferior to another.

We stand in awe of our Creator, who made us and gives to all "life, breath, and all things" (v.25). Equal in God's sight, we together praise and honor Him. —Anne Cetas

Every life has been created—
God's handiwork displayed;
When we cherish His creation,
We value what He's made. —*Sper*

God loves each of us as if there were only one of us.

June 9
Tuesday

Obedience Is Worship

Read:
1 Samuel 15:13-23

To obey is better than sacrifice.
—1 Samuel 15:22

The Bible In One Year:
■ 2 Chronicles 32–33
■ John 18:19-40

While I was traveling with a chorale from a Christian high school, it was great to see the students praise God as they led in worship in the churches we visited. What happened away from church was even better to see. One day the group discovered that a woman had no money for gas—and they spontaneously felt led by God to take up a collection. They were able to give her enough money for several tankfuls of gas.

It's one thing to worship and praise God at church; it's quite another to move out into the real world and worship Him through daily obedience.

The students' example causes us to think about our own lives. Do we confine our worship to church? Or do we continue to worship Him by obeying Him in our daily life, looking for opportunities to serve?

In 1 Samuel 15 we see that Saul was asked by the Lord to do a task; but when we review what he did (vv.20-21), we discover that he used worship (sacrifice) as an excuse for his failure to obey God. God's response was, "To obey is better than sacrifice" (v.22).

It's good to be involved in worship at church. But let's also ask God to show us ways to continue to give Him the praise He deserves through our obedience. —Dave Branon

Lord, I want my worship of You to extend beyond
the walls of my church. Help me to listen to
Your prompting and to serve others wherever
I can—no matter what day it is.

Our worship should not be confined to times and places; it should be the spirit of our lives.

June 10
Wednesday

A Letter From C. S. Lewis

Read:
1 John 2:9-17

I write to you, little children, because your sins are forgiven you for His name's sake.
—1 John 2:12

The Bible In One Year:
■ 2 Chronicles 34–36
■ John 19:1-22

In September 1961, Harvey Karlsen, a high school student in Brooklyn, New York, wrote to C. S. Lewis in England. Harvey had read Lewis' book *The Screwtape Letters* and asked the author, "When you wrote this book, did Satan give you any trouble, and if he did, what did you do about it?"

Three weeks later, Lewis penned a reply in which he affirmed that he still had plenty of temptations. He said that in facing them, "Perhaps . . . the most important thing is to *keep on;* not to be discouraged however often one yields to the temptation, but always to pick yourself up again and ask forgiveness."

The New Testament letters of John are filled with encouragement to persevere in the face of temptation. "I write to you, little children, because your sins are forgiven you for His name's sake. I write to you, fathers, because you have known Him who is from the beginning. I write to you, young men, because you have overcome the wicked one" (1 John 2:12-13).

Whatever our age or experience, we are in a spiritual battle together. "The world is passing away, and the lust of it; but he who does the will of God abides forever" (v.17).

Let us cling to God and *keep on*! —David McCasland

Lord, I get discouraged when I've given in again to one of Satan's schemes. I'm thankful, though, that Christ paid for that sin on the cross. Help me to confess it and then to keep on relying on You for my spiritual growth.

To master temptation, let Christ master you.

June 11
Thursday

Savor Every Bite

Read:
Psalm 119:97-104

How sweet are Your words to my taste, sweeter than honey to my mouth!
—Psalm 119:103

The Bible In One Year:
- **Ezra 1–2**
- **John 19:23-42**

My wife Martie often tells me, "Joe, you eat too fast! Slow down and enjoy your meal." I'm usually done long before she is, because she takes the time to savor every bite.

I wonder how many of us rush through reading God's Word without really savoring it. The psalmist said about it, "How sweet are Your words to my taste, sweeter than honey to my mouth!" (Ps. 119:103). That sounds good to me!

What are the benefits of delighting in the rich food of Scripture? A daily meal of God's Word helps to keep anxiety, pride, fear, and temptation from plaguing our undernourished hearts, and strengthens us for a victorious journey. The Word gives us wisdom and understanding (vv.98-100). And it helps restrain our feet from evil (v.101). Just as our digestive system distributes nutrients to our bodies, God's Word, when digested, nourishes our minds, our emotions, and our will.

Rather than grabbing the Word on the run just before dashing out the door, it's important to read it at a time and in a place where we can really fellowship with God.

Take the time and enjoy savoring the richness of God's Word. —Joe Stowell

Thank You, Father, for the gift of Your Word. Please forgive us for the times when we've rushed through reading without taking the time to savor the richness of its meaning. Help us to listen to Your voice.

God's Word provides the ingredients we need to thrive spiritually.

June 12
Friday

Unfinished Business

Read:
Luke 23:32-43

Lord, remember me when You come into Your kingdom.
—Luke 23:42

The Bible In One Year:
- Ezra 3–5
- John 20

At age 99, Leo Plass received his college diploma from Eastern Oregon University. He had stopped working on his teaching degree during the 1930s when he left college to earn an income in the logging industry. Seventy-nine years later, he completed the three credits necessary to graduate and resolve this important unfinished business in his life.

Many of us can relate to Leo. Our unfinished business may include apologies left unsaid or, even more important, unfinished spiritual decisions. One of the criminals who was crucified with Jesus needed desperately to make such a decision. Just a few breaths away from eternity, he realized who Jesus was and wanted to be with Him in heaven. He recognized his sin and Jesus' innocence, and said, "Lord, remember me when You come into Your kingdom" (Luke 23:42). Jesus replied, "Assuredly, . . . today you will be with Me in Paradise" (v.43).

God does not want anyone to perish (2 Peter 3:9). His offer of salvation is open to anyone, regardless of age, health, or stage in life. His offer is open to you. Don't delay receiving Jesus as Savior (2 Cor. 6:2). Resolve this important, unfinished business, and you'll look forward to eternity with Him. —Jennifer Benson Schuldt

Time after time, He has waited before,
And now He is waiting again
To see if you're willing to open the door;
Oh, how He wants to come in! —Carmichael

To be saved here means to be safe hereafter.

June 13
Saturday

Stay Connected

Read:
Psalm 119:33-40

Your Word is a lamp to my feet and a light to my path.
—Psalm 119:105

The Bible In One Year:
- **Ezra 6–8**
- **John 21**

I woke up one morning and discovered that my Internet connection was not working. My service provider conducted some tests and concluded that my modem needed to be replaced, but the earliest they could do so was the next day. I panicked a little when I thought about being without the Internet connection for 24 hours! I thought, *How am I going to survive without it?*

Then I asked myself, *Would I also panic if my connection with God was disrupted for a day?* We keep our connection with God alive by spending time in His Word and in prayer. Then we are to be "doers of the Word" (James 1:22-24).

The writer of Psalm 119 recognized the importance of a connection to God. He asked God to teach him His statutes and give him understanding of His law (vv.33-34). Then he prayed that he would observe it with his whole heart (v.34), walk in the path of God's commandments (v.35), and turn away his eyes from looking at worthless things (v.37). By meditating on God's Word and then applying it, the psalmist stayed "connected" to God.

God has given us His Word as a lamp to our feet and a light to our path to lead us to Him. —C. P. Hia

May the mind of Christ my Savior
Live in me from day to day,
By His love and power controlling
All I do and say. —*Wilkinson*

To recharge your spiritual battery, plug into the Source.

June 14
Sunday

Imaginary Friend?

Read:
Romans 1:18-25

Abraham believed God . . . and he was called the friend of God.
—James 2:23

The Bible In One Year:
- Ezra 9–10
- Acts 1

Not long ago, I heard about this billboard along the highway: "God is an imaginary friend—choose reality. It will be better for all of us."

Obviously, the bold statement compares Christians to children whose vivid imaginations invent a make-believe companion. But is that what God is—an imaginary friend?

Actually, the evidence favors His reality. Ponder these ideas: The creation of the world shows there is a Designer behind the universe (Rom. 1:18-20). The conscience indicates a Lawgiver behind each human's sense of right and wrong (Rom. 2:14-15). The creativity we express in music and art reflect the same attribute that the Creator possesses (Ex. 35:31-32). Christ reveals what God is like in human form (Heb. 1:1-4). And the communion or fellowship of the Spirit in the Christian heart manifests the reality of God (Gal. 5:22-23).

The Bible tells us there will be those who deny the reality of God (2 Peter 3:4-6). But James reminds us of His reality and how an Old Testament believer befriended Him: " 'Abraham believed God, and it was accounted to him for righteousness.' And he was called the friend of God" (James 2:23). Have you met the redeeming God? He gave His Son to become your real, eternal Friend (John 15:15). —Dennis Fisher

I've found a Friend, O such a Friend!
He loved me ere I knew Him;
He drew me with the cords of love,
And thus He bound me to Him. —*Small*

The dearest friend on earth is but a mere shadow compared to Jesus. —Chambers

June 15
Monday

To God Be The Glory

Read:
1 Chronicles 25:1-8

Chenaniah, leader of the Levites, was instructor in charge of the music, because he was skillful.
—1 Chronicles 15:22

The Bible In One Year:
- **Nehemiah 1–3**
- **Acts 2:1-21**

When Jason was asked to sing at a church he was visiting, he was delighted to participate even though he wasn't asked until a few minutes before the service started. He chose a familiar hymn, "To God Be the Glory," because it was a song that was especially meaningful to him. He practiced it a few times in the church basement and sang it without accompaniment in the church service.

Several weeks later, Jason learned that some people in the church didn't appreciate his ministry. They thought he was showing off. Because they did not know him, they wrongly assumed that he was singing to impress them, not to honor the Lord.

From the Old Testament we learn that God appointed people with skill to be involved in temple worship. From construction workers to worship leaders—people were chosen based on their skill (1 Chron. 15:22; 25:1,7).

The Lord gave each of us different talents and spiritual gifts to be used for His glory (Col. 3:23-24). When we serve with that purpose, not to lift up ourselves, we don't need to be concerned with what others think. God gave His very best to us—His Son Jesus—and we honor Him by giving our best to Him. —Julie Ackerman Link

The Master needs what you have to offer,
No matter if you think it's small;
His work on earth is done through His children,
So give Him your best, give your all. —*Hess*

We are at our best when we serve God from our hearts.

June 16
Tuesday

Greedy Birds

Read:
2 Corinthians 9:6-15

God is able to make all grace abound toward you, that you . . . may have an abundance for every good work.
—2 Corinthians 9:8

The Bible In One Year:
- **Nehemiah 4–6**
- **Acts 2:22-47**

Every year when I put out the hummingbird feeder, the busy little birds start battling for position. Even though there are four places at the "table," the birds fight for whatever place one of their neighbors is using. The source of food at each place is the same—a reservoir of syrup in the bottom of the feeder. Knowing that all the feeding stations are equal, I shake my head at their greediness.

But then I wonder, *Why is it so much easier to see the greed of the birds than it is to see my own?* I often want the place at "God's table" that someone else has, even though I know all good things come from the same source—God—and that His supply will never run out. Since God can prepare a table for us even in the presence of our enemies (Ps. 23:5), why be concerned that someone else might have the station in life that we want?

The Lord is able to give us "all sufficiency in all things" so that we will have "an abundance for every good work" (2 Cor. 9:8). When we recognize the importance of our work as ministers of the grace of God (1 Peter 4:10), we'll stop fighting to take over someone else's position and be grateful for the place God has given us to serve others on His behalf. —Julie Ackerman Link

Thank You for the privilege we have to serve You by
serving others, Lord. Help us to be content to fill
the place where You have put us, so that
You might be glorified through us.

Resentment comes from looking at others;
contentment comes from looking at God.

June 17
Wednesday

No Risk

Read:
Ephesians 2:1-10

For by grace you have been saved through faith, and that not of yourselves; it is the gift of God.
—Ephesians 2:8

The Bible In One Year:
- Nehemiah 7–9
- Acts 3

A colleague recently shared an experience I don't intend to try personally—bungee jumping. I found his description of the event both fascinating and terrifying. To think of jumping headfirst from a bridge hundreds of feet in the air suspended only by a giant rubber band is not my idea of a good time. But his leap was not without support. He described not one, but two heavy-duty harnesses that secured him to his lifeline—and to safety. The careful design and proven testing of those harnesses gave him great confidence as he jumped into the air.

As I listened, it occurred to me that for the follower of Christ, living in a sinful world is not a blind "leap of faith." We too have a pair of protections that can secure us in even the darkest times of life. In Ephesians 2:8-9, Paul wrote these words, "For by grace you have been saved through faith, and that not of yourselves; it is the gift of God, not of works, lest anyone should boast."

It's in these twin harnesses—God's grace and faith in the finished work of Jesus—that our relationship with God safely rests. In the strength of these provisions, salvation is not a risky leap into the void. It's an exercise of confidence in God's Word and His unfailing love and protection. —Bill Crowder

'Twas grace that taught my heart to fear,
And grace my fears relieved;
How precious did that grace appear
The hour I first believed! —Newton

We can expect God's peace when we accept God's grace.

June 18
Thursday

Every Word Matters

Read:
Deuteronomy 4:1-10

You shall not add to the word which I command you, nor take from it, that you may keep the commandments of the Lord your God.
—Deuteronomy 4:2

The Bible In One Year:
- Nehemiah 10–11
- Acts 4:1-22

Kim Peek was a savant (a person with extraordinary memory) who memorized all of Shakespeare's plays. During a performance of *Twelfth Night,* Peek noticed that the actor had skipped a word from one of the lines. Peek suddenly stood up and shouted, "Stop!" The actor apologized and said he didn't think anyone would mind. Peek replied, "Shakespeare would."

Words matter. But especially when they are the very words of God. Moses warned Israel, "You shall not add to the word which I command you, nor take from it, that you may keep the commandments of the Lord your God" (Deut. 4:2). Moses often reminded Israel of God's mercy and faithfulness to them in the past. But he also stressed the importance of obedience to God's commands as they prepared to enter the Promised Land. He told them that obedience would result in blessings of life and a rich inheritance (vv.39-40). Every command and regulation mattered to God. The value His people placed on God's Word showed their view of Him.

Today, when we value God's Word, handle it with great care, and obey what it says, we give God the reverence He truly deserves. —Marvin Williams

The Bible stands, and it will forever
When the world has passed away;
By inspiration it has been given—
All its precepts I will obey. —*Lillenas*

God's Word needs no additions or subtractions.

June 19
Friday

PLAY IN PAIN

READ:
Lamentations 3:1-3, 25-33

Though He causes grief, yet He will show compassion.
—Lamentations 3:32

THE BIBLE IN ONE YEAR:
- Nehemiah 12–13
- Acts 4:23-37

Baseball Hall-of-Fame catcher Gary Carter was a follower of Jesus. During his 19-year career, he drew strength and endurance from his faith in God to compete day after day. In an article that appeared in the *Wall Street Journal* shortly after Carter died of brain cancer at age 57, writer Andrew Klavan told how Carter had influenced his life.

In the late 1980s, Klavan had sunk to a low point in his life. His mind dwelt on suicide. Then he heard Carter interviewed after a game. His team, the New York Mets, had won, and the aging catcher had helped by running hard at a critical point in the game. Carter was asked how he could do that with his aching knees. Klavan heard him say something like this: "Sometimes you just have to play in pain." That simple statement helped draw Klavan out of his depression. "I can do that!" he declared. Encouraged, he found hope—and later became a believer in Christ.

The comforting truth behind Carter's statement comes from Lamentations. We may face sorrow, pain, and hardship, but we don't have to sink into self-pity. The same God who allows our suffering also showers us with His compassion (Lam. 3:32). With God's love lifting us up, we can—if we have to—"play" in pain. —Dave Egner

Along life's pathway troubles come
That God will help us bear;
Then we can look beyond the pain
To those who need our care. —*Branon*

God will either spare you from suffering or give you the grace to bear it.

June 20
Saturday

Rock Of Refuge

Read:
Psalm 94:3-23

The Lord has been my defense, and my God the rock of my refuge. —Psalm 94:22

The Bible In One Year:
- Esther 1–2
- Acts 5:1-21

One year during my vacation, I walked along the shoreline of a large lake. As I approached a pile of boulders, I noticed a small alcove between the rocks and observed that a tiny plant had taken root there. The plant appeared to be absorbing the right amount of sunlight and water, and it was also getting something else: protection. No downpour or windstorm would ruffle its tender leaves.

The plant's secure habitat reminded me of these familiar hymn lyrics: "Rock of Ages, cleft for me, let me hide myself in Thee." Those words express what many of us want when we encounter people with evil intentions—people characterized by pride, cruelty, and a lack of regard for God (Ps. 94:4-7). When we are the target of someone's wrongdoing, we can remember the testimony of the psalmist: "The Lord has been my defense, and my God the rock of my refuge" (v.22).

As our rock, God is dependable and strong. As our refuge, He can provide safety until problems pass. The psalmist reminds us: "Under His wings you shall take refuge" (Ps. 91:4). With God as our defender, we don't have to fear what others will do. We can trust that God will support us when trouble comes. —Jennifer Benson Schuldt

Thank You, God, for Your stable and unchanging nature. Help us to hide ourselves in You when trouble comes our way. Remind us that we don't have to fight our own battles.

Refuge can be found in the Rock of Ages.

June 21
Sunday

Strength Of A Man

Read:
1 Corinthians 16:9-13

Watch, stand fast in the faith, be brave, be strong.
—1 Corinthians 16:13

The Bible In One Year:
■ Esther 3–5
■ Acts 5:22-42

Some years ago I found myself in an elevator with a couple of men. It was late at night, and we all looked weary. The elevator came to a stop, and a larger-than-life cowboy ambled in, wearing a battered hat, an old, stained sheepskin coat, and rundown logger boots. He looked us up and down, met our eyes, and growled, "Good evening, *men*." All of us straightened up and squared our shoulders. We were trying to live up to the name.

On this day, which is given over to honoring guys, let's talk about living up to the name *man*. We try to be strong and macho, but often it's just a façade. For all our effort, we realize we don't measure up. Underneath the bravado we harbor a host of fears, insecurities, and shortcomings. Much of our manliness is pure bluff.

Paul was man enough to admit it: "We also are weak," he said (2 Cor. 13:4). That's not pious chatter; it's a humbling fact. Yet in what seems to be a contradiction, Paul insisted that we are to be "men of courage" (1 Cor. 16:13 NIV).

How can we be the strong person that God meant for us to be? Only by putting ourselves in God's hands and asking Him to make us that way through His power and enablement. —David Roper

Come, Lord, and give me courage,
Thy conquering Spirit give;
Make me an overcomer—
In power within me live. —*Anon.*

True strength is the power of God in the soul.

June 22
Monday

Hanging On Nothing

Read:
Job 26:5-14

He stretches out the north over empty space; He hangs the earth on nothing.
—Job 26:7

The Bible In One Year:
- Esther 6–8
- Acts 6

A world map published by the National Geographic Society has this notation: "Earth's mass is 6.6 sextillion tons." And what supports all that weight? Nothing. The planet we inhabit spins on its axis at 1,000 miles per hour as it hurtles through space in its orbit around the sun. But it's easy for that to remain unnoticed in the midst of our daily concerns about health, relationships, and how to pay the bills.

The Old Testament character Job repeatedly considered God's creation in his struggle to make sense of the numbing loss of his health, his wealth, and his children. "[God] stretches out the north over empty space," Job said. "He hangs the earth on nothing" (Job 26:7). Job marveled at the clouds that did not break under the heavy water inside them (v.8) and the horizon "at the boundary of light and darkness" (v.10), but called them "the mere edges of His ways" (v.14).

Creation itself did not answer Job's questions, but the heavens and the earth pointed him to God the Creator, who alone could respond with help and hope.

The Lord who upholds the universe by the "word of His power" (Heb. 1:3; Col. 1:17) is in control of our everyday lives. Experiences that seem "empty places" are all undergirded by our heavenly Father's power and love. —David McCasland

Dear Lord, we praise You for Your infinite power.
You created the world out of nothing and uphold
it by Your word. Help me to remember that You
are also in control of every part of my life.

When we reflect on the power of God's creation, we see the power of His care for us.

June 23
Tuesday

WATER PROBLEMS

READ:
Romans 13:1-7

There is no authority except from God, and the authorities that exist are appointed by God. —Romans 13:1

THE BIBLE IN ONE YEAR:
- Esther 9–10
- Acts 7:1-21

Our church family was excited to see work begin on our new sanctuary. Each Sunday we eagerly looked at the big hole in the ground. But progress seemed slow.

It all came down to water. Too much in one place and not enough in another. An underground spring was one problem. Construction could not continue until inspectors were satisfied that water was being directed away from the site. At the same time, city officials said we didn't have enough water coming into the building for a sprinkler system—so new lines for water had to be added. None of us wanted the project to be slowed down by these rulings, but we realized that if codes weren't followed, we would face serious problems in the future.

Sometimes we grumble about government and other officials. But a proper respect for authority honors God. Paul, who had his own problems with those in charge, wrote, "Let every soul be subject to the governing authorities" (Rom. 13:1). And later, "Do what is good, and you will have praise from [the authorities]" (v.3).

As we let God's Spirit teach us, we can have a healthy attitude toward government. It's for our good, the testimony of our faith, and most of all for God's honor. —Dave Branon

Thank You, Lord, for people who are willing to serve in our local, state, and national governments. We pray that they will seek righteousness and justice and that You will help us to respect those You have placed over us.

Respect for authority brings glory to God.

June 24
Wednesday

Flight Simulator

Read:
John 16:25-33

These things I have spoken to you, that in Me you may have peace. —John 16:33

The Bible In One Year:
- Job 1–2
- Acts 7:22-43

When airplane pilots are training, they spend many hours in flight simulators. These simulators give the students a chance to experience the challenges and dangers of flying an aircraft—but without the risk. The pilots don't have to leave the ground, and if they crash in the simulation, they can calmly walk away.

Simulators are tremendous teaching tools—helpful in preparing the aspiring pilot to take command of an actual aircraft. The devices, however, have a shortcoming. They create an artificial experience in which the full-blown pressures of handling a real cockpit cannot be fully replicated.

Real life is like that, isn't it? It cannot be simulated. There is no safe, risk-free environment in which we can experience life's ups and downs unharmed. The risks and dangers of living in a broken world are inescapable. That's why the words of Jesus are so reassuring. He said, "These things I have spoken to you, that in Me you may have peace. In the world you will have tribulation; but be of good cheer, I have overcome the world" (John 16:33).

Although we can't avoid the dangers of life in a fallen world, we can have peace through a relationship with Jesus. He has secured our ultimate victory. —Bill Crowder

Outward troubles may not cease,
But this your joy will be:
"Thou wilt keep him in perfect peace
Whose mind is stayed on Thee." —*Anon.*

No life is more secure than a life surrendered to God.

June 25
Thursday

Country Doctor

Read:
Philippians 2:1-11

Let nothing be done through selfish ambition or conceit, but in lowliness of mind let each esteem others better than himself. —Phil. 2:3

The Bible In One Year:
- **Job 3–4**
- **Acts 7:44-60**

Sinclair Lewis' novel *Main Street* tells the story of Carol, a sophisticated city woman who marries a country doctor. She feels superior to others in her new small-town environment. But her husband's response to a medical crisis challenges her snobbery. An immigrant farmer terribly injures his arm, which needs to be amputated. Carol watches with admiration as her husband speaks comforting words to the injured man and his distraught wife. The physician's warmth and servant attitude challenges Carol's prideful mindset.

In all of our relationships as Jesus' followers, we can choose to think we're superior or we can humbly serve the interests of others. Paul, the apostle, tells us, "Let nothing be done through selfish ambition or conceit, but in lowliness of mind let each esteem others better than himself. Let each of you look out not only for his own interests, but also for the interests of others" (Phil. 2:3-4).

We can learn to consider others' needs more important than our own as we focus on Jesus' example. He took "the form of a bondservant," and gave Himself up for us (vv.5-8). When we fail in valuing others, His sacrifice for us shows us the humble, better way. —Dennis Fisher

More like the Master I would ever be,
More of His meekness, more humility;
More zeal to labor, more courage to be true,
More consecration for work He bids me do. —*Gabriel*

Joy comes from putting another's welfare ahead of your own.

June 26
Friday

Her Worst Day Ever

Read:
Job 7:11-21

I will speak in the anguish of my spirit; I will complain in the bitterness of my soul. —Job 7:11

The Bible In One Year:
- Job 5–7
- Acts 8:1-25

In May 2011, a young woman took cover in a bathtub during a tornado that devastated her city of Joplin, Missouri. Her husband covered her body with his and took the blows from flying debris. He died, and she survived because of his heroism. She naturally wrestles with the question, "Why?" But a year after the tornado, she said that she finds comfort because even on her worst day ever, she was loved.

When I think about "worst days ever," I think of Job right away. A man who loved God, he lost his animals, his servants, and his 10 children in one day! (Job 1:13-19). Job mourned deeply, and he also asked the "Why?" questions. He cried out, "Have I sinned? What have I done to You . . . ? Why have You set me as Your target?" (7:20). Job's friends accused him of sinning and thought he deserved his difficulties, but God said of his friends: "You have not spoken of Me what is right, as My servant Job has" (42:7). God did not give him the reasons for his suffering, but He listened to Job and did not fault him for his questions. God assured him of His control over everything, and Job trusted Him (42:1-6).

The Lord may not give us the reasons for our trials. But, thankfully, even on our worst day ever, we can know for sure we are loved by Him (Rom. 8:35-39). —Anne Cetas

We're grateful, Father, that You know our hearts
with our pain and joy. Thank You that You never
leave us nor forsake us, as Your Word tells
us. Please hold us close during our trials.

God's love does not keep us from trials, but sees us through them.

June 27
Saturday

Let's Stick Together

Read:
1 Corinthians 12:12-27

For in fact the body is not one member but many.
—1 Corinthians 12:14

The Bible In One Year:
- Job 8–10
- Acts 8:26-40

Most regions of the world are familiar with the amazing phenomenon of snow. Snowflakes are beautiful, uniquely crafted ice crystals. Individual snowflakes are fragile, and they quickly melt if they land on your hand. Yet, en masse they create a force to be reckoned with. They can shut down major cities while creating beautiful landscapes of snow-laden trees whose pictures decorate calendars and become the subject of artwork. They provide pleasure on the ski slopes and joy for children as they make snowmen and ammunition for snowball fights. All because they stick together.

So it is with those of us who follow Christ. Each of us has been uniquely gifted with the capacity to make a contribution to the work of Christ. We were never intended to live in isolation but to work together to become a great force for God and the advance of His cause. As Paul reminds us, the body of Christ "is not one member but many" (1 Cor. 12:14). All of us are to use our gifts to serve one another so that together we can make a significant difference in our world.

Put your giftedness to work, joyfully cooperate with the giftedness of those around you, and let the wind of the Spirit use you for His glory! —Joe Stowell

Lord, teach us to use our strengths in cooperation with the strengths of others. Help us to serve as one so that we might know the joy of the power of our togetherness for Your name's sake and the advance of Your kingdom.

We can accomplish more together than we can alone.

June 28
Sunday

MISERABLE SUCCESS

READ:
Luke 9:18-27

If anyone desires to come after Me, let him deny himself, and take up his cross daily, and follow Me. —Luke 9:23

THE BIBLE IN ONE YEAR:
■ Job 11–13
■ Acts 9:1-21

In whatever a man does without God, he must fail miserably—or succeed more miserably," wrote George MacDonald (1824–1905), a Scottish novelist, poet, and Christian minister. This intriguing statement is often cited by modern speakers and writers and appears in MacDonald's book *Unspoken Sermons.*

MacDonald was dealing with the difficult subject of a Christian's self-denial and how we are to apply this teaching of Jesus: "If anyone desires to come after Me, let him deny himself, and take up his cross daily, and follow Me. For whoever desires to save his life will lose it, but whoever loses his life for My sake will save it" (Luke 9:23-24).

Rather than merely trying to suppress our natural desires, MacDonald said that true self-denial means "we must see things as [Christ] saw them, regard them as He regarded them; we must take the will of God as the very life of our being . . . . We are no more to think, 'What should I like to do?' but 'What would the Living One have me do?' "

Getting only what *we* want is succeeding miserably. True success is found in "losing" our lives for Jesus' sake and finding them again full and free in His will. —David McCasland

More like the Master I would live and grow,
More of His love to others I would show;
More self-denial, like His in Galilee,
More like the Master I long to ever be. —*Gabriel*

The spirit of humility and self-denial precedes a deeper and closer walk with God.

June 29
Monday

Love And Prayer

Read:
Psalm 92

They shall still bear fruit in old age; they shall be fresh and flourishing.
—Psalm 92:14

The Bible In One Year:
- **Job 14–16**
- **Acts 9:22-43**

In a popular children's book, Winnie the Pooh watches Kanga bound away. *I wish I could jump like that,* he thinks. *Some can and some can't. That's how it is.*

We see younger or more able men and women doing extraordinary things that we cannot do. They can; we can't. That's how it is. It's easy to feel useless when we can't do the things we were once capable of doing.

It's true that we may not be able to "jump" like we once did, but we can love and we can pray. These are the works that time and experience have prepared us to do well.

Love is the very best gift we have to give to God and to others. It is no small matter, for love is the means by which we fulfill our whole duty to God and our neighbor. Our love for one person may seem to be a small action, but love is the greatest gift of all (1 Cor. 13:13).

And we can pray. Paul encouraged the Colossians to "continue earnestly in prayer, being vigilant in it with thanksgiving" (Col. 4:2). Our prayers are a powerful force in the universe!

Love and prayer are mighty works indeed, the mightiest works for any of us. Why? Because our God, who wants to use us, is an all-loving and all-powerful God. —David Roper

Begin the day with God;
Kneel down to Him in prayer;
Lift up thy heart to His abode,
And seek His love to share. —*Dann*

God pours His love into our hearts that it might flow out to others.

June 30
Tuesday

LATE ARRIVALS WELCOME

READ:
Matthew 20:1-16

I wish to give to this last man the same as to you. —Matthew 20:14

THE BIBLE IN ONE YEAR:
- Job 17–19
- Acts 10:1-23

One night when I visited a nursing home, a resident named Tom slipped out quietly from his room, hoping to catch me to chat. After we talked awhile, he asked, "Won't God be insulted if I become a Christian this late in life?" Tom's question wasn't a surprise. As a chaplain, I often hear it in varying forms from the elderly, from those who struggle with addictions, from former prisoners. They think they have a legitimate reason to believe it's too late for them to know God or to be used by Him.

Tom and I spent time exploring people in Scripture who, because of their past, could have thought it was too late for them to know God. But Rahab, a prostitute (Josh. 2:12-14; Heb. 11:31), and Zacchaeus, a tax collector (Luke 19:1-8), chose faith in God despite their past.

We also looked at Jesus' parable of workers in the vineyard (Matt. 20:1-16). The earlier the hire, the more labor they were able to give the vineyard owner (vv.2-7), but those hired later discovered they had equal value in the owner's eyes and would be rewarded equally (vv.8-16). The vineyard owner chose to be gracious to them all.

No matter our past or present, God longs to show us His grace and bring us into relationship with Him. —Randy Kilgore

Father, we are amazed at Your grace! Thank You that we can come to You at any time for forgiveness and be restored to relationship with You. Thank You that we can now be used by You to touch the lives of others.

To give your life to Christ now is to keep it forever.

July 1
Wednesday

Bouncing Back

Read:
1 John 1:5–2:2

**If we confess our sins, He is faithful and just to forgive us our sins and to cleanse us from all unrighteousness.
—1 John 1:9**

The Bible In One Year:
■ Job 20–21
■ Acts 10:24-48

On January 18, 2012, the longest winning streak in US intercollegiate varsity sports history—252 consecutive victories—ended when Trinity College lost a squash match to Yale. The morning after the team's first loss in 14 years, Trinity's coach, Paul Assaiante, received an e-mail from a friend, a prominent professional football coach, who wrote, "Well, now you get to bounce back." Ten days later, that football coach's team lost in one of the most widely seen athletic events—the NFL Super Bowl. All of us must cope with defeat.

The feeling of failure after an athletic loss mirrors our greater self-condemnation following a spiritual collapse. How can we recover from grieving God and others, along with disappointing ourselves? The apostle John wrote, "If we say that we have no sin, we deceive ourselves, and the truth is not in us. If we confess our sins, He is faithful and just to forgive us our sins and to cleanse us from all unrighteousness" (1 John 1:8-9). God forgives us because Jesus Christ paid the price for our sins (2:2).

God's pardon sets us free to begin again and focus on today's opportunity rather than yesterday's defeat. His faithful cleansing allows us to start over with a pure heart. Today, God invites and enables us to bounce back. —David McCasland

When you've trusted Jesus and walked His way,
When you've felt His hand lead you day by day,
But your steps now take you another way,
Start over. —*Kroll*

Instead of living in the shadows of yesterday, walk in the light of today and the hope of tomorrow.

July 2
Thursday

A FLYING MIRACLE

READ:
Psalm 104:10-24

O LORD, how manifold are Your works! In wisdom You have made them all. The earth is full of Your possessions. —Psalm 104:24

THE BIBLE IN ONE YEAR:
- Job 22–24
- Acts 11

Among God's creatures, the butterfly is one of the most stunningly beautiful! Its gentle flight, colorful wings, and amazing migratory patterns are traits that make the butterfly a masterpiece of the natural world.

This flying insect, while supplying us with visual enjoyment, also supplies us with amazing examples of the marvels of God's creative work.

For instance, the majestic monarch butterfly can travel 3,000 miles on its migration to Central America—only to end up at the same tree its parents or even grandparents landed on a generation or two earlier. It does this guided by a brain the size of a pinhead.

Or consider the monarch's metamorphosis. After the caterpillar builds a chrysalis around itself, it releases a chemical that turns its insides to mush—no perceptible parts. Somehow from this emerges the brain, internal parts, head, legs, and wings of a butterfly.

One butterfly expert said, "The creation of the body of a caterpillar into the body and wings of a butterfly is, without doubt, one of the wonders of life on earth." Another expert feels that this metamorphosis is "rightly regarded as a miracle."

"How manifold are [God's] works!" (Ps. 104:24)—and the butterfly is but one of them. —Dave Branon

We stand amazed, God, at the awesome creation You
allow us to enjoy. From distant galaxies to beautiful
butterflies, You have given us a world that speaks loudly
of Your love for us. Thank You, Lord, for creation.

Creation's design points to the Master Designer.

July 3
Friday

Service And Witness

Read:
2 Corinthians 4:1-12

We do not preach ourselves, but Christ Jesus the Lord, and ourselves your bondservants for Jesus' sake.
—2 Corinthians 4:5

The Bible In One Year:
- Job 25–27
- Acts 12

While serving as a maid in London, England, in the early part of the 20th century, Gladys Aylward had other dreams. Her goal was to be a missionary to China. Having been rejected by a Christian missionary organization as "unqualified," Gladys decided to go there on her own. At the age of 28, she used her life savings to purchase a one-way ticket to Yangcheng, a remote village in China. There she established an inn for trade caravans where she shared Bible stories. Gladys served in other villages as well and became known as *Ai-weh-deh,* Chinese for "virtuous one."

The apostle Paul also spread the gospel to distant regions of the world. He extended himself as a servant to meet the needs of others (2 Cor. 11:16-29). He wrote this about serving: "We do not preach ourselves, but Christ Jesus the Lord, and ourselves your bondservants for Jesus' sake" (4:5).

Not all of us are called to endure hardship to spread the gospel in distant lands. But each of us is responsible as a servant of God to share Christ with people in our sphere of influence. It's our privilege to help our neighbors, friends, and relatives. Ask God for openings to serve and to talk about Jesus who gave Himself for us. —Dennis Fisher

My life is a painting created by God,
And as such I've nothing to boast;
Reflecting the image of Christ to the world
Is what I desire the most. —*Sper*

We serve God by sharing His Word with others.

July 4
Saturday

Eternal Eyesight

Read:
2 Corinthians 4:16–5:8

We do not look at the things which are seen, but at the things which are not seen.
—2 Corinthians 4:18

The Bible In One Year:
- Job 28–29
- Acts 13:1-25

I received good news at my eye checkup last month—my faraway vision has improved. Well, I thought it was good news until a friend informed me: "Faraway vision can improve as we age; close-up vision may diminish."

The report made me think of another kind of improved faraway vision that I have observed in some Christians. Those who have known the Lord for a long time or who have gone through great trials seem to have a better heavenly vision than the rest of us. Their eternal eyesight has gotten better and their close-up "earthly" vision is diminishing.

Because the apostle Paul had that type of eternal vision, he encouraged the church in Corinth: "Our light affliction, which is but for a moment, is working for us a far more exceeding and eternal weight of glory . . . . The things which are seen are temporary, but the things which are not seen are eternal" (2 Cor. 4:17-18).

For now we struggle with our "eyesight." There's a tension between enjoying all that God has given us in this life, yet still believing what theologian Jonathan Edwards said about our future: "To go to heaven, fully to enjoy God, is infinitely better than the most pleasant accommodations here." Seeing Him will bring perfect vision. —Anne Cetas

Lord, we know that our life on this earth is but
a moment compared to eternity. Help us to enjoy
the time we've been given, and use us to tell of Your
love and goodness until that day when we see You.

Keep your eyes fixed on the prize.

July 5
Sunday

BATTLING EGO

READ:
James 4:6-17

God resists the proud, but gives grace to the humble. —James 4:6

THE BIBLE IN ONE YEAR:
■ Job 30–31
■ Acts 13:26-52

When a general returned from a victorious battle, ancient Rome would stage a parade to welcome the conqueror home. The parade would include the general's troops, as well as trophy captives who had been brought along as evidence of the victory. As the parade made its way through the city, the crowds would cheer their hero's success.

To prevent the general's ego from becoming unduly swollen, a slave rode along with him in his chariot. Why? So that as the Roman throngs heaped praise on the general, the slave could continually whisper in his ear, "You too are mortal."

When successful, we too may lose sight of our own frailty and allow our hearts to fill with destructive pride. James pointed us away from the danger of pride by pointing us to humility and to God. He wrote, "God resists the proud, but gives grace to the humble" (James 4:6). The key to that statement is *grace*. Nothing is more wonderful! The Lord alone deserves thanks and praise—especially for the grace He has lavished on us.

Our achievements, success, or greatness are not rooted in ourselves. They are the product of God's matchless grace, upon which we are eternally dependent. —Bill Crowder

New mercies every morning,
Grace for every day,
New hope for every trial,
And courage all the way. —*Mc Veigh*

God's grace is infinite love
expressing itself through infinite goodness.

July 6
Monday

Avoid Dehydration

Read:
John 7:37-39

If anyone thirsts, let him come to Me and drink. —John 7:37

The Bible In One Year:
■ **Job 32–33**
■ **Acts 14**

A couple of times in the past few years I've experienced dehydration and, believe me, it is not something I want to repeat. It happened once after I suffered a torn hamstring while cross-country skiing, and another time in the 115-degree heat of an Israeli desert. Both times I experienced dizziness, disorientation, loss of clear vision, and a host of other symptoms. I learned the hard way that water is vital to maintaining my well-being.

My experience with dehydration gives me a new appreciation for Jesus' invitation: "If anyone thirsts, let him come to Me and drink" (John 7:37). His announcement was dramatic, particularly in terms of the timing. John notes that it was the last day of the "great feast"—the annual festival commemorating the wandering of the Jews in the wilderness—which climaxed with a ceremonial pouring of water down the temple steps to recall God's provision of water for the thirsty wanderers. At that point, Jesus rose and proclaimed that He is the water we all desperately need.

Living like we really need Jesus—talking to Him and depending on His wisdom—is vital to our spiritual well-being. So, stay connected to Jesus, for He alone can satisfy your thirsty soul! —Joe Stowell

Dear Lord, forgive me for thinking that I can do life without the water of Your presence, advice, counsel, comfort, and conviction. Thank You that You are indeed the living water that I so desperately need.

Come to Jesus for the refreshing power of His living water.

July 7
Tuesday

Welcome To All!

Read:
Isaiah 55:1-9

Man looks at the outward appearance, but the Lord looks at the heart.
—1 Samuel 16:7

The Bible In One Year:
- **Job 34–35**
- **Acts 15:1-21**

A beautifying project on the main road of my town prompted the demolition of a church built in the 1930s. Although the windows of the empty church had been removed, the doors remained in place for several days, even as bulldozers began knocking down walls. Each set of doors around the church building held a message written in giant, fluorescent-orange block letters: **KEEP OUT!**

Unfortunately, some churches whose doors are open convey that same message to visitors whose appearance doesn't measure up to their standards. No fluorescent, giant-size letters needed. With a single disapproving glance, some people communicate: "You're Not Welcome Here!"

How people look on the outside, of course, is not an indicator of what is in their hearts. God's focus is on the inner life of people. He looks far below the surface of someone's appearance (1 Sam. 16:7) and that's what He desires for us to do as well. He also knows the hearts of those who appear to be "righteous" but are "full of hypocrisy" on the inside (Matt. 23:28).

God's message of welcome, which we are to show to others, is clear. He says to all who seek Him: "Everyone who thirsts, come to the waters" (Isa. 55:1). —Cindy Hess Kasper

Thank You, Lord, that You welcome all into Your family,
and You have welcomed me. Show me how
to be as accepting of others as You are.
May I reveal Your heart of love.

No one will know what you mean when you say, "God is love"—unless you show it.

July 8
Wednesday

Jesus Loves Me

Read:
Romans 8:31-39

Keep yourselves in the love of God.
—Jude 1:21

The Bible In One Year:
■ Job 36–37
■ Acts 15:22-41

On cold days, our old dog moves around the yard, finding a sunny spot to stretch out on the grass to keep herself in the warmth of the sun.

This reminds me that we must "keep" ourselves in the love of God (Jude 1:21). That doesn't mean we have to act in some special way to make God love us (although our desire is to please Him). Because we are His children we're loved no matter what we do or fail to do. It means instead that we should think about His love and bask in its radiance and warmth all day long.

"[Nothing] shall be able to separate us from the love of God" (Rom. 8:39). He loved us before we were born, and He loves us now. This is our identity in Christ; it is who we are—God's beloved children. That's something to think about throughout the day.

Five times in John's gospel he described himself as the disciple Jesus loved (13:23; 19:26; 20:2; 21:7,20). Jesus loved His other disciples too, but John reveled in the fact that Jesus loved him! We can adopt John's theme—"I am the disciple Jesus loves!"—and repeat it to ourselves all day long. Or we can sing that familiar children's song in our hearts, "Jesus loves me, this I know." As we carry that truth with us throughout the day, we'll bask in the warmth of His love! —David Roper

I am so glad that our Father in heaven
Tells of His love in the Book He has given;
Wonderful things in the Bible I see—
This is the dearest, that Jesus loves me. —*Bliss*

God loves us not because of who we are, but because of who He is.

July 9
Thursday

Space Music

Read:
Job 38:1-7

Who laid [earth's] cornerstone, when the morning stars sang together, and all the sons of God shouted for joy? —Job 38:6-7

The Bible In One Year:
- **Job 38–40**
- **Acts 16:1-21**

One of NASA's observatories has discovered a giant black hole that hums. Located in the Perseus cluster of galaxies about 250 million light years from Earth, the black hole vibrates at the frequency of a B flat. But it is too low a pitch to be picked up by the human ear. Scientific instruments have placed the note at 57 octaves below middle C on a piano.

The idea of music and heavenly bodies is not new. In fact, when God revealed Himself to Job, He asked: "Where were you when I laid the foundations of the earth? . . . When the morning stars sang together, and all the sons of God shouted for joy?" (Job 38:4,7). We are told that at the creation of our marvelous universe, songs of praise and shouts of joy resounded to God's glory.

A wonderful hymn by St. Francis of Assisi captures the awe and worship we feel when beholding the radiant sun by day or the star-studded sky at night.

All creatures of our God and King,
Lift up your voice and with us sing Alleluia, Alleluia!
Thou burning sun with golden beam,
Thou silver moon with softer gleam:
O praise Him, O praise Him!
Alleluia! Alleluia! Alleluia!

"The heavens declare the glory of God; and the firmament shows His handiwork" (Ps. 19:1).

Let's praise the One who made such beauty for us to enjoy! —Dennis Fisher

---

The beauty of creation gives us reasons to sing God's praise.

July 10
Friday

Stand Firm

Read:
Colossians 1:19-27

Be steadfast, immovable, always abounding in the work of the Lord, knowing that your labor is not in vain in the Lord.
—1 Corinthians 15:58

The Bible In One Year:
- **Job 41–42**
- **Acts 16:22-40**

As our final project for a high school earth science class, a friend and I built a stream table. With extensive help from my father, we built a long plywood box with a hinge in the middle. Then we lined it with plastic and filled it with sand. At one end we attached a hose. At the other end was a drainage hole. After assembling all of it, we raised one end of the stream table, turned on the water, and watched as it created a path directly to the hole at the other end. The next part of the experiment was to place a rock in the stream and watch how it changed the path of the water.

This project taught me as much about life as it did about science. I learned that I can't change the direction things are going if I'm on the bank of the river. I have to step into the stream of life and stand there to divert the flow. That's what Jesus did. The Bible refers to salvation as a rock (2 Sam. 22:47; Ps. 62:2,6-7), and the apostle Paul clarifies that Christ is that Rock (1 Cor. 10:4). God placed Jesus in the stream of history to change its course.

When we remain steadfast in Christ, abounding in the work of the Lord, God uses us to change the course of history through acts of obedience that turn others to Him. —Julie Ackerman Link

The Master is seeking a harvest
In lives He's redeemed by His blood;
He seeks for the fruit of the Spirit
And works that will glorify God. —*Lehman*

Be sure to put your feet in the right place, then stand firm. —Abraham Lincoln

July 11
Saturday

The Winding Road

Read:
Psalm 121

He will not allow your foot to be moved; He who keeps you will not slumber.
—Psalm 121:3

The Bible In One Year:
- Psalms 1–3
- Acts 17:1-15

In his book *A Sweet and Bitter Providence,* John Piper offers these thoughts about God's providence and guidance: "Life is not a straight line leading from one blessing to the next and then finally to heaven. Life is a winding and troubled road. . . . God is not just showing up after the trouble and cleaning it up. He is plotting the course and managing the troubles with far-reaching purposes for our good and for the glory of Jesus Christ."

The Jews journeying to Jerusalem for the annual feasts (Deut. 16:16) had the assurance of knowing that the Lord was plotting their course and managing the winding and troubled roads for them. They expressed this assurance in Psalm 121, a pilgrim song. The question, "From whence comes my help?" did not express doubt but affirmation in the Lord who rules supreme (vv.1-2). Unlike a guard who sometimes slumbered, or the god Baal who needed to be rustled out of his stupor (1 Kings 18:27), the Lord is fully alert and secured the journey of His people with providential care (vv.3-4). The Lord, who rescued Israel, would continue to help, preserve, and walk with His people.

Life is a winding road with unknown perils and troubles, but we can be certain of God's providence, security, and care. —Marvin Williams

Dear Lord, sometimes life seems to be full of perilous and winding roads. Thank You for giving us the assurance that You have our course plotted and are watching over our every step.

Troubles are unknown; God's providence is certain.

July 12
Sunday

THAT'S JESUS!

READ:
Isaiah 53:4-12

He was wounded for our transgressions, He was bruised for our iniquities.
—Isaiah 53:5

THE BIBLE IN ONE YEAR:
- Psalms 4–6
- Acts 17:16-34

As a Jewish kid growing up in New York, Michael Brown had no interest in spiritual things. His life revolved around being a drummer for a band, and he got mixed up with drugs. But then some friends invited him to church, where he found the love and prayers of the people to be irresistible. After a short spiritual struggle, Michael trusted Jesus as Savior.

This was a monumental change for a wayward Jewish teen. One day he told his dad he had heard about Old Testament texts describing Jesus. His dad, incredulous, asked, "Where?" When Michael opened his Bible, it fell to Isaiah 53. They read it, and Michael exclaimed, "That's Him! That's Jesus!"

Indeed, it *is* Jesus. Through the help of Christians and the guidance of the Holy Spirit, Brown (today a Bible scholar and an author) came to recognize the Messiah of Isaiah 53. He experienced the salvation that changes lives, forgives sin, and gives abundant life to all who trust the "Man of sorrows" (v.3). Jesus is the One who was "wounded for our transgressions" and who died for us on the cross (v.5).

The Bible reveals Jesus, who alone has the power to change lives. —Dave Branon

God, I struggle with this idea of Jesus as Savior. I know He's a good man, but I need to see that He is more than that. Please show me—through others or through the Bible—how I can know for sure who Jesus is.

The Spirit of God uses the Word of God to change hearts.

July 13
Monday

The Life We'd Like To See

Read:
Luke 6:27-36

Just as you want men to do to you, you also do to them likewise.
—Luke 6:31

The Bible In One Year:
- **Psalms 7–9**
- **Acts 18**

The annual Texas Book Festival in Austin draws thousands of people who enjoy browsing for books, attending discussions led by acclaimed authors, and gleaning advice from professional writers. At one such festival, an author of young adult fiction told aspiring writers, "Write the book that you want to find on the shelf." That's a powerful recommendation for writing and for living. What if we decided to live the way we want everyone else to live?

In Luke 6:27-36, Jesus urged His followers to pursue a lifestyle that demonstrates God's mercy to all: "Love your enemies, do good to those who hate you, bless those who curse you, and pray for those who spitefully use you" (vv.27-28). He also said that generosity and a lack of retaliation should characterize our reaction to unreasonable treatment (vv.29-30). Jesus concluded, "Just as you want men to do to you, you also do to them likewise" (v.31).

Impossible? Yes, if we rely on our own strength and resolve. The strength comes from the Spirit. And the resolve comes from remembering how God has treated us: "He is kind to the unthankful and evil. Therefore be merciful, just as your Father also is merciful" (vv.35-36). That's a life we all long to see.

—David McCasland

All the way my Savior leads me—
What have I to ask beside?
Can I doubt His tender mercy,
Who through life has been my Guide? —*Crosby*

Christianity is not just Christ in you, but Christ living His life through you.

July 14
Tuesday

Warning Sign

Read:
Hebrews 3:1-13

Beware, brethren, lest there be in any of you an evil heart of unbelief in departing from the living God.
—Hebrews 3:12

The Bible In One Year:
- **Psalms 10–12**
- **Acts 19:1-20**

On a sandy beach in Uruguay, giant concrete fingers partially submerged in sand reach up toward the sky. It is called the Monument to the Drowned. Locals just call it *La Mano,* "The Hand." It was created by Chilean artist Mario Irarrázabal as a warning to swimmers about the danger of drowning. "The Hand" has become a tourist attraction, but its real purpose remains to remind swimmers about the perils of the sea.

The Word of God contains its own kind of warning signs. The book of Hebrews especially provides cautions about perils to the soul. "Beware, brethren, lest there be in any of you an evil heart of unbelief in departing from the living God; but exhort one another daily, while it is called 'Today,' lest any of you be hardened through the deceitfulness of sin" (Heb. 3:12-13).

The context of the verse is a review of the unbelief and rebellion of Israel in the wilderness. Though this happened centuries before the book of Hebrews was written, the spiritual principle applies today. We are to exhort one another to resist the hardening of our hearts that comes with sin.

Warning signs are given to us for our safety. Praise God that He has given us protective warnings in His Word because of His great love for us. —Dennis Fisher

Lord, thank You for the warnings in Your Word
that are intended to protect and preserve my life.
Help me to heed Your reproofs and instruction
that I may live a life that is pleasing to You.

God gives us loving warnings in His Word to protect and preserve us.

July 15
Wednesday

Read Backwards

Read:
Revelation 21:1-7

He who overcomes shall inherit all things, and I will be his God and he shall be My son.
—Revelation 21:7

The Bible In One Year:
- Psalms 13–15
- Acts 19:21-41

I confess that I sometimes read the end of a book before I read the beginning. Doing so allows me to know which characters live and which characters don't. When I know how it will turn out, I'm able to relax and thoroughly appreciate and enjoy the story and the characters.

In a similar way, reading the final book of the Bible, the book of Revelation, can be an encouragement and comfort for the followers of Jesus. Time and again, Christians are called to be overcomers (1 John 4:4; 5:4; Rev. 2:7,11,17,26; 3:5,12,21). We can be overcomers now and will be for all eternity.

As the apostle John talks about the revealing of the new heaven and the new earth in Revelation (21:1), he describes what the final victory will look like for those who have received Jesus as Savior. At that time, we will see the end of death, tears, sorrow, and pain (v.4). The Lord declares: "He who overcomes shall inherit all things, and I will be his God and he shall be My son" (v.7). He will dwell with us (v.3), and He will "make all things new" (v.5).

When the trials of today seem more daunting than your strength, let the Lord show you the end of the story when you will be in His presence forever! —Randy Kilgore

Stand up, stand up for Jesus, the strife will not be long;
This day the noise of battle—the next the victor's song.
To him that overcometh a crown of life shall be;
He with the King of glory shall reign eternally. —*Duffield*

For hope today, remember the end of the story—eternity with God.

July 16
Thursday

Hard Way To Strength

Read:
2 Corinthians 12:1-10

My strength is made perfect in weakness.
—2 Corinthians 12:9

The Bible In One Year:
- Psalms 16–17
- Acts 20:1-16

Diamonds are beautiful and valuable gemstones, but their beginning is common carbon—black, dirty, and combustible. Through years of intense heat and high pressure, they become pure and strong. This makes them a good metaphor for spiritual strength; God uses intense outside forces to rid us of impurities and to perfect His strength in us.

God's strength is made perfect in our weakness, says the apostle Paul (2 Cor. 12:9). I wish this were not true because I hate being weak. Chemotherapy and radiation treatments taught me more than I ever wanted to know about physical weakness. Then a minor event plunged me into a state of emotional weakness that caught me off guard. After losing 3 feet of hair and being bald for nearly a year, one bad haircut should not have been a big deal. But it was, and I felt silly for being so weak. Some of us are able to create an illusion of strength and self-sufficiency. But sudden loss of health, employment, or a treasured relationship is a startling reminder of our total dependence on God.

When we experience the fiery furnace of suffering—whether physical or emotional, whether persecution from without or humiliation from within—God's loving purpose is to make us pure and strong. —Julie Ackerman Link

God uses testing in our lives
To rid us of impurity
And teach us that our strength's in Him
And not in self-sufficiency. —*Sper*

Suffering is the fire that God uses to purify and strengthen us.

July 17
Friday

What We Talk About

Read:
Psalm 19

Let the words of my mouth and the meditation of my heart be acceptable in Your sight, O Lord. —Psalm 19:14

The Bible In One Year:
- **Psalms 18–19**
- **Acts 20:17-38**

Perhaps you are familiar with the saying, "Great minds discuss ideas; average minds discuss events; small minds discuss people." Admittedly, there are ways to speak of people that can honor them. But this saying highlights our darker experiences. In a world of ever-present media—social and professional—we are continually confronted with people's lives at a level of intimacy that can be inappropriate.

Worse, this tidal wave of personal information about others could become grist for our conversational mills to the point that gossip becomes the norm—and not just about the rich and famous. People in our workplaces, churches, neighborhoods, and families can also be targets of sharp tongues and feel the pain of discussions that never should have happened.

How can we escape our inclination to use words to hurt others? By recognizing that the ultimate Hearer of our words is God, who longs for us to be better than that. With the psalmist, we can pray, "Let the words of my mouth and the meditation of my heart be acceptable in Your sight, O Lord" (Ps. 19:14). When we seek to please God with our conversations about others, we honor Him. With His help, we can glorify Him through what we talk about. —Bill Crowder

Forgive me, Father, for the times my speech
crosses the line of that which is appropriate.
Help me to understand the power of words,
and give me the wisdom to use them well.

It is better to bite your tongue than to make a biting remark.

July 18
Saturday

Creating Your Life

Read:
Mark 10:35-45

Whoever of you desires to be first shall be slave of all. —Mark 10:44

The Bible In One Year:
- **Psalms 20–22**
- **Acts 21:1-17**

The advice that I read in a self-help book sounded good: Do only what you're great at because that's when you'll feel most fulfilled. The author was trying to help readers create the kind of life they wanted. I don't know about you, but if I did only what I was great at, I wouldn't accomplish much!

In Mark 10, we read about two disciples, James and John, who had some plans for the kind of life they wanted for themselves someday. They asked to be at Jesus' right and left hand in His kingdom (v.37). The other 10 disciples were "greatly displeased" with them for asking (v.41). (Possibly because that was the kind of position they wanted for themselves!)

But Jesus used the opportunity to teach His followers about another kind of life—one of serving others. He said, "Whoever desires to become great among you shall be your servant. And whoever of you desires to be first shall be slave of all" (vv.43-44). It appears that service for others is God's design for us.

Even Jesus, the Son of God, "did not come to be served, but to serve" (v.45). As we look at Christ's example and depend on the Holy Spirit's help, we too can be servants and will create a fulfilling life. —Anne Cetas

I admit, Lord, that my eyes do get focused
on myself. But I really do want to live from a heart of
love for You. Teach me to be a servant
and to look for my fulfillment in You.

Great occasions for serving God come seldom,
but little ones surround us daily.

July 19
Sunday

Don't Forget

Read:
Deuteronomy 8:7-18

Beware that you do not forget the Lord your God.
—Deuteronomy 8:11

The Bible In One Year:
- **Psalms 23–25**
- **Acts 21:18-40**

I don't agree with those who rail against material things and say that owning stuff is inherently evil. And I have to admit that I'm a consumer—often tempted to pad my pile of treasures with items I think I need.

But I do recognize that one of the dangers of owning a lot of stuff is that it can lead to spiritual loss. The more we have and the more we feel as if we have all we need, the more prone we are to forget our need for God and even our desire for Him. Yet, ironically, everything we have comes ultimately from God, who "gives us richly all things to enjoy" (1 Tim. 6:17).

Sadly, our enjoyment of God's provisions might just mean that we end up loving the gift and forgetting the Giver. This is why, when God was getting ready to give His people a life full of bounty in the Promised Land of good and plenty, He warned, "Beware that you do not forget the Lord your God" (Deut. 8:11).

If God has allowed you to enjoy material abundance, remind yourself where it came from. In fact, all of us, whether rich in this world's goods or not, have much to be thankful for. Let's heed the warning not to forget the Lord and praise Him for His abundant goodness. —Joe Stowell

I'd rather have Jesus than silver or gold,
I'd rather be His than have riches untold;
I'd rather have Jesus than anything
This world affords today. —*Miller*

Love the Giver more than the gifts!

July 20
Monday

EARWORMS

READ:
Philippians 4:4-9

**If there is any virtue and if there is anything praiseworthy—meditate on these things.
—Philippians 4:8**

THE BIBLE IN ONE YEAR:
- Psalms 26–28
- Acts 22

They burrow. They bore in. They attach themselves inside your head. *Earworms*, a term once used exclusively for insects, is now the name for those unrelenting tunes that you can't get out of your head. Songs like, "The Lion Sleeps Tonight," the "Barney" song, or my personal nightmare: "It's a Small World After All."

They say the only way to rid yourself of the insidious infestation is to replace it with another tune—your "cleaner" song. New words and a fresh tune can crowd out the old.

Maybe we could use a cleaner song for our thought-life as well. When lustful or vengeful thoughts creep into our minds, reading and meditating on God's Word can help to clean up our thinking.

Scripture tells us to love the Lord "with all [our] heart, with all [our] soul, and with all [our] mind" (Matt. 22:37) and not to "be conformed to this world" but to "be transformed by the renewing of [our] mind" (Rom. 12:2). It instructs us to think about things that are true, noble, right, pure, lovely, admirable, excellent, and praiseworthy (Phil. 4:8).

When our minds wander to evil, the best "cleaner" is to allow the wisdom of the Bible to permeate our thoughts and hearts (2 Tim. 3:16). —Cindy Hess Kasper

Dear Lord, our desire is to spend time in Your Word.
We know that meditating on Your Word fills our minds
with thoughts of You and helps to keep our
thinking from wandering to evil. Help us to do so.

Character is the sum total of all our thoughts, words, and deeds.

July 21
Tuesday

ARROGANCE AND PRIDE

READ:
Proverbs 8:12-21

Pride and arrogance and the evil way and the perverse mouth I hate. —Proverbs 8:13

THE BIBLE IN ONE YEAR:
- **Psalms 29–30**
- **Acts 23:1-15**

In *The Screwtape Letters* written by C. S. Lewis, a senior devil urges his young protégé to divert a Christian's thoughts away from God and focus instead on the faults of the people around him at church.

During a Sunday service, I found myself distracted and somewhat annoyed by a person near me who sang loudly off key and was out of sync during the unison readings. But when we bowed our heads for a time of silent prayer, it struck me that the Lord must surely be more pleased with that other person's heart than with the judgmental feelings He saw in mine.

A few days later I happened to read Proverbs 8 and was struck by verse 13: "Pride and arrogance and the evil way and the perverse mouth I hate." Throughout this chapter, wisdom calls to us to gain an understanding heart (v.5) and to find life and obtain favor from the Lord (v.35). The alternative is to go through life with a superior attitude while dying inside in the process (v.36).

Pride is a sword that wounds the person who uses it along with those against whom it is used. Arrogance robs us of all God longs to give us, but "by humility and the fear of the LORD are riches and honor and life" (22:4). —David McCasland

Oh, just a bit of Thy meekness, my Savior,
To be the least when of self I would boast;
Finding my glory and strength in Thy favor,
Know in my weakness Thy grace can do most. —*Bosch*

Pride brings shame. Humility brings wisdom.

July 22
Wednesday

More, More, More

Read:
Luke 12:13-21

Take heed and beware of covetousness, for one's life does not consist in the abundance of the things he possesses. —Luke 12:15

The Bible In One Year:
■ Psalms 31–32
■ Acts 23:16-35

Some people love to shop. They have a perpetual desire to buy, buy, buy. The craze to find the latest deal is worldwide. There are huge shopping malls in China, Saudi Arabia, Canada, the Philippines, the United States, and around the world. A rise in store purchases and online buying show that buying is a global phenomenon.

Shopping can be fun. Certainly, there is nothing wrong with trying to find a real deal and to enjoy the things God has given to us. But when we become preoccupied with obtaining material goods, we lose focus.

Jesus challenged His listeners with these words: "Take heed and beware of covetousness, for one's life does not consist in the abundance of the things he possesses" (Luke 12:15). He went on to tell a parable about a man "who lays up treasure for himself," but is not concerned about his relationship with God (v.21).

How can we learn to be content with what we have and not be consumed with amassing more? Here are some ways: View material goods as given by God to be used wisely (Matt. 25:14-30). Work hard to earn and save money (Prov. 6:6-11). Give to the Lord's work and those in need (2 Cor. 9:7; Prov. 19:17). And always remember to be thankful and to enjoy what God gives (1 Tim. 6:17). —Dennis Fisher

Lord, our hearts often run after "stuff." Teach
us not to be obsessed with collecting more and
more material goods. May we instead learn
what it means to be "rich" toward You.

To be rich in God is far better than to be rich in goods.

July 23
Thursday

ROAD CONSTRUCTION

READ:
Jeremiah 31:31-34

We have been delivered from the law, . . . so that we should serve in the newness of the Spirit. —Romans 7:6

THE BIBLE IN ONE YEAR:
- **Psalms 33–34**
- **Acts 24**

Here in Michigan we joke that we have two seasons: winter and road construction. Harsh winters damage road surfaces, so repair crews begin their work as soon as the ice melts and the ground thaws. Although we call this work "construction," much of what they do looks like "destruction." In some cases, simply patching holes is not an option. Workers have to replace the old road with a new one.

That's what it can feel like when God is at work in our lives. Throughout the Old Testament, God told His people to expect some major renovation on the road between Him and them (Isa. 62:10-11; Jer. 31:31). When God sent Jesus, it seemed to the Jews as if their way to God was being destroyed. But Jesus wasn't destroying anything. He was completing it (Matt. 5:17). The old way paved with laws became a new way paved with the sacrificial love of Jesus.

God is still at work replacing old ways of sin and legalism with the way of love that Jesus completed. When He removes our old ways of thinking and behaving, it may feel as if everything familiar is being destroyed. But God is not destroying anything; He is building a better way. And we can be confident that the end result will be smoother relationships with others and a closer relationship with Him. —Julie Ackerman Link

Free from the law—O happy condition!
Jesus has bled, and there is remission;
Cursed by the law and bruised by the fall,
Grace has redeemed us once for all. —*Bliss*

Upheaval often precedes spiritual progress.

July 24
Friday

Too Blessed

Read:
Psalm 107:1-8

Oh, that men would give thanks to the Lord for His goodness, and for His wonderful works to the children of men! —Psalm 107:8

The Bible In One Year:
- **Psalms 35–36**
- **Acts 25**

On my daily commute to and from the office, I have plenty of time for reading—bumper stickers on cars, that is. Some are surly, others clever, and still others downright distasteful. One bumper sticker I saw recently, however, gently challenged my heart about the way I often engage life. The sticker simply said, "Too blessed to complain."

I must confess that I felt convicted as I pondered those words. Too often I find myself lamenting moments in life that don't go my way, rather than focusing on the wonderful gifts my heavenly Father has given me. Reading that simple message that day brought me a renewed commitment to be more actively and intentionally grateful because my God has been good to me in more ways than I could ever count.

Psalm 107 is a song that seeks to rectify thankless thinking. The psalmist (who many think was King David) makes a plea to hearts grown cold with ingratitude, repeating four times, "Oh, that men would give thanks to the Lord for His goodness, and for His wonderful works to the children of men!" (vv.8,15,21,31). Even in the worst of times, we have much to be thankful for. May we learn to thank God for His goodness to us! —Bill Crowder

Count your blessings—name them one by one;
Count your blessings—see what God hath done;
Count your blessings—name them one by one;
Count your many blessings—see what God hath done. —Oatman

We don't need more to be thankful for, we just need to be more thankful.

July 25
Saturday

Where Can Wisdom Be Found?

Read:
James 3:13-17

If any of you lacks wisdom, let him ask of God. —James 1:5

The Bible In One Year:
- **Psalms 37–39**
- **Acts 26**

Wisdom is the beauty of holiness. James says wisdom is reasonable; flexible; forgiving; peaceful; caring; given to friendly visits, small acts of courtesy, and kind words. It is humble, transparent, simple, gentle, and gracious to the core (James 3:17).

Where can wisdom be found? It comes from heaven (1:5). "Wisdom," wrote Charles Spurgeon, "is a beauty of life that can only be produced by God's workmanship in us."

It's good to ask from time to time: "Am I growing in wisdom?" After all, life is relentlessly dynamic. We're either growing sweeter and wiser as the days go by, or we're growing into foolish or even sour-faced curmudgeons. Into what are we growing?

It's never too late to begin growing in wisdom. God loves us with an ardent, intense affection that can deliver us from our foolishness if we yield ourselves to Him. His love can make the most difficult nature into a miracle of astonishing beauty. It may hurt a little and it may take a while, but God relentlessly seeks our transformation. When we ask, His wisdom will begin to rise in us and pour itself out to others.

We have this promise: "If any of you lacks wisdom, let him ask of God, who gives to all liberally and without reproach, and it will be given to [you]" (1:5). —David Roper

Lord, please put an end to our foolishness and
turn our hearts toward the wisdom that comes
only from You. We ask You now to take our
lives and transform them into Your likeness.

True wisdom begins and ends with God.

July 26
Sunday

TAKING ROOT

READ:
Matthew 13:1-9

Some fell on stony places, where they did not have much earth; and they immediately sprang up.
—Matthew 13:5

THE BIBLE IN ONE YEAR:
- **Psalms 40–42**
- **Acts 27:1-26**

A small area of my yard just couldn't seem to get going. The grass always seemed sparse in that spot, no matter how well I watered it.

So one day I stuck a shovel into this troublesome real estate and discovered the problem: Just below the surface was a layer of stones about three inches deep. This led me to replace the stones with rich topsoil in which new seeds could take root.

Jesus talked about seed and soils. In a parable in Matthew 13 about what happens when the seed of the gospel is sown on various kinds of ground, He said that seeds that land on stones and "not much earth" grow quickly but then die in the sun (vv.5-6). He was speaking of one who has heard and received the gospel, but in whose life the message doesn't take root. When trouble comes, this person—who is not a genuine believer—falls away.

How grateful we can be for Jesus' words that conclude this parable: "He who received seed on the good ground is he who hears the Word and understands it, who indeed bears fruit" (v.23). What a reminder of both the privilege and the responsibility that accompanies our salvation.

Praise God for the seed of the gospel and the soil of spiritual growth. —Dave Branon

Lord, I would be soil in which You can plant
Your Word with its promise of fruit;
I want to be open to You every day,
So what You have planted takes root. —*Hess*

A heart open to God is soil in which the seed of His Word can flourish.

July 27
Monday

The Rules Of Disengagement

Read:
Genesis 50:15-21
John 8:31-36

If the Son makes you free, you shall be free indeed. —John 8:36

The Bible In One Year:
- Psalms 43–45
- Acts 27:27-44

In her book *Throw Out Fifty Things,* Gail Blanke outlines four "Rules of Disengagement" to help people clear the clutter from their lives. The first rule states: "If it . . . weighs you down, clogs you up, or just plain makes you feel bad about yourself, throw it out, give it away, sell it, let it go, move on."

I think this Rule of Disengagement has a spiritual application too: We don't have to stay connected to past sin. Joseph's brothers struggled with this. Years after they sold Joseph into slavery, they recalled their cruelty and feared revenge (Gen. 50:15). So they sent a message to Joseph, begging for forgiveness (vv.16-17). They did this despite previous merciful actions and reassurances from their brother (45:4-15).

Many of us remain connected to age-old offenses despite mercy and forgiveness from those we may have hurt. However, true freedom comes when we confess our wrongdoing to God. He forgives it (1 John 1:9) and separates us from it (Ps. 103:12). As one verse puts it, He throws our sin into the depths of the sea! (Micah 7:19). Because of this, we can remind ourselves that the Son has made us free, and we are free indeed (John 8:36). —Jennifer Benson Schuldt

'Twas a glad day when Jesus found me,
When His strong arms were thrown around me;
When my sins He buried in the deepest sea,
And my soul He filled with joy and victory. —Reitz

The price of our freedom from sin was paid by Jesus' blood.

July 28
Tuesday

THE WISDOM OF CROWDS

READ:
1 Corinthians 1:18-25

Where there is no counsel, the people fall; but in the multitude of counselors there is safety.
—Proverbs 11:14

THE BIBLE IN ONE YEAR:
- **Psalms 46–48**
- **Acts 28**

The online description of *The Wisdom of Crowds* reads, "In this fascinating book, *New Yorker* business columnist James Surowiecki explores a deceptively simple idea: Large groups of people are smarter than an elite few, no matter how brilliant—better at solving problems, fostering innovation, coming to wise decisions, even predicting the future."

The author uses a variety of things, ranging from pop culture to politics, to present one basic thought: More often than not, the crowd gets it right. It's an interesting theory, but one that would probably be debated during election years or when someone's favorite contestant is voted off a reality TV show.

While the Bible makes it clear that the wisdom of crowds may not be reliable and can be dangerous (Matt. 7:13-14), there is another way collective wisdom can be helpful. In Proverbs 11:14, we read, "Where there is no counsel, the people fall; but in the multitude of counselors there is safety." One of the benefits of the body of Christ is that we can assist one another—in part by working together to seek God's wisdom. When we join together to pursue God's purposes, we find safety in His provision of each other and receive His wisdom for the challenges of life. —Bill Crowder

Immortal, invisible, God only wise,
In light inaccessible hid from our eyes,
Most blessed, most glorious, the Ancient of Days,
Almighty, victorious, Thy great name we praise. —*Smith*

We best pursue the wisdom of God when we pursue it together.

July 29
Wednesday

What's Love?

Read:
Psalm 103:1-14

In this is love, not that we loved God, but that He loved us and sent His Son. —1 John 4:10

The Bible In One Year:
- **Psalms 49–50**
- **Romans 1**

When asked "What's love?" children have some great answers. Noelle, age 7, said, "Love is when you tell a guy you like his shirt, then he wears it every day." Rebecca, who is 8, answered, "Since my grandmother got arthritis, she can't bend over and polish her toenails anymore. So my grandfather does it for her all the time, even after his hands got arthritis too. That's love." Jessica, also 8, concluded, "You really shouldn't say 'I love you' unless you mean it. But if you mean it, you should say it a lot. People forget."

Sometimes we need reminding that God loves us. We focus on the difficulties of life and wonder, *Where's the love?* But if we pause and consider all that God has done for us, we remember how much we are loved by God, who *is* love (1 John 4:8-10).

Psalm 103 lists the "benefits" God showers on us in love: He forgives our sin (v.3), satisfies us with good things (v.5), and executes righteousness and justice (v.6). He is slow to anger and abounds in mercy (v.8). He doesn't deal with us as our sins deserve (v.10) and has removed our sin as far as the east is from the west (v.12). He has not forgotten us!

What's love? God is love, and He's pouring out that love on you and me. —Anne Cetas

Our God is God—
His truth, His love remains each day the same,
He's faithful to His matchless name,
For God is God—He does not change. —D. DeHaan

The death of Christ is the measure of God's love for you.

July 30
Thursday

A PERSON OF INFLUENCE

READ:
2 Kings 5:1-15

She said to her mistress, "If only my master were with the prophet who is in Samaria! For he would heal him of his leprosy." —2 Kings 5:3

THE BIBLE IN ONE YEAR:
- Psalms 51–53
- Romans 2

If you Google "person of influence," the search will take you to various lists of "the most influential people in the world." These lists usually include political leaders; business entrepreneurs and athletes; along with people in science, the arts, and entertainment. You will not find the names of cooks and cleaners who work for them. Yet those in so-called lowly positions often influence the people they serve.

The story of Naaman, a high-ranking military commander, includes two kings and a prophet of God (2 Kings 5:1-15). Yet it was the servants in the background whose words led to Naaman being cured of leprosy, a career-ending, life-changing disease.

A young servant girl taken captive from Israel told Naaman's wife that a prophet in Samaria could heal him (vv.2-3). When Elisha's instructions to bathe in the Jordan River angered Naaman, his servants urged him to follow the prophet's orders. The result was Naaman's restoration to health and his declaration, "Now I know that there is no God in all the earth, except in Israel" (v.15).

What a beautiful picture of our role as followers of Jesus Christ! We are called to be people of influence—the Lord's servants who point others to the One whose touch can change their lives. —David McCasland

Lord, I would like to live a life of influence like
Naaman's servant girl—to be brave and bold
to touch the lives of others by pointing them to
You. Fill me, Holy Spirit, with Your power.

Christ sends us out to bring others in.

July 31
Friday

Your Flight Is Confirmed

Read:
Romans 3:21-26

For as in Adam all die, even so in Christ all shall be made alive.
—1 Corinthians 15:22

The Bible In One Year:
■ Psalms 54–56
■ Romans 3

A heavy thunderstorm delayed our flight to Frankfurt, causing us to miss our connecting flight. We were told that we had been confirmed on another flight the next evening. But when we arrived at the gate, we were told that we were on standby. The flight was full.

When I learned this, I wondered if this was mere miscommunication or if this was how they dealt with missed flights. If passengers had been told up front that they were only on standby, they would have been unhappy. Perhaps they saved the truth until later.

Thankfully, God doesn't work that way. He clearly tells us everything we need to know to get to heaven. The Bible declares that "all have sinned and fall short of the glory of God" (Rom. 3:23). God gave us the full picture of our sin nature from Genesis 3 so that He could give us His full and complete solution.

God's solution in Romans 3:24 is that we are "justified freely by His grace through the redemption that is in Christ Jesus." God sent His own sinless Son to die for our sins. His sacrifice on the cross provided us forgiveness. All we need to do is receive that free gift through faith. I'm so glad God told us the truth up front! He hasn't left us to find our own way. —C. P. Hia

Thank You, Almighty God, that You don't hide the truth from us. You showed us how completely sin has affected our lives in order to reinforce just how much Jesus Christ has delivered us from.

Christ's work makes us safe;
God's Word makes us sure.

August 1
Saturday

SNAPPING, SNARLING THOUGHTS

READ:
Psalm 59

You have been my defense and refuge in the day of my trouble.
—Psalm 59:16

THE BIBLE IN ONE YEAR:
- **Psalms 57–59**
- **Romans 4**

Many years ago, my father and I hiked through Big Bend in Texas. It's a national park now, but in those days it was rough country.

One night we were rolling out our sleeping bags when a couple with a dog asked if they could camp nearby. We welcomed their company and turned in for the night. They tethered their dog to a stake beside their tent.

Some hours later my father nudged me awake and turned his flashlight into the darkness. Illuminated by the light, we saw pairs of yellow eyes peering out of the shadows. A pack of snapping and snarling coyotes were closing in on the dog. Although we chased them off and our neighbors put the dog in their tent, we slept fitfully.

I think of that night when I read Psalm 59 and David's twice-repeated imagery: "At evening they return, they growl like a dog" (vv.6,14). David was thinking of Saul's army that was closing in on him. I think, however, of the thoughts that return to menace us. They come back at nightfall, snapping and snarling: "You're stupid." "You're a failure." "You're useless." "Who needs you?"

When we have such thoughts, we can revel in God's unconditional, unending love. His steady devotion is our refuge in the dark night of self-doubt and fear (v.16). —David Roper

Dear Lord, I am so thankful that You love me unconditionally. Please chase away destructive thoughts that keep returning to take away my confidence in You and Your work in me. I want to rest in You and Your love.

Knowing that God loves us can dispel doubt.

August 2
Sunday

Pass It On

Read:
2 Corinthians 1:3-7

As you are partakers of the sufferings, so also you will partake of the consolation.
—2 Corinthians 1:7

The Bible In One Year:
- **Psalms 60–62**
- **Romans 5**

I've noticed through the years that those who have suffered are quick to comfort other sufferers. When a young couple suffers the loss of a child, another couple who also lost a child in the past asks if they can help. If a couple loses their main income, almost immediately another couple steps forward to offer their aid, remembering their own journey through foreclosure years earlier. Again and again we see the body of Christ supporting and encouraging one another. These Christians have learned that they can use the trials they've been through to reach out to others going through similar difficulties.

Have you been sick? Lost a loved one? Been imprisoned? Unfairly treated? In all of our trials, God promises to bring something good out of even our darkest moments (James 1:2-4). One key way this takes place is when we share the comfort He offered us with those who are now going through trials.

As Paul points out in 2 Corinthians 1:3-7, we are comforted by a Savior who knows our suffering, and we honor Him when we pass His comfort on to still others.

May we never leave someone to suffer alone. If we know the trail another is on, God will help us to guide that person to His presence—the surest comfort of all. —Randy Kilgore

Dear Lord, help us to step forward when others around us are suffering trials similar to what we've been through. Enable us to be a comfort, as You have been to us in the past.

God comforts us so that we can comfort others.

August 3
Monday

Corine

Read:
1 Peter 4:7-11

Be hospitable to one another without grumbling.
—1 Peter 4:9

The Bible In One Year:
- **Psalms 63–65**
- **Romans 6**

A group of us were helping to put together packets of material at an *Our Daily Bread* event in Orlando last winter when Corine greeted us. It was mid-morning, and she was sure we must be hungry and thirsty. I told her we were "fine," and she replied, "I know you're fine, but you need something to eat." A few minutes later she came back with cold water and snacks.

Throughout the 2 days we were there, Corine came by to check on us, bring us food or water, and take away our trash. On one occasion, I thanked her and said, "You have the gift of hospitality, don't you, Corine!" She looked down and replied, "I don't know. But you write the devotional articles, and I'll clean up. And God will be glorified."

Corine's desire is to bring God glory by helping people. She definitely has the gift of hospitality and practices it well. God has graced each of His children with skills and abilities so that He can minister to others through us. You can find those gifts listed in Romans 12:4-13, 1 Corinthians 12:27-31, Ephesians 4:7-12, and 1 Peter 4:9-11.

The Lord has gifted us "that in all things God may be glorified through Jesus Christ, to whom belong the glory and the dominion forever and ever" (1 Peter 4:11). —Anne Cetas

All Christians have been gifted
By grace from God above,
Equipped to build and strengthen
The church in faith and love. —*Fitzhugh*

You are one of a kind—
designed to glorify God as only you can.

August 4
Tuesday

Take Time To Ponder

Read:
Luke 2:8-19

Mary kept all these things and pondered them in her heart.
—Luke 2:19

The Bible In One Year:
- **Psalms 66–67**
- **Romans 7**

Parents love to remember the developmental milestones of their children. They will record in a baby book when their little ones first roll over, then crawl, and take their first steps. Often they will take photographs and save baby clothing to bring back the memories of those precious experiences.

According to Luke 2:19, Mary, the mother of Jesus, kept a baby book of sorts—in her heart. She treasured the promises that had been given about her Son and "pondered them." The Greek word for "ponder" means "placing together for comparison." Mary had heard of great things concerning her Son from angels and shepherds (1:32; 2:17-18). As His life unfolded, she would compare those promises with how her Son acted to fulfill them.

Our faith will be strengthened and we will be encouraged when we meditate on what the Scriptures say about God and compare it with the way He works in our own lives (John 14:21). He is a God who answers prayer (1 John 5:14-15), comforts us in our suffering (2 Cor. 1:3-4), and provides for our needs (Phil. 4:19).

When we take time to ponder, we will see the faithfulness of our great God. —Dennis Fisher

Pardon for sin and a peace that endureth,
Thine own dear presence to cheer and to guide,
Strength for today and bright hope for tomorrow—
Blessings all mine, with ten thousand beside! —*Chisholm*

God gives by promise that we may take by faith.

August 5
Wednesday

The Other Eighty Percent

Read:
Psalm 69:29-36

Let heaven and earth praise Him, the seas and everything that moves in them.
—Psalm 69:34

The Bible In One Year:
- **Psalms 68–69**
- **Romans 8:1-21**

Recently I saw a billboard stating that 80 percent of all life on Earth is found in the seas. That staggering number is difficult to process, largely because most of that life is out of sight.

As I considered this, it reminded me of how much greater God's creation is than we typically appreciate. While we can easily have our breath taken away by a majestic mountain range or a panoramic sunset, we sometimes fail to see His extraordinary work in the details that require more careful study and examination. Not only is much of God's creation hidden by the oceans, but other parts are also too small for our eyes to observe. From the microscopically small to the unsearched reaches of the universe, it is all the work of our Creator. In those magnificent structures—seen and unseen—God's creative glory is revealed (Rom. 1:20).

As we grow to understand the wonder of creation, it must always point us to the Creator Himself—and call us to worship Him. As the psalmist said, "Let heaven and earth praise Him, the seas and everything that moves in them" (Ps. 69:34). If creation itself gives praise to the Creator, we can and should certainly join the chorus. What a mighty God we serve! —Bill Crowder

O Lord my God, when I in awesome wonder,
Consider all the worlds Thy hands have made,
I see the stars, I hear the rolling thunder,
Thy power throughout the universe displayed! —*Boberg*

The wonder of creation causes us to say, "What a wonderful God!"

August 6
Thursday

THE STANDOFF

READ:
1 John 4:1-6

**He who is in you is greater than he who is in the world.
—1 John 4:4**

THE BIBLE IN ONE YEAR:
- Psalms 70–71
- Romans 8:22-39

When a local bookstore rearranged its shelves, I noticed an increase in the number of titles relating to sorcery and witchcraft. In fact, the religion section had become a virtual "standoff" between light and darkness. Christian titles flanked one side of the aisle, while roughly the same number of occult books lined the other side.

Sometimes we may think of God and Satan in the same way I thought of the books in that bookstore. We see them as opposing but equal forces with the same unlimited power. However, God is God and Satan is not. God is stronger than any force of darkness. He does what He pleases (Ps. 135:6), while Satan's power is limited to what God allows. When Satan supposed that misfortune would make Job curse God, God told Satan, "Behold, all that [Job] has is in your power; only do not lay a hand on his person" (Job 1:12). Satan had to play by God's rules.

Because God is in charge over everything, as Christ's followers we don't need to be paralyzed by fear of Satan's power over our lives or the lives of the believers around us. He tempts us and tries to influence us, but the Bible assures us, "He who is in [us] is greater than he who is in the world" (1 John 4:4). —Jennifer Benson Schuldt

All hail the pow'r of Jesus' name!
Let angels prostrate fall;
Bring forth the royal diadem,
And crown Him Lord of all! —Perronet

The powers of evil around you are no match for the power of Jesus within you.

August 7
Friday

Childhood Beginnings

Read:
2 Timothy 3:14-17

Even the Son of Man did not come to be served, but to serve.
—Mark 10:45

The Bible In One Year:
■ Psalms 72–73
■ Romans 9:1-15

Last summer, our church invited a young man to join the staff. As Caleb shared how he grew up in Costa Rica while his family was serving Christ there, he reflected on the words of 2 Timothy 3:14-17. From his childhood, he reminisced, he had known the Bible. His mother and father had taught him the truths of the Scriptures that were "able to make [him] wise for salvation through faith which is in Christ Jesus" (v.15). He acknowledged that his preparation to be a pastor had begun when he was still a child.

Our congregation had the opportunity to "meet" his family in Costa Rica via a video-conferencing call. Caleb's dad challenged his son using the words of Jesus about Himself in Mark 10:45. He said, "Caleb, remember our family motto, 'We are here to serve, not to be served.'" It was easy to understand how this young man had developed his maturity of faith.

The children God has entrusted to us are precious gifts. A good foundation will help them to develop into mature believers who are "complete, thoroughly equipped for every good work" (2 Tim. 3:17). With God's help we can pass on the baton of faith to future generations. What a great privilege to be servants like Jesus. —Cindy Hess Kasper

Begin to train them early
To fear and love the Lord,
To carry on life's pathway
God's lamp, His holy Word. —*Fennema*

Children are God's precious jewels—
help them shine for Christ.

August 8
Saturday

Reflections On Windows

Read:
Psalm 34:1-10

Open my eyes, that I may see wondrous things from Your law.
—Psalm 119:18

The Bible In One Year:
- **Psalms 74–76**
- **Romans 9:16-33**

Much of the scenery I saw during our vacation in Alaska was through the windows of moving vehicles. I was thankful for glass that allowed me to see the beauty while remaining warm and dry. But the windows also presented a challenge. When it rained, water drops on the outside obscured the view. When the temperature changed, condensation caused fog to develop on the inside.

Those challenges help me understand why it is impossible for us to see life the way God intended it. Sin obscures the beauty of life that God wants us to enjoy. Sometimes sin is inside—our selfishness creates a fog that makes us see ourselves as more important than we are and causes us to forget about others' interests. Sometimes sin is outside. The injustice of others causes our tears to fall like rain, preventing us from seeing the goodness of God. Sin of any kind keeps us from seeing the wonder and glory of life as God designed it.

For now, even though "we see things imperfectly, like puzzling reflections in a mirror" (1 Cor. 13:12 NLT), we see enough to know that God is good (Ps. 34:8). The many wonderful things that God has revealed will help us to forsake sin and work to minimize its consequences in the world. —Julie Ackerman Link

Lord, improve our vision. Clear the fog that comes from self-centered thinking. Help us to uphold justice, to offer comfort to others, and to wipe away the tears that have been left by the storms of life.

The only way to see life clearly is to focus on Christ.

August 9
Sunday

BELONGING

READ:
John 14:1-11

In my Father's house are many mansions . . . . I go to prepare a place for you.
—John 14:2

THE BIBLE IN ONE YEAR:
- **Psalms 77–78**
- **Romans 10**

My dad was full of stories about his hometown. So you can imagine how excited I was as a child when he took our family there every summer. We fished the St. Joseph River together and visited his boyhood farm where all of his stories came to life. Although that place was never really *my* home, whenever I visit that town—now with grown children and grandchildren of my own—it fills me with a nostalgic sense of belonging.

Jesus talked with His disciples about His home in heaven, which He left to come and live among us. What a joy it must have been for Him to tell His disciples, "In my Father's house are many mansions . . . . I go to prepare a place for you, . . . that where I am, there you may be also" (John 14:2-3). No doubt Jesus, "who for the joy that was set before Him endured the cross" (Heb. 12:2), was looking forward to returning to His heavenly home and taking His Father's sons and daughters there to be with Him.

The thought of Jesus taking us to His Father's home fills us with great anticipation and compels us to tell others the good news about the Son who came to rescue us from this fallen place. —Joe Stowell

Now I belong to Jesus;
Jesus belongs to me—
Not for the years of time alone,
But for eternity. —*Clayton*

Only Jesus can fill us with a sense of belonging like we've never known before.

August 10
Monday

The Power Of Compassion

Read:
Isaiah 42:1-9

A bruised reed He will not break, and smoking flax He will not quench.
—Isaiah 42:3

The Bible In One Year:
- **Psalms 79–80**
- **Romans 11:1-18**

Francis Schaeffer, author and Christian apologist, struggled to spell words correctly because of dyslexia. At the college he attended, spelling errors lowered the grade on all written assignments. During his first year, a professor told Schaeffer, "This is the best philosophy paper I've ever read, but it's the worst spelling. What am I going to do? I can't pass you."

Francis replied, "Sir, I could never spell. Could you please just read what I'm saying and not worry about the spelling?"

After a long pause, the professor replied, "You know, Mr. Schaeffer, I think we'll do that." His wise, compassionate response encouraged a gifted young man who would later help many of the searching generation during the 1960s and 70s to find their way to faith in Christ.

Isaiah said of the promised Messiah, "A bruised reed He will not break, and smoking flax He will not quench; He will bring forth justice for truth" (Isa. 42:3). The image is of a gentle, yet powerful Person who sets prisoners free and encourages those who are fainthearted and tempted to despair.

Jesus came to free us from sin, not to condemn us for our condition. Today, He offers salvation and encouragement to all who turn to Him. —David McCasland

No condemnation now I dread,
I am my Lord's and He is mine;
Alive in Him, my living Head,
And clothed in righteousness divine. —*Wesley*

When we come to Christ in our brokenness, He makes us whole.

August 11
Tuesday

"I'm . . . Uh . . . Sorry"

Read:
Psalm 51:1-17

Blot out my transgressions. Wash me thoroughly from my iniquity, and cleanse me from my sin.
—Psalm 51:1-2

The Bible In One Year:
- Psalms 81–83
- Romans 11:19-36

The news is quick to report all the details of famous people's wrongdoings and their subsequent confessions. Perhaps it's an athlete who was arrested for driving while drunk. Or it could be a politician caught in an indiscretion. Only God knows the heart, but when we hear a stuttered "I'm . . . uh . . . sorry," we may wonder if they are truly repentant or just sorry they got caught.

When we read the confession of the famous King David we see what looks like genuine contriteness. In his public discussion of his sins in Psalm 51, this disgraced monarch—who had an embarrassing record of flagrant sins which he had kept hidden (2 Sam. 12:1-13; Ps. 32:3-5)—pleads for mercy.

He recognized that his sin was an affront to God—not just to people—and that God alone can judge him (Ps. 51:1-6). He realized that he must be cleansed by God (vv.7-10), and he celebrated his restoration through service and worship (vv.11-17).

All of us sin and fall short of God's glory. When we feel the heavy burden of sin weighing us down, we have the blessing of confession and forgiveness (1 John 1:9) to lift us up. Isn't it just like our great God to turn even our sins into an opportunity to grow in His grace and power and love! —Dave Branon

Dear Lord, please give me a humble heart
and the courage to confess my sins before You
and others. Thank You for Your promise to be
faithful to forgive my sins and to cleanse me.

Confession is agreeing with God about our sin.

August 12
Wednesday

The Blessed Hope

Read:
2 Peter 3:10-18

[We look] for the blessed hope and glorious appearing of our great God and Savior Jesus Christ. —Titus 2:13

The Bible In One Year:
- **Psalms 84–86**
- **Romans 12**

So many predictions of the end of the world have come and gone. Those predictions are unsettling and often fill people with fear. Yet the Bible does refer to a time called "the day of the Lord" when He will return. It will happen, but only God knows when.

It's a day that Jesus' followers can look forward to. In light of that time to come, the apostle Peter tells us how the believer can live with a joyful purpose (2 Peter 3:10-18). We can look upward by living Christ-honoring lives (v.11). We can look inward by making every effort to be found at peace with God (v.14). And we can look outward by being on guard so we aren't carried away by the wrong influence of others (v.17).

How do we do this? By "grow[ing] in the grace and knowledge of our Lord and Savior Jesus Christ" (v.18). When we grow in character through His written Word, we begin to relate more closely to Jesus, the Living Word. The Holy Spirit takes God's Word and guides us in the way to live.

The day of the Lord shouldn't be a fearful day for Jesus' followers. Our King will return to make all things right and to rule forever. We wait for that time with great anticipation. It is our "blessed hope" (Titus 2:13). —C. P. Hia

And for the hope of His return,
Dear Lord, Your name we praise;
With longing hearts we watch and wait
For that great day of days! —Sherwood

One day Jesus will return to rule and reign!

August 13
Thursday

LOOKING DOWN

READ:
Luke 18:9-14

I say . . . to everyone who is among you, not to think of himself more highly than he ought to think, but to think soberly.
—Romans 12:3

THE BIBLE IN ONE YEAR:
- Psalms 87–88
- Romans 13

After I had minor eye surgery, the nurse told me, "Don't look down for the next 2 weeks. No cooking or cleaning." The last part of those instructions was a little easier to take than the first part! The incisions needed to heal, and she didn't want me to put any unnecessary pressure on them by looking down.

C. S. Lewis wrote about another kind of looking down that we may have a problem with: "In God you come up against something which is in every respect immeasurably superior to yourself. . . . As long as you are proud you cannot know God. A proud man is always looking down on things and people: and, of course, as long as you are looking down, you cannot see something that is above you" (*Mere Christianity*).

Jesus told a parable about a Pharisee who felt superior to others. In a prideful prayer, he thanked God that he was not like other men (Luke 18:11). He looked down on extortioners, the unjust, adulterers, and the tax collector who was also praying in the temple. By contrast, the tax collector knew he was a sinner before God and asked for His mercy (v.13).

Pride can be an issue for all of us. May we not look down on others but instead see the God who is far above us all.
—Anne Cetas

When I survey the wondrous cross
On which the Prince of Glory died,
My richest gain I count but loss,
And pour contempt on all my pride. —*Watts*

Spiritual pride is the most arrogant of all kinds of pride.

August 14
Friday

The Joy Of Disappointment

Read:
Proverbs 3:1-12

Trust in the Lord with all your heart, and lean not on your own understanding.
—Proverbs 3:5

The Bible In One Year:
- **Psalms 89–90**
- **Romans 14**

While in Bible college, I auditioned for one of the school's traveling musical teams. I was excited about the thought of being able to be involved in that ministry, but was crushed when I failed to make the team. In my disappointment, I could only trust that God's purposes were greater than mine.

Months later, I had the opportunity to join a different musical team, but as the Bible teacher. The results were more than I could have imagined. Not only was my future wife a part of that team, allowing us to serve Christ together, but it also gave me many opportunities to preach over the next 3 years—priceless preparation for a life of ministry in the Word.

Many times we struggle with the reality that our Father knows what is best. We assume our way is right. But, as we rest in Him, His purposes always prove to be for our good and His praise. To be honest, that's easy to see when the outcome is better than we had hoped, but difficult when we can't see the good right now or maybe won't till heaven.

As wise King Solomon said, "Trust in the Lord with all your heart, and lean not on your own understanding; in all your ways acknowledge Him, and He shall direct your paths" (Prov. 3:5-6). —Bill Crowder

Guide me, O Thou great Jehovah,
Pilgrim through this barren land.
I am weak, but Thou art mighty;
Hold me with Thy powerful hand. —*Williams*

God's purpose for today's events may not be seen until tomorrow.

August 15
Saturday

The Anchor Of Our Hope

Read:
Hebrews 6:13-20

This hope we have as an anchor of the soul, both sure and steadfast.
—Hebrews 6:19

The Bible In One Year:
- Psalms 91–93
- Romans 15:1-13

Frank, Ted, and I were fishing for bluegill on Rice Lake in Ontario, Canada. We were on a pontoon boat, and the fish were really biting. Busy baiting and hooking, we slowly became aware that the action had slacked off. Then we realized why: The boat was no longer sitting where we had put it. A strong wind had come up and pushed it across the water. The anchor could not hold us and was sliding across the lake bottom. We hauled it up, returned to our hot spot, and re-anchored. We were moved away again. After a third try, we went back to shore. We could not get our anchor to grab and stick.

When it comes to our salvation, our hope is anchored in the promise of God and the work of Jesus Christ. The winds and waves of doubt, discouragement, and spiritual attack by the evil one can cause us to think that we are adrift and salvation from God is not secure. Not so! God has given His promise that our salvation is sure, and He cannot lie (Heb. 6:18-19). Our hope is securely fastened in Jesus Christ who redeemed us once and for all when He died, rose again, and ascended to heaven.

Our anchor is the Rock unmovable—Jesus Christ. His limitless love holds us sure and steadfast. —David Egner

We have an anchor that keeps the soul,
Steadfast and sure while the billows roll;
Fastened to the Rock which cannot move,
Grounded firm and deep in the Savior's love. —*Owens*

Our anchor is the Rock, Jesus Christ.

August 16
Sunday

Contained But Not Extinguished

Read:
Hebrews 10:19-39

For yet a little while, and He who is coming will come and will not tarry. —Hebrews 10:37

The Bible In One Year:
- **Psalms 94–96**
- **Romans 15:14-33**

In June 2012, the Waldo Canyon fire destroyed 346 homes in Colorado Springs, Colorado, and burned more than 18,000 acres of mountain forest. The fire was declared 100-percent contained when perimeter lines had been built around the entire area of the blaze. It had been confined to a defined area until it could be fully extinguished. A fire information official warned residents that they might continue to see smoke in the burn area because even though the fire was fully contained it "is not controlled and it is not out."

When our world is rocked by tragic events and evil acts, we long for the day when evil will finally be destroyed and God will bring history to a close and fully establish His kingdom. Until that time, however, the Lord gives us His grace to live purposeful lives of faith as we await His coming. In Hebrews 10, we are urged to draw near to God with sincere hearts (v.22); hold fast to the hope we profess (v.23); spur each other on to love and good works (v.24); and continue meeting together for encouragement "and so much the more as you see the Day approaching" (v.25).

Until the time God extinguishes the fires of evil forever, He gives us His grace and strength to endure the trials of life as we look forward to His return. —David McCasland

Dear Lord, thank You for the grace You give us to live each day for Your glory. We look forward to the day when You return, all evil will be extinguished, and we will live with You in perfect harmony forever.

Jesus is coming—perhaps today!

August 17
Monday

SLACK TIDE

READ:
Mark 6:30-32

He said to them, "Come aside by yourselves to a deserted place and rest a while." —Mark 6:31

THE BIBLE IN ONE YEAR:
- Psalms 97–99
- Romans 16

I find it fascinating to consider pull of the moon on our gre oceans, which creates high and low tides. At the changing of the tide, there is a brief period of time called "slack tide" when the water is neither high nor low. According to scientists, this is when the water is "unstressed." It is a quiet pause before the surging of tidal flow begins again.

Sometimes in our busy schedules we may feel pulled in different directions by competing responsibilities. In Jesus' ministry, we see how He understood the demands made on His followers and the need for rest. Returning from a traveling ministry in teams of two, the Twelve reported the wonderful things that God had done through them (Mark 6:7-13,30). But Jesus responded: "'Come aside by yourselves to a deserted place and rest a while.' For there were many coming and going, and they did not even have time to eat. So they departed to a deserted place in the boat by themselves" (vv.31-32).

What responsibilities are pulling on you today? It is certainly acceptable to plan some rest and relaxation time to rejuvenate your body and soul for more fruitful service to others. Jesus advised it, and we all need it. He will meet you there. —Dennis Fisher

My Shepherd is the Lord
Who knows my needs, and I am blest;
By quiet streams, in pastures green,
He leads and makes me rest. —*Psalter*

Spending quiet time with God can bring quiet rest from God.

18

Always An Upgrade

Read:
Colossians 3:12-17

Put on tender mercies, kindness, humility, meekness, longsuffering; . . . but above all these things put on love.
—Colossians 3:12,14

The Bible In One Year:
- **Psalms 100–102**
- **1 Corinthians 1**

When I'm about to leave the house, sometimes my wife, Martie, stops me and says, "You can't go to the office dressed like that!" It's usually something about the tie not matching the jacket or the color of the slacks being out of sync with the sportcoat. Though being questioned about my fashion choices may feel like an affront to my good taste, I have realized that her correcting influence is always an upgrade.

Scripture often calls us to "put on" attitudes and actions that match our identity in Christ. Sometimes we are known by the clothes we wear, but we can make Jesus known by wearing attitudes and actions that reveal His presence in our lives. The apostle Paul advised us to set the fashion standard by modeling the wardrobe of Jesus' compassion, kindness, humility, meekness, patience, and forgiveness (Col. 3:12). And, he added, "above all these things put on love . . . . And let the peace of God rule in your hearts" (vv.14-15).

Clothing ourselves in Jesus' likeness begins with spending time with Him. If you hear Him say, "You can't go out like that!" let Him lovingly take you back to the closet so He can clothe you with His likeness. It's always an upgrade!
—Joe Stowell

Lord, help us to see ourselves the way You see us.
By Your Spirit teach us to adorn our lives with the
attitudes and actions You have designed for us as
a public statement about our identity with You.

Clothing ourselves with Jesus' attitudes and actions shows His presence in our lives.

August 19
Wednesday

The Gift Of Remembering

Read:
Genesis 40:1-14,23

Yet the chief butler did not remember Joseph, but forgot him.
—Genesis 40:23

The Bible In One Year:
- Psalms 103–104
- 1 Corinthians 2

During seminary, I worked in a nursing home. As I spent time talking to these men and women, at some point nearly every patient would describe the loneliness of their present lives and the realization that they were outliving their peers. Most wondered if anyone would remember them when they passed from this life.

It isn't just the elderly who can feel lonely and forgotten. In fact, many of us feel trapped and alone, set aside by circumstances fair and unfair. Sometimes we even experience what the Old Testament character Joseph did: people failing to remember us when there's every reason they should.

Genesis 40 describes Joseph's experiences as he's trapped in prison. The cupbearer had been freed and returned to the king's service, just as Joseph told him would happen (vv.9-13). Joseph had asked to be mentioned to Pharaoh, but the cupbearer forgot him (vv.14,23).

We may feel forgotten. Yet, like Joseph, we are not (42:9-13). Jesus sits at the right hand of God, and our prayers reach the throne of the King without fail because our Savior is our Mediator. When we feel alone, let's remember to rest in the confidence of Jesus' promise to be with us forever (Matt. 28:20). —Randy Kilgore

Lord, let me be found serving others, as Joseph did, in those hours when I feel most forgotten. May I never be the "cupbearer" who fails to bring the lonely and hurting to Your attention in prayer.

Jesus never abandons or forgets His own.

August 20
Thursday

IMAGE CONSCIOUS

READ:
2 Corinthians 3:1-3, 17-18

We all . . . are being transformed . . . by the Spirit of the Lord.
—2 Corinthians 3:18

THE BIBLE IN ONE YEAR:
- **Psalms 105–106**
- **1 Corinthians 3**

When going through old family photos, my cousins and I joke about which physical characteristics we've inherited. We notice primarily the negative ones: short legs, crooked teeth, unruly cowlicks. All of us can easily identify in our ancestors our own least favorite body part. In addition to physical attributes, we also inherited character traits—some good, some not so good. But we don't always pay as much attention to those.

According to my unscientific observations, people try all kinds of methods to overcome physical imperfections—exercise routines, weight-loss programs, makeup, hair coloring, cosmetic surgery. But instead of trying to overcome our character flaws, we tend to use them as an excuse for behaving badly. I suppose this is because changing our looks is easier than changing our character. But imagine how much better off we'd be if we put our energy into character development.

As God's children, we're not limited by our genetic makeup. We can surrender our flaws to Him and allow Him to fulfill the potential He had in mind when He created us as unique expressions of His love. The power of God's Spirit and the life of God's Son are at work in us, conforming us to His image (2 Cor. 3:18). —Julie Ackerman Link

I know, Lord, that You're more interested in the condition of my heart than my outward appearance. Please make me into the person You want me to be— filled with kindness, patience, integrity, and love.

The Spirit develops in us the clear image of Christ.

August 21
Friday

Living Beyond The Odds

Read:
Acts 12:1-11

Constant prayer was offered to God for [Peter] by the church.
—Acts 12:5

The Bible In One Year:
- Psalms 107–109
- 1 Corinthians 4

Many of us make daily decisions based on the odds. If there's a 20 percent chance of rain, we may ignore it. If there's a 90 percent chance, we'll take an umbrella. The greater the odds, the more our behavior is affected because we want to choose wisely and be successful.

Acts 12:1-6 describes a situation in which Peter's odds of survival were very low. He was in prison, "bound with two chains between two soldiers" while others guarded the door (v.6). Herod had already executed James, one of Jesus' closest followers, and he had the same fate in mind for Peter (vv.1-3). A gambler would not have put any money on Peter getting out of this alive.

Yet God's plan for Peter included a miraculous deliverance that even those who were interceding for him found hard to believe (vv.13-16). They were astonished when he showed up at their prayer meeting.

God can operate outside the odds because He is all-powerful. Nothing is too hard for Him. The One who loves us and gave Himself for us is in charge of our lives. In ordinary circumstances and impossible situations, God can reveal His power. Whether we are showered with success or sustained in sorrow, He is with us. —David McCasland

Dear God, we're so thankful that nothing is too difficult for You. You can do amazing things! Help us to trust that You are always with us and always in control. We love You, Lord.

God is always in control behind the scenes.

August 22
Saturday

Thumbs Up

Read:
Matthew 5:17-20

The entirety of Your Word is truth.
—Psalm 119:160

The Bible In One Year:
- **Psalms 110–112**
- **1 Corinthians 5**

Pandora is one of the musical marvels of the Internet age. It helps you create your own personal radio station by allowing you to "customize" your music. It plays a song and you then click a thumbs up or thumbs down sign to indicate whether or not you like it. You end up with a grouping of only songs that you like.

Unfortunately, sometimes we do that with the Bible too. People may choose some Scripture passages they especially like and ignore others, and so they "customize" it to their preferences. The psalmist looked at God's Word this way: "The entirety of Your Word is truth" (Ps. 119:160). And the apostle Paul told Timothy, a young pastor, "All Scripture is given by inspiration of God, and is profitable" (2 Tim. 3:16).

The Scriptures were important to Jesus (Matt. 5:17-18), but He looked at them differently than the religious leaders of His day. To Him, "You shall not murder" was on the level of being "angry with [a] brother without a cause" (vv.21-22). Far from customizing Scripture, He was concerned about the motivation of people's hearts in applying all of it.

As we embrace God's Word more fully, we'll know Him more deeply and desire to honor Him. —Marvin Williams

Lord, I don't want to treat Your Word lightly or to dismiss what seems too difficult. Show me my heart and help me to obey from the heart whatever You tell me. In Jesus' name, amen.

When you open your Bible,
ask the Author to open your heart.

August 23
Sunday

The Gift Of Light

Read:
John 8:12-20

I am the light of the world. He who follows Me shall not walk in darkness, but have the light of life. —John 8:12

The Bible In One Year:
- Psalms 113–115
- 1 Corinthians 6

Sir Christopher Wren designed and built more than 50 church buildings in London during the late 1600s. His design style had two prominent features—the first of which was sturdy, tall steeples. The second, however, was more profound. Wren was convinced that all of the windows in his churches must use clear glass as opposed to the stained glass so popular in churches of that era. In part, his reason for the clear glass is found in words attributed to him: "God's greatest gift to man is light." Allowing light to bathe people as they worshiped was, to Wren, a celebration of that gift.

In the Genesis account, on the first day of creation God made light (1:3). The light God created is even more than just a means by which to see. It's a picture of what Christ brought when He entered this darkened world. In John 8:12, our Lord said, "I am the light of the world. He who follows Me shall not walk in darkness, but have the light of life." To the follower of Christ, light is one of the great reminders of the character of our Savior and the quality of the life He has given us through His sacrifice on the cross.

Wren was right. God's greatest gift to man is light—Jesus Christ, the Light of the world! —Bill Crowder

Creator God, I thank You that You spoke light into the darkness of the universe, and I thank You that You brought light into the darkness of my heart through Your Son, Jesus Christ.

Jesus came to give light to a dark world.

August 24
Monday

On My Side

Read:
Psalm 118:1-6

The Lord is on my side; I will not fear.
—Psalm 118:6

The Bible In One Year:
■ Psalms 116–118
■ 1 Corinthians 7:1-19

After Olympic gymnast Gabby Douglas captured two gold medals in the 2012 London Games, she made this proclamation: "God will never fail you. He's always on your side."

Sometimes this kind of statement by an athlete can be misunderstood. It can be taken to mean that if I'm competing against you in a sports contest and I have God's help, there is no way I can lose. But if we turn to Psalm 118:5-6, we get the true picture of what this line means—and what Gabby meant. The psalmist wrote, "I called on the Lord in distress; the Lord answered me and set me in a broad place. The Lord is on my side; I will not fear."

Another version translates verse 6 as "the Lord is with me" (NIV). It's the idea that when trouble comes into our lives, God, who is full of mercy and love (which "endures forever," v.4) will always be attentive to us and provide the protection we need.

We can learn from this heroic Olympic champion. When the economy falters and our finances can't keep up, listen to Gabby: "God will never fail you." When a relationship we cherished falls apart; indeed, no matter what our situation, as Christ-followers we know where to find help. "The Lord is on my side." —Dave Branon

Be still, my soul—the Lord is on thy side!
Bear patiently the cross of grief or pain;
Leave to thy God to order and provide—
In every change He faithful will remain. —*von Schlegel*

In the midst of every trial,
God is on our side.

August 25
Tuesday

THE NEXT CHAPTER

READ:
Hebrews 12:1-11

Let us run with endurance the race that is set before us, looking unto Jesus, the author and finisher of our faith.
—Hebrews 12:1-2

THE BIBLE IN ONE YEAR:
■ Psalm 119:1-88
■ 1 Corinthians 7:20-40

Steve was almost 5 when his father, missionary pilot Nate Saint, was killed in 1956, along with four other men, by the Waodani tribe in Ecuador. But as a result of the love and forgiveness demonstrated by the families of the martyred men, there is now a growing community of believers among the Waodani.

As an adult, Steve moved back to Ecuador and became friends with Mincaye, one of the men who killed his father. Steve's motto is: "Let God Write Your Story." He says, "You have a lot of people . . . who want to write their own story and have God be their editor when [it] goes wrong. I decided long ago to let God write my story." When Steve suffered a serious accident in 2012, he reassured his family: "Let's let God write *this* chapter too." His faith continues to carry him toward recovery.

The story continues to unfold for all followers of Jesus Christ. None of us knows how the next chapter of our life will read. But as we look to Jesus and "run with endurance the race that is set before us," we can trust Him—the author and finisher of our faith (Heb. 12:1-2). Jesus wrote the beginning of our story, and He'll write the next chapter and the ending as well. —Cindy Hess Kasper

When we stand with Christ in glory,
Looking o'er life's finished story,
Then, Lord, shall I fully know—
Not till then—how much I owe. —McCheyne

Let your life tell the story of Christ's love and mercy to the world around you.

August 26
Wednesday

What's At Stake?

Read:
Proverbs 19:15-25

Listen to counsel and receive instruction, that you may be wise in your latter days.
—Proverbs 19:20

The Bible In One Year:
- **Psalm 119:89-176**
- **1 Corinthians 8**

To stake or not to stake? That's the question Marilyn faced when she planted a tree sapling last summer. The salesman said, "Stake it for one year so it will be supported in strong winds. Then remove them so it can grow deep roots on its own." But a neighbor told her, "Staking may cause more harm than good. The tree needs to start building strong roots right away, or it may never. Not staking is best for long-term health."

We wonder about that question in relationships too. For instance, if someone has gotten himself into trouble, do we "stake him down" by rescuing him, or do we let the person "grow strong roots" on his own by allowing him to face the consequences of his choices? Obviously it depends on what seems best for the person's long-term spiritual health. What does love do, and when does it do it? Proverbs 19 gives opposite thoughts: We are to have "pity" and lend our assistance (v.17), yet there are dangers in rescuing another because you might need to do it again (v.19). Providing the right help requires wisdom beyond our own.

God hasn't left us on our own. He will give us the wisdom when we ask Him. And as we lean on Him, our own roots will grow deep in Him as well. —Anne Cetas

We lack wisdom, Lord, in many situations.
We know we'll make mistakes, but teach us to
be dependent on You. Thank You that You will
be faithful. Grow our roots deep in You.

Real wisdom is looking at the world from God's point of view.

August 27
Thursday

Surrounded By Mercy

Read:
Psalm 32

He who trusts in the Lord, mercy shall surround him.
—Psalm 32:10

The Bible In One Year:
- **Psalms 120–122**
- **1 Corinthians 9**

It was almost impossible not to see the giant billboard with the red background and huge white letters that shouted: "This year thousands of men will die from stubbornness." Later I learned that the billboard was one of hundreds just like it targeted at middle-aged men who typically avoid routine medical screenings and often die from preventable conditions.

Psalm 32 deals with the spiritual disease of sin, which can be treated by honest acknowledgment and repentance. The first five verses express the anguish of hiding our guilt and then celebrate the joyful release of confessing our transgressions to God and being forgiven.

This psalm goes on to show that the Lord longs for us to seek His help in difficulty (vv.6-8) and receive His guidance. "I will instruct you and teach you in the way you should go; I will guide you with My eye" (v.8). We are hindered, though, when we stubbornly refuse to follow His direction and repent from our sin.

God's Word urges us, "Do not be like the horse or like the mule, . . . which must be harnessed with bit and bridle, else they will not come near you" (v.9). Rather than hold on to our sin, the Lord offers an alternative: When we humbly confess, His mercy shall surround us (v.10). —David McCasland

Heavenly Father, help us now
At Thy feet to humbly bow;
Take away all thought of sin,
Make us clean and pure within. —*Bartels*

The first step to receiving God's forgiveness is to admit that we need it.

August 28
Friday

A Way Of Escape

Read:
1 Cor. 10:12-13
Matthew 4:1-11

[God will] make the way of escape, that [we] may be able to bear it.
—1 Corinthians 10:13

The Bible In One Year:
- **Psalms 123–125**
- **1 Corinthians 10:1-18**

Highway 77, which passes through the Appalachian Mountains in West Virginia, features a series of runaway truck ramps. These semi-paved exits appear in an area of the highway where the altitude drops nearly 1,300 feet over the course of about 6 miles. This steep descent combined with the road's winding path can create problems for motorists—especially truck drivers.

Just as a runaway truck needs an escape route from a highway, we also need "a way of escape" when out-of-control desires threaten our spiritual well-being. When we face temptation, "[God will] make the way of escape, that [we] may be able to bear it" (1 Cor. 10:13). God enables us to say "no" to enticement through the power of His Word. Jesus conquered Satan's temptation relating to food, authority, and trust by quoting verses from Deuteronomy (Matt. 4:4-10). Scripture helped Him resist the devil despite the effects of a 40-day fast in the wilderness.

When we are tempted, we may feel like disaster is just around the bend. Memories of past failure and isolation from others can intensify this feeling. However, we can trust God in moments of temptation; He is faithful. He will provide a way for us to resist sin's allure. —Jennifer Benson Schuldt

I need Thee every hour, stay Thou near by;
Temptations lose their pow'r when Thou art nigh.
I need Thee, O I need Thee;
Every hour I need Thee. —*Hawks/Lowry*

The best way to escape temptation is to run to God.

August 29
Saturday

Overwhelming Concern

Read:
John 13:31-35

A new commandment I give to you, that you love one another.
—John 13:34

The Bible In One Year:
- Psalms 126–128
- 1 Corinthians 10:19-33

A while ago, I wrote an article about my wife, Marlene, and her struggles with vertigo. When the article appeared, I was unprepared for the tidal wave of response from readers offering encouragement, help, suggestions and, mostly, concern for her well-being. These messages came from all over the world, from people in all walks of life. Expressions of loving concern for my wife poured in to the point where we could not even begin to answer them all. It was overwhelming in the best kind of way to see the body of Christ respond to Marlene's struggle. We were, and remain, deeply grateful.

At its core, this is how the body is supposed to work. Loving concern for our brothers and sisters in Christ becomes the evidence that we have experienced His love. While addressing the disciples at the Last Supper, Jesus said, "A new commandment I give to you, that you love one another; as I have loved you, that you also love one another. By this all will know that you are My disciples" (John 13:34-35).

Marlene and I experienced a sampling of Christlike love and concern in those letters we received. With the help of our Savior and as a way of praising Him, may we show others that kind of love as well. —Bill Crowder

Bearing people's heavy burdens,
Shouldering their pain and grief,
Shows the love of Christ to others,
Bringing them His sure relief. —*Anon.*

The height of our love for God is indicated by the depth of our love for one another. —Morley

August 30
Sunday

Risks and Rescue

Read:
Romans 16:1-7

Greet Priscilla and Aquila . . . who risked their own necks for my life. —Romans 16:3-4

The Bible In One Year:
- Psalms 129–131
- 1 Corinthians 11:1-16

On September 7, 1838, Grace Darling, the daughter of an English lighthouse keeper, spotted a shipwreck and survivors offshore. Together, she and her father courageously rowed their boat a mile through rough waters to rescue several people. Grace became a legend for her compassionate heart and steady hand in risking her life to rescue others.

The apostle Paul tells us of another man and woman team who took risks to rescue others. He wrote about Priscilla and Aquila, his fellow workers in Christ, who "risked their own necks for my life, to whom not only I give thanks, but also all the churches of the Gentiles" (Rom. 16:3-4).

We are not told exactly what "risk" Paul was referring to, but with beatings, imprisonment, shipwrecks, and threats of death so common to Paul's ministry, it's not hard to see how this couple could have put themselves in harm's way to help their friend. Apparently, Paul's rescue was more important to them than their own safety.

Rescuing others—whether from physical or spiritual danger—often carries a risk. But when we take a risk by reaching out to others, we reflect the heart of our Savior who gave up so much for us. —Dennis Fisher

The hand of God protects our way
When we would do His will;
And even when we take a risk,
We know He's with us still. —D. DeHaan

When you've been rescued,
you'll want to rescue others.

August 31
Monday

The Real Deal

Read:
1 Corinthians 15:1-21

[Christ] rose again the third day . . . [and] was seen by over five hundred brethren.
—1 Corinthians 15:4-6

The Bible In One Year:
Psalms 132–134
1 Corinthians 11:17-34

Sometimes cleaning out Grandpa's attic pays off. For an Ohio man, it paid off in the discovery of a more than 100-year-old set of mint-condition baseball cards. Appraisers placed the cards' value at $3 million.

One key to the high value of those cards was the fact that they were well-preserved. But beyond that, the true worth of the cards rested in the fact that they were authentic. If they had been fakes or counterfeits—no matter how good they looked—they wouldn't have been worth the cardboard they were printed on.

The apostle Paul had something similar to say about Christianity. He said that our faith would be completely worthless and counterfeit if Jesus' resurrection were not the real deal. It took bravery and confidence in God's plan for Paul to say, "If Christ is not risen, then our preaching is empty and your faith is also empty" (1 Cor. 15:14) and "If Christ is not risen, your faith is futile; you are still in your sins!" (v.17).

The Christian faith rests on the authenticity of this story: Jesus died on the cross and was raised from the dead. Praise God for the clear evidence of Jesus' death and resurrection (vv.3-8). It's the real deal, and we can stake our eternity and our total dependence on God on its truth. —Dave Branon

Lord, we're eternally thankful for the truth
confirmed in Your Word and in our hearts
that You died and rose again for us. We love
You, Lord, and lift our voices in praise!

God is the only true God.

September 1
Tuesday

A Slower Pace

Read:
Exodus 20:8-11

Six days you shall labor and do all your work, but the seventh day is the Sabbath of the Lord your God. In it you shall do no work.
—Exodus 20:9-10

The Bible In One Year:
- Psalms 135–136
- 1 Corinthians 12

When writer Bruce Feiler was diagnosed with bone cancer in his thigh, he couldn't walk without some help for over a year. Learning to get around on crutches caused him to appreciate a slower pace of life. Feiler said, "The idea of slowing down became the number one lesson I learned from my experience."

After God's people were liberated from Egypt, He gave them a commandment that would cause them to slow down and view Him and the world "in pause." The fourth commandment introduced a dramatic contrast to the Israelites' slavery under Pharaoh when they had no break in their daily work routine.

The commandment insisted that God's people set aside one day a week to remember several important things: God's work in creation (Gen. 2:2), their liberation from Egyptian bondage (Deut. 5:12-15), their relationship with God (6:4-6), and their need for personal refreshment (Exod. 31:12-18). This was not to be a day of laziness, but one where God's people acknowledged, worshiped, and rested in Him.

We too are called to slow down, to be refreshed physically, mentally, and emotionally, and to behold God in His good creation. —Marvin Williams

Lord, I need spiritual and physical rest. Help me to deliberately take the time to spend with You. Please remove any obstacle that keeps me from having a more balanced rhythm to my life.

Living for God begins with resting in Him.

September 2
Wednesday

CUPBEARER TO THE KING

READ:
Nehemiah 2:1-8

Why is your face sad? . . . What do you request?
—Nehemiah 2:2,4

THE BIBLE IN ONE YEAR:
- **Psalms 137–139**
- **1 Corinthians 13**

One of my favorite Bible passages that applies to work is Nehemiah 1–2. King Artaxerxes' employee Nehemiah had been such an exemplary worker that the king wanted to honor him by helping him when he was sad that Jerusalem was still in ruins. He asked Nehemiah, "Why is your face sad? . . . . What do you request?" (2:2,4). He wasn't just any worker for the king, he was the cupbearer, the man who tasted the king's drink to protect him from being poisoned. In order to have earned such a position, he apparently worked hard and honored God in everything he did. And the king granted his requests.

God cares about the way we work. Colossians 3:23 tells us, "Whatever you do, do it heartily, as to the Lord and not to men." We can follow Nehemiah's example in these ways: Be such a competent and trusted worker that God is honored (Neh. 1:11–2:6). Care passionately about others and what's important to them. Take action, occasionally even risky action, to honor what's important to God and to fellow believers (2:3-6).

When we honor God in work, our employers may notice. But even if they don't, our heart's desire and purpose should be to honor the One we really serve—the Lord our God (Col. 3:17,23). —Randy Kilgore

O Lord, may the way I serve tell Your story!
I want to bring You all the glory in my work,
at home, and everywhere I go. Fill me and use
me to bless others and honor You today.

God honors faith because faith honors God.

September 3
Thursday

NOT INTERESTED IN RELIGION

READ:
John 5:18,37-47

How often I wanted to gather your children together, as a hen gathers her chicks under her wings, but you were not willing! —Matthew 23:37

THE BIBLE IN ONE YEAR:
■ Psalms 140–142
■ 1 Corinthians 14:1-20

A radio ad for a church caught my attention: "Because you've heard about Christianity, you might not be interested in religion. Well, it might surprise you—Jesus wasn't interested in religion either. But He was big on relationship and teaching us to love one another." It continued, "You may not like everything about our church, but we offer authentic relationship, and we're learning to love God and each other. You're welcome to visit."

This church may have overstated things about Jesus and religion because Scripture does speak of "true religion" in James 1:27 as helpful deeds toward others. But Jesus did have difficulties with religious people of His day. He said the Pharisees, guided by tradition and rules not by love for the Lord, "outwardly appear righteous to men, but inside [they] are full of hypocrisy and lawlessness" (Matt. 23:28). They didn't have the love of God in their hearts (John 5:42). Jesus wanted relationship with them, but they were "not willing to come to [Him]" (v.40).

If being "religious" means following a set of rules so we can look good—instead of enjoying a relationship with the Savior—Jesus isn't interested. He offers forgiveness and love to all who want an intimate relationship with Him. —Anne Cetas

True religion is to know
The love that Christ imparts;
True religion is to show
This love to burdened hearts. —*D. DeHaan*

There is a longing in every heart that only Jesus can satisfy.

September 4
Friday

A Special Day

Read:
Luke 11:1-4

This is the day the Lord has made.
—Psalm 118:24

The Bible In One Year:
■ Psalms 143–145
■ 1 Corinthians 14:21-40

What's special about September 4? Perhaps it's your birthday or anniversary. That would make it special. Or maybe you could celebrate the historic events of this day. For instance, in 1781, the city of Los Angeles, California, was founded. Or this: In 1993, Jim Abbott, a pitcher for the New York Yankees, didn't let anyone get a hit off his pitches—and he was born without a right hand. Or if you're a TV fan: In 1951, the first live US coast-to-coast television broadcast was aired from San Francisco.

But what if none of these events and facts seem to make your September 4 special? Try these ideas:

Today God gives you a new opportunity to praise Him. Psalm 118:24 says, "This is the day the Lord has made; we will rejoice and be glad in it."

Today God provides for you and wants your trust. "Give us day by day our daily bread" (Luke 11:3).

Today God wants to speak to you through His Word. The believers at Berea "searched the Scriptures daily" (Acts 17:11).

Today God desires to renew your inner person. "The inward man is being renewed day by day" (2 Cor. 4:16).

With God as your guide, September 4—and every day—can be special. —Dave Branon

This is the day the Lord hath made,
He calls the hours His own;
Let heaven rejoice, let earth be glad,
And praise surround the throne. —*Watts*

Each new day gives us new reasons to praise the Lord.

September 5
Saturday

Almost Content?

Read:
1 Timothy 6:6-12

Be content with such things as you have. For He Himself has said, "I will never leave you nor forsake you." —Hebrews 13:5

The Bible In One Year:
- Psalms 146–147
- 1 Corinthians 15:1-28

As I stepped into the restaurant parking lot after lunch, I saw a pickup truck speeding through the parked vehicles. While observing the driver's reckless behavior, I noticed the words on the truck's front license plate. It read, "Almost Content." After thinking about that message and the sentiment it tried to communicate, I concluded that the concept "almost content" doesn't exist. Either we are content or we are not.

Admittedly, contentment is a tough needle to thread. We live in a world that feeds our desire for more and more—until we find it almost impossible to be content with anything. But this is nothing new. The book of Hebrews addressed this issue, saying, "Let your conduct be without covetousness; be content with such things as you have. For He Himself has said, 'I will never leave you nor forsake you' " (13:5). The only remedy for hearts that "want it all" is the contentment found in the presence of the living God. He is sufficient for our needs and longings, and He alone can bring us the peace and contentment we'll never find in the pursuits of this life.

Almost content? There is no such thing. In Christ we can know true contentment. —Bill Crowder

I find contentment in His wondrous grace,
No cloud or shadow can obscure His face;
When great temptations I must bear,
I find the secret place of prayer. —*Dunlop*

Contentment is not getting what we want but being satisfied with what we have.

September 6
Sunday

Longing To Grow

Read:
1 Peter 1:22–2:3

As newborn babes, desire the pure milk of the Word, that you may grow thereby.
—1 Peter 2:2

The Bible In One Year:
- Psalms 148–150
- 1 Corinthians 15:29-58

The 2010 documentary film *Babies* followed four infants who were born into very different circumstances in Namibia, Mongolia, Tokyo, and San Francisco. There is no narration or dialogue from adults in the film, only the sounds babies make as they begin to discover the world into which they have been born. They coo and laugh when they're happy; they cry when they are hurt or hungry. And all of them like milk! The fascination of the film lies in watching them grow.

As a baby craves milk, followers of Christ are to crave the "pure milk of the Word" that leads to spiritual growth. The apostle Peter says, "Long to grow up into the fullness of your salvation; cry for this as a baby cries for his milk" (1 Peter 2:2 TLB). Peter wrote to encourage a group of Christ-followers who had been scattered by persecution. He urged them to set aside feelings of anger and jealousy toward each other, along with talking one way and living another (v.1), and "as newborn babes, desire the pure milk of the Word, that you may grow thereby" (v.2).

The Lord invites us to drink all that we need from His bountiful supply. He loves to watch His children grow!
—David McCasland

Lord, I want to be more like You.
Please give me a fervent desire to drink of
Your Word. Grow me into a person who
resembles You in all I say and do.

The more we dig into God's Word, the more we grow.

September 7
Monday

GodAware

Read:
Psalm 139:1-10

Oh, the depth of the riches both of the wisdom and knowledge of God!
—Romans 11:33

The Bible In One Year:
- Proverbs 1–2
- 1 Corinthians 16

On the FlightAware Web site, Kathy checked the progress of the small plane her husband Chuck was piloting to Chicago. With a few clicks, she could track when he took off, where his flight was at any moment, and exactly when he would land. A few decades earlier when Chuck was a pilot in West Africa, Kathy's only contact had been a high-frequency radio. She recalls one occasion when 3 days had passed before she was able to reach him. She had no way of knowing that he was safe but unable to fly because the airplane had been damaged.

But God was always aware of exactly where Chuck was and what he was doing, just as He is with us (Job 34:21). Nothing is hidden from His sight (Heb. 4:13). He knows our thoughts and our words (1 Chron. 28:9; Ps. 139:4). And He knows what will happen in the future (Isa. 46:10).

God knows *everything* (1 John 3:20), and He knows you and me intimately (Ps. 139:1-10). He is aware of each temptation, each broken heart, each illness, each worry, each sorrow we face.

What a comfort to experience care from the One of whom it is said, "Oh, the depth of the riches both of the wisdom and knowledge of God!" (Rom. 11:33). —Cindy Hess Kasper

Beneath His watchful eye
His saints securely dwell;
That hand which bears all nature up
Shall guard His children well. —*Doddridge*

We can trust our all-knowing God.

September 8
Tuesday

Light Up The Night

Read:
Daniel 12:1-3

Those who are wise shall shine like the brightness of the firmament.
—Daniel 12:3

The Bible In One Year:
- Proverbs 3–5
- 2 Corinthians 1

On a mild fall evening when the sky was dark and the moon was full, thousands of people in my hometown gathered along the banks of the river to light sky lanterns. They released them into the darkness, and watched as the lights rose to join the moon in a dazzling display that turned the night sky into a sparkling work of art.

When I saw pictures of the event, I was disappointed that I was out of town and had missed it. But a few days later I realized that what had happened in Grand Rapids could be seen as a symbol of the conference I was attending in New York City. More than 1,000 people from 100 cities around the world had gathered there to plan a "work of art"—how to light up the darkness of their own cities by planting churches and reaching thousands of people with the gospel of Christ, the Light of the world.

The prophet Daniel wrote about a time when those who turn others to the Lord will shine like stars forever (Dan. 12:3). We can all join in that great event. When we shine the light of Christ in dark places where we live and work, He is lighting up the night sky with stars that never will go out.
—Julie Ackerman Link

I want to shine for You in my world, Lord. Show me how to lift You up, the Light of the world. I look forward to that day when I will gather with people from all nations to bow at Your feet and worship You.

When the Light of the world illuminates the earth, His beauty will attract people from every nation.

September 9
Wednesday

All Through This Hour

Read:
Psalm 25:1-11

Lead me in Your truth and teach me, for You are the God of my salvation; on You I wait all the day. —Psalm 25:5

The Bible In One Year:
- **Proverbs 6–7**
- **2 Corinthians 2**

The majestic chime of London's Great Clock of Westminster, commonly known as Big Ben, is familiar to many. In fact, some of us may have clocks in our homes that sound the same hourly chime. It is traditionally thought that the melody was taken from Handel's *Messiah*. And the lyrics inscribed in the Big Ben clock room have a time significance:

All through this hour,
Lord, be my guide;
And by Thy power,
No foot shall slide.

These lyrics are a good reminder of our constant need for God's guidance. King David recognized that he needed guidance all through the day as he faced the challenges of life. In Psalm 25 he says: "Lead me in Your truth and teach me, for You are the God of my salvation; on You I wait all the day" (v.5). Wanting to be a teachable follower of God, David looked to his Redeemer for direction. His heart's desire was to wait on God with dependent faith throughout the entire day.

May this be our desire as well. Our requests for God's help often begin the day, but then competing distractions can pull our attention away from Him. Lord, remind us to pray: "All through this hour, Lord, be my guide." —Dennis Fisher

There's never a day nor a season
That prayer may not bless every hour,
And never a prayer need be helpless
When linked with God's infinite power. —Morton

Let Christ be first in your thoughts in the morning, and last in your thoughts at night.

September 10
Thursday

THE POWER OF AFFIRMATION

READ:
1 Corinthians 1:4-9

I thank my God always concerning you for the grace of God which was given to you by Christ Jesus.
—1 Corinthians 1:4

THE BIBLE IN ONE YEAR:
- Proverbs 8–9
- 2 Corinthians 3

During a recent study, 200,000 employees were interviewed to discover the missing ingredient in their productivity. The study concluded that appreciation and affirmation topped the list of what they wanted most from their superiors. This research implies that receiving affirmation is a basic human need.

The apostle Paul seemed to realize this basic need in the Corinthian believers, so before he peppered them with firm words of discipline, he showered them with affirmation. As their spiritual leader, Paul began his letter with thanksgiving to God for the grace being displayed in their lives.

Once far from God, these believers were now participating in His grace through the death and resurrection of Christ. United with Jesus, they were drawing their spiritual life from Him, and the fruit of this union was their spiritual growth in godliness (1 Cor. 1:4-7). Paul deliberately and continually thanked God for His work in the Corinthian believers' lives. I imagine that they were better able to bear firm criticism from Paul because of his tender affirmation.

When we see people who are obeying God, let's take time to affirm them and to thank God for what He's doing through them. —Marvin Williams

Lord, You are at work in so many ways in my life
and in the people around me. Help me to encourage
my brothers and sisters in Christ by telling them
how I am blessed to see Your work in them.

Praise loudly—correct softly.

September 11
Friday

It's All About The Love

Read:
1 John 4:7-19

We have known and believed the love that God has for us. God is love. —1 John 4:16

The Bible In One Year:
■ Proverbs 10–12
■ 2 Corinthians 4

I saw a sign in front of a church that seems to me to be a great motto for relationships: Receive love. Give love. Repeat.

The greatest love that we *receive* is the love of God. He loved us so much that He gave His Son Jesus to live, die, and rise again to redeem us (1 John 4:9). We receive His love when we receive Jesus as our Savior and Lord. "As many as received Him, to them He gave the right to become children of God, to those who believe in His name" (John 1:12).

After we've experienced God's love, we then can learn to *give* love. "Let us love one another, for love is of God" (1 John 4:7).

God's love enables us to love our brothers and sisters in Christ. We teach, encourage, and rebuke. We weep and rejoice. The love we give is tender and tough and supportive. We are taught by Jesus even to love our enemies: "Do good to those who hate you, and pray for those who spitefully use you and persecute you" (Matt. 5:44). Giving love to others can be challenging in some situations, but it's possible because of the love God has first given to us.

A good plan for our lives today: Receive love. Give love. Repeat. —Anne Cetas

For Further Study

How do we experience the love of Christ? (John 15:10). What is the evidence of God's love in our lives? (1 John 4:16-21). How can we show God's love today?

Receive love. Give love. Repeat.

September 12
Saturday

Beneficial Power

Read:
2 Chronicles 16:6-13

The eyes of the Lord run to and fro . . . , to show Himself strong on behalf of those whose heart is loyal to Him.
—2 Chronicles 16:9

The Bible In One Year:
■ Proverbs 13–15
■ 2 Corinthians 5

Boxing and strong-man competitions have a unique aspect to them. In the events, the athletes compete individually for the purpose of demonstrating their superior strength. It's like arm wrestling—you do it to prove that you are the strongest person in the room.

One aspect of God's glory is His almighty power. But how does He show His strength? He doesn't do it by rearranging the galaxies before our very eyes, changing the color of the sun at a whim, or freezing a lightning bolt as a trophy to His strength. Instead, in His love and compassion for needy people like ourselves, God has chosen to "show Himself strong on behalf of those whose heart is loyal to Him" (2 Chron. 16:9).

The pattern is consistent throughout Scripture. From the dividing of the Red Sea, to the marvel of manna in the wilderness, to the miraculous virgin birth, and ultimately to the power of the resurrection, our Almighty God has chosen to demonstrate His strength to bless, preserve, and protect His people.

Be assured that He delights in showing Himself strong in the challenges of our life. And when He proves His power on our behalf, let's remember to give Him the glory! —Joe Stowell

Lord, thank You for choosing to expend Your divine power on the needs of my life. When my strength is weak, teach me to trust that Your mighty arm is able to guard, protect, and deliver!

All of God's promises are backed by His wisdom, love, and power.

September 13
Sunday

A Father To Follow

Read:
2 Chronicles 17:1-10

[Jehoshaphat] sought the God of his father, and walked in His commandments.
—2 Chronicles 17:4

The Bible In One Year:
- Proverbs 16–18
- 2 Corinthians 6

When I think of my father, I think of this saying: "He didn't tell me how to live; he lived, and he let me watch him do it." During my youth, I watched my dad walk with God. He participated in Sunday morning church services, taught an adult Bible-study class, helped with counting the offering, and served as a deacon. Outside of church, he faithfully defended the gospel and read his Bible. I saw him express his love for the Lord through outward actions.

Asa, king of Judah, modeled devotion to God for a season in his life (2 Chron. 14:2). He removed the idols from his kingdom, restored the altar of the Lord, and led the people into a covenant with God (15:8-12). Asa's son Jehoshaphat carried on this legacy by seeking "the God of his father and walk[ing] in His commandments" (17:4). Jehoshaphat purged the land of idol worship (v.6) and sent out priests and Levites to teach God's law in all of the cities of Judah (vv.7-9).

Jehoshaphat's reign resembled that of his father; he faithfully honored Asa's godly example. Yet even more important, Jehoshaphat's "heart took delight in the ways of the Lord" (v.6). Today, if you're looking for a father to follow, remember your heavenly Father and take delight in His ways. —Jennifer Benson Schuldt

We magnify our Father God
With songs of thoughtful praise;
As grateful children we confess
How perfect are His ways. —*Ball*

We honor God's name when we call Him our Father and live like His Son.

September 14
Monday

Unfailing Mercy

Read:
Luke 22:54-62

Through the Lord's mercies we are not consumed, because His compassions fail not. . . . Great is Your faithfulness.
—Lamentations 3:22-23

The Bible In One Year:
■ Proverbs 19–21
■ 2 Corinthians 7

As I strolled through Chicago's O'Hare airport, something caught my eye—a hat worn by someone racing through the concourse. What caught my attention was the message it conveyed in just two words: "Deny Everything." I wondered what it meant. Don't ever admit to guilt? Or deny yourself the pleasures and luxuries of life? I scratched my head at the mystery of those two simple words, "Deny Everything."

One of Jesus' followers, Simon Peter, did some denying. In a critical moment, he denied three times that He even knew Jesus! (Luke 22:57, 58,60). His fear-filled act of denial caused him such guilt and heartache that, broken by his spiritual failure, he could only go out and weep bitterly (v.62).

But Peter's denial of Christ, like our own moments of spiritual denial, could never diminish the compassion of God. The prophet Jeremiah wrote, "Through the Lord's mercies we are not consumed, because His compassions fail not. They are new every morning; great is Your faithfulness" (Lam. 3:22-23). We can take heart that even when we fail, our faithful God comes to us in mercy and compassion that never fails! —Bill Crowder

Thank You, Father, for Your new and never-failing mercies. Forgive me for the times I deny You and fail others, and teach me to run to You for Your overflowing compassion.

Being imperfect emphasizes our dependence on God's mercy.

September 15
Tuesday

A Life That Shined

Read:
Matthew 5:3-16

Let your light so shine before men, that they may see your good works and glorify your Father in heaven.
—Matthew 5:16

The Bible In One Year:
■ Proverbs 22–24
■ 2 Corinthians 8

According to the International Basketball Federation, basketball is the world's second-most popular sport, with an estimated 450 million followers in countries around the globe. In the US, the annual NCAA tournament in March often brings mention of legendary coach John Wooden. During his 27 years at UCLA, Wooden's teams won an unprecedented 10 National Championship titles. Yet, today, John Wooden, who died in 2010, is remembered not just for what he accomplished but for the person he was.

Wooden lived out his Christian faith and his genuine concern for others in an environment often obsessed with winning. In his autobiography, *They Call Me Coach,* he wrote, "I always tried to make it clear that basketball is not the ultimate. It is of small importance in comparison to the total life we live. There is only one kind of life that truly wins, and that is the one that places faith in the hands of the Savior. Until that is done, we are on an aimless course that runs in circles and goes nowhere."

John Wooden honored God in all he did, and his example challenges us to do the same. Jesus said, "Let your light so shine before men, that they may see your good works and glorify your Father in heaven" (Matt. 5:16). —David McCasland

Show me the way, Lord, let my light shine
As an example of good to mankind;
Help them to see the patterns of Thee,
Shining in beauty, lived out in me. —*Neuer*

Let your light shine—whether you're a candle in a corner or a lighthouse on a hill.

September 16
Wednesday

GOD'S WILL

READ:
Psalm 37:23-40

The steps of a good man are ordered by the LORD, and He delights in his way.
—Psalm 37:23

THE BIBLE IN ONE YEAR:
- Proverbs 25–26
- 2 Corinthians 9

We're often looking for God's will—especially when we're in a difficult situation. We wonder, *What will happen to me here? Should I stay or does God want me somewhere else?* The only way to know for sure is to do what He asks you to do right now—the duty of the present moment—and wait for God to reveal the next step.

As you obey what you know, you will be strengthened to take the next step and the next. Step by step, one step at a time. That's how we learn to walk with God.

But you say, "Suppose I take the first step. What will happen next?" That's God's business. Your task and mine is to obey this day and leave the future to Him. The psalmist says our steps are "ordered by the LORD" (37:23). This day's direction is all we need. Tomorrow's instruction is of no use to us at all. George MacDonald said, "We do not understand the next page of God's lesson book; we see only the one before us. Nor shall we be allowed to turn the leaf until we have learned its lesson."

If we concern ourselves with God's will and obey each day the directions and warnings He gives, if we walk by faith and step out in the path of obedience, we will find that God will lead us through this day. As Jesus put it, "Tomorrow will worry about its own things" (Matt. 6:34). —David Roper

God knows each winding way I take,
And every sorrow, pain, and ache;
His children He will not forsake—
He knows and loves His own. —*Bosch*

Blessed is the person who finds out which way God is moving and then goes in that direction.

September 17
Thursday

Seeing God In Familiar Places

Read:
Isaiah 6:1-6

The whole earth is full of His glory! —Isaiah 6:3

The Bible In One Year:
■ Proverbs 27–29
■ 2 Corinthians 10

Because of where I live, I'm treated to spectacular displays of the magnificent, creative glory of God. Recently, on a drive through the woods, I was struck with a breathtaking display of deep rich reds and a variety of yellows that decorated the trees of autumn—all artfully arranged against the backdrop of a brilliant blue sky.

And soon, as the temperatures plummet and winter blows in, I'll be reminded that no two snowflakes are ever the same as they pile on top of one another to create a rolling landscape of pristine white drifts. After that will come the miracle of spring, when that which seemed hopelessly dead bursts into life with buds and blossoms that will grace the meadows with a multiplicity of colors.

Wherever we look in the world around us, we see evidence that "the whole earth is full of His glory!" (Isa. 6:3). What is amazing is that the creation that surrounds us is damaged by sin (see Rom. 8:18-22), yet God has seen fit to grace our fallen landscape with these loving brushstrokes of His creative hand. It serves as a daily reminder that the beauty of His grace covers our sin and that His love for that which is fallen is always available to us. —Joe Stowell

Lord, may we be ever mindful of Your grace and love in all that surrounds us. Thank You for making Yourself visible through the beauty of Your creation. Teach us to look beyond the beauty to see Your hand at work.

Never pass up an opportunity to enjoy nature's beauty—it's the handwriting of God.

September 18
Friday

God Had Other Plans

Read:
1 Peter 1:1-9

A man's heart plans his way, but the Lord directs his steps.
—Proverbs 16:9

The Bible In One Year:
- **Proverbs 30–31**
- **2 Corinthians 11:1-15**

My friend Linda grew up planning to become a medical missionary. She loves the Lord and wanted to serve Him as a doctor by taking the gospel to sick people in parts of the world where medical care is hard to find. But God had other plans. Linda has indeed become a medical missionary, but not the way she expected.

At age 14, Linda developed a chronic health problem that required her to be hospitalized for major surgery several times a year. She survived bacterial meningitis that left her in a coma for 2 weeks and blind for 6 months. She once celebrated two birthdays in a row in the hospital—without going home in between. She has had several experiences when she was not expected to live. But yet Linda is the most vibrant, grateful, and cheerful person you will ever meet. She once told me that her mission field, as she hoped and planned, is the hospital. But instead of serving God as a doctor, she serves Him as a patient. No matter how sick she is, the light of the Lord radiates from her.

Linda exemplifies the teaching of the apostle Peter. Despite her trials, she rejoices, and the genuineness of her faith brings "praise, honor, and glory" to Jesus Christ (1 Peter 1:6-7). —Julie Ackerman Link

Lord, I'm so thankful that no matter where
we are, we can serve You. Help me to reflect
Your image in my current situation, even
if it's not where I hoped I would be.

Write your plans in pencil and remember that God has the eraser.

September 19
Saturday

Time For A Change

Read:
Genesis 12:1-8

There he built an altar to the Lord and called on the name of the Lord. —Genesis 12:8

The Bible In One Year:
■ Ecclesiastes 1–3
■ 2 Corinthians 11:16-33

Many believers long to spend daily time with God, praying and reading His Word. Ironically, they are often distracted by a busy schedule. Frustrations mount as busyness seems to crowd out an opening in their schedule.

Oswald Chambers has wisely commented on the transforming power of even 5 minutes in the presence of the Lord. Indeed, even a short time spent in intercession and the Word still has great value: "It is not the thing on which we spend the most time that moulds us, but the thing that exerts the greatest power. Five minutes with God and His Word is worth more than all the rest of the day." Now, it may sound like Chambers has made an overstatement. Yet powerful results can come from even a short time of prayer, because *God* is powerful.

Sometimes our days are filled with busy demands that crowd out time spent in listening to and responding to God. But no matter where we are, any time taken to build our own spiritual "altar" to the Lord as Abram did (Gen. 12:8) opens the door to His transforming power. If you are having trouble establishing a time with God, you could start with just 5 minutes and see where it leads. Our God longs to meet with us and show His power in our lives. —Dennis Fisher

Lord, it's amazing to me that You, Almighty God,
would want to spend time with me! Thank You.
I stumble with my words at times but am in awe of
You. Thank You that You want to hear from me.

Talk with God—He wants to hear your heart.

September 20
Sunday

A Difficult Place

Read:
Acts 8:4-8,26-35

I will never leave you nor forsake you.
—Hebrews 13:5

The Bible In One Year:
- **Ecclesiastes 4–6**
- **2 Corinthians 12**

When a sudden change in technology made his job obsolete, a highly trained scientist found himself working in a fast-food restaurant. One evening after our Bible study he described the situation as difficult and humbling. He said, "One good thing I can say is that the young people there seem very interested in my faith." A member of the group responded, "I admire you for being humble. I know your faith must have something to do with it."

Like my acquaintance, Philip may have wondered why God would pull him off an assignment in Samaria (Acts 8:4-8) and plop him in the middle of the desert (v.26). But then he found that the Ethiopian needed help understanding the Scriptures (vv.27-35), and his place made sense.

When Jesus promised He would never leave us alone (Matt. 28:20; Heb. 13:5), He meant in the hard times as well as in the good times. Our mission in the difficult seasons of life is to work or serve remembering we are doing it for God, and then to watch as God works to accomplish His purposes.

Look for God in your difficult place and discover what He's doing in and through you there. —Randy Kilgore

Disappointment—His appointment,
No good thing will He withhold;
From denials oft we gather
Treasures of His love untold. —Young

What's better than answers to our why questions?
Trusting a good God who has His reasons.

September 21
Monday

A Prize For Peace

Read:
Ephesians 2:11-18

These things I have spoken to you, that in Me you may have peace. —John 16:33

The Bible In One Year:
■ Ecclesiastes 7–9
■ 2 Corinthians 13

Alfred Nobel made a fortune from the invention of dynamite, which changed the course of warfare. Perhaps because of the horrors that wars inflicted with the use of dynamite, he made a provision in his will for a prize to be given annually to those who work to promote peace. Today it's called the Nobel Peace Prize.

God's expression of peace to the world was His Son. When Jesus was born, the angels' clear, unmistakable message to the shepherds was "on earth peace, goodwill toward men" (Luke 2:14).

The biblical definition of *peace* is, first of all, peace *with* God (Rom. 5:1). Sin makes us enemies with God (v.10), but Jesus' coming to this earth and dying on the cross turned away God's wrath. We can now be reconciled with Him. Having put right our relationship with God, Jesus now enables us to work at breaking down the barriers between us and others.

Another kind of peace is having the peace *of* God (Phil. 4:7). There is no need to be anxious about anything, for we are told that we can make our requests known to Him.

Having brought peace, Jesus is now seated at the right hand of the Father (Heb. 12:2). Today, we can have peace *with* God and the peace *of* God. —C. P. Hia

Hark! The herald angels sing,
"Glory to the newborn King;
Peace on earth, and mercy mild—
God and sinners reconciled!" —*Wesley*

True peace is not the absence of war; it is the presence of God. —Loveless

September 22
Tuesday

The Good And The Bad

Read:
1 Kings 14:7-16

My servant David . . . followed Me with all his heart.
—1 Kings 14:8

The Bible In One Year:
- **Ecclesiastes 10–12**
- **Galatians 1**

Recently, I began studying the kings of the Old Testament with some friends. I noticed on the chart that we were using that a few of the leaders of the kingdoms of Israel and Judah are labeled *good,* but most of them are labeled *bad, mostly bad, extra bad,* and *the worst.*

King David is described as a good king who "followed [God] with all his heart" (1 Kings 14:8) and is an example to follow (3:14; 11:38). The bad kings are noted for their willful rejection of God and for leading their subjects into idolatry. King Jeroboam, the first king to rule Israel after the kingdom was divided, has the legacy of being remembered as one of the worst kings—"who sinned and who made Israel sin" (14:16). Because of his bad example, many kings who came after him are compared to him and are described as being as evil as he was (16:2,19,26,31; 22:52).

Each of us has a unique sphere of influence, and that influence can be used for evil or for good. An unfettered faithfulness to God is a light that will shine brightly and leave a legacy of good.

It's our privilege to bring glory to the Lord. May others see His light shining through us and be drawn to His goodness. —Cindy Hess Kasper

Oh, make me, Lord, so much like Thee,
My life controlled by power divine,
That I a shining light may be
From which Thy grace may ever shine. —*Robertson*

The smallest light still shines in the darkest night.

September 23
Wednesday

CONFIDENCE IN TROUBLED TIMES

READ:
Psalm 91

He who dwells in the secret place of the Most High shall abide under the shadow of the Almighty. —Psalm 91:1

THE BIBLE IN ONE YEAR:
- Song of Solomon 1–3
- Galatians 2

Some kids love to brag about their dads. If you eavesdrop on neighborhood conversations, you'll hear children saying, "My dad is bigger than your dad!" or "My dad is smarter than your dad!" But the best brag of all is, "My dad is stronger than your dad!" This boast is usually in the context of a warning that if kids are threatening you, they'd better beware, because your dad can come and take them all down, including their dads!

Believing your dad is the strongest guy on the block inspires a lot of confidence in the face of danger. This is why I love the fact that God our Father is almighty. That means that no one can match His strength and power. Better still, it means that you and I "abide under the shadow of the Almighty" (Ps. 91:1). So, it's no wonder the psalmist can confidently say that he will not "be afraid of the terror by night, nor of the arrow that flies by day" (v.5).

Regardless of what today may bring or the trouble you are now going through, don't forget that your God is stronger than anything in your life. So, be confident! The shadow of His all-prevailing presence guarantees that His power can turn even the worst situation into something good. —Joe Stowell

Father God, in the midst of my trouble, teach me to rest in the fact that You are almighty. Thank You for the confidence I have that You are stronger than anything that threatens my life.

God is greater than our greatest problem.

September 24
Thursday

A Friend In Need

Read:
1 John 3:11-18

My little children, let us not love in word or in tongue, but in deed and in truth. —1 John 3:18

The Bible In One Year:
■ Song of Solomon 4–5
■ Galatians 3

Not long ago my wife, Janet, and I bought a quantity of beef from a friend who raised cattle on a small farm. It was less expensive than meat from a grocery store, and we put it in the freezer to use throughout the coming months.

Then a terrible lightning storm cut power throughout our area. For the first 24 hours we were confident that the freezer would keep the meat frozen. But when the second day came with still no word of getting our power back, we began to be concerned.

We contacted Ted, a member of our Bible-study group, to see if he had any advice. He canceled an appointment he had and showed up at our doorstep with a generator to provide power for the freezer. We were thankful that Ted helped us, and we knew it was because of his love for Christ.

The old saying "a friend in need is a friend indeed" took on new meaning for us. John reminds us in 1 John 3:18, "My little children, let us not love in word or in tongue, but in deed and in truth." Sometimes this means inconveniencing ourselves to care for the interests of others or receiving that help when we ourselves are in need. After all Christ has done for us, it's a blessing to be His hands and feet in loving one another. —Dennis Fisher

Father, thank You for making me a part of Your family by giving Your Son Jesus for me. Help me to accept the care of others and also to serve them out of gratitude and out of my love for You.

When we love Christ, we love others.

September 25
Friday

INSIGNIFICANT

READ:
Luke 3:2-6,15-18

The Word of God came to John the son of Zacharias in the wilderness. —Luke 3:2

THE BIBLE IN ONE YEAR:
- Song of Solomon 6–8
- Galatians 4

"Movers and shakers" are people climbing the ladder of influence and success. Luke 3 mentions seven prominent leaders who exercised control in the society of their time. Roman Emperor Tiberias Caesar held the power of life and death over people in his far-flung empire. Pontius Pilate represented Rome as governor of Judea; while Herod, Philip, and Lysanias kept people in line at the regional level. Annas and Caiaphas served as high priests, taking their religious authority seriously.

While these power brokers flexed their political muscles, "the Word of God came to John the son of Zacharias in the wilderness" (v.2). Who could seem less important than this obscure man living in the desert and listening for God's voice? What could John the Baptist possibly accomplish by "preaching a baptism of repentance for the remission of sins"? (v.3). Yet multitudes came to John seeking truth, turning from their wrongs, and wondering if he could be the Messiah (vv.7,15). John told them, "One mightier than I is coming . . . . He will baptize you with the Holy Spirit and fire" (v.16).

John's life helps us understand what it means to be significant in God's eyes. Like John, may everything we say and do point others to Jesus. —David McCasland

Lord, help us to surrender our desire for influence
and success to You. May our heart's desire ever be
to be used by You to further Your kingdom.
Make our lives a living testimony of You.

Our surrender to God precedes His significant work in our life.

September 26
Saturday

The Path Of Wisdom

Read:
Psalm 38:1-15

In You, O Lord, I hope; You will hear, O Lord my God.
—Psalm 38:15

The Bible In One Year:
- Isaiah 1–2
- Galatians 5

Albert Einstein was heard to say, "Only two things are infinite, the universe and human stupidity, and I'm not sure about the former." Sadly, it does seem that far too often there is no limit to the foolishness we get ourselves into—or the damage we create by our foolishness and the choices it fosters.

It was in such a season of regret that David poured out his struggle and complaint to God in Psalm 38. As he recounted his own failings, as well as the painful consequences he was enduring because of those failings, the shepherd-king made an insightful comment: "My wounds are foul and festering because of my foolishness" (v.5). Although the psalmist does not give us the details of those choices or of his worsening wounds, one thing is clear—David recognized his own foolishness as their root cause.

The answer for such destructive foolishness is to embrace the wisdom of God. Proverbs 9:10 reminds us, "The fear of the Lord is the beginning of wisdom, and the knowledge of the Holy One is understanding." Only by allowing God to transform us can we overcome the foolish decisions that cause so much trouble. With His loving guidance, we can follow the pathway of godly wisdom. —Bill Crowder

Loving Father, forgive me for the seemingly limitless capacity I have to be foolish. Teach me in Your wisdom, so that my life might be pleasing to You and a blessing to others around me.

God's wisdom is given to those who humbly ask Him for it.

September 27
Sunday

FIRE AND RAIN

READ:
Isaiah 16:1-5

**In mercy the throne will be established; and One will sit on it in truth . . . judging and seeking justice and hastening righteousness.
—Isaiah 16:5**

THE BIBLE IN ONE YEAR:
- Isaiah 3–4
- Galatians 6

When a wildfire raged through the beautiful canyons near Colorado Springs, Colorado, it destroyed the habitat of all kinds of wildlife and hundreds of homes. People across the nation cried out to God, pleading with Him to send rain to douse the flames, put an end to the destruction, and give firefighters relief. Some people's prayers had an interesting condition attached to them. They asked God to show mercy and send rain without lightning, which they feared would start even more fires.

This reminds me of how we live in tension between things that save us and kill us. With fire, we cook our food and keep warm, but in it we can be consumed. With water, we keep our bodies hydrated and our planet cooled, but in it we also can drown. Too much or too little of either is life-threatening.

We see the same principle at work spiritually. To thrive, civilizations need the seemingly opposite qualities of mercy and justice (Zech. 7:9). Jesus scolded the Pharisees for being sticklers about the law but neglecting these "weightier matters" (Matt. 23:23).

We may lean toward justice or mercy, but Jesus keeps them in perfect balance (Isa. 16:5; 42:1-4). His death satisfies God's need for justice and our need for mercy. —Julie Ackerman Link

Father, for personal reasons I sometimes lean toward showing mercy, and sometimes I just want justice now. Teach me the balance as I look at Your character and give me the wisdom I need in specific situations.

God's justice and mercy met at the cross.

September 28
Monday

WHO AM I?

READ:
Exodus 3:7-15

Moses said to God, "Who am I that I should go to Pharaoh?" —Exodus 3:11

THE BIBLE IN ONE YEAR:
■ Isaiah 5–6
■ Ephesians 1

Years ago, world-famous evangelist Billy Graham was scheduled to speak at Cambridge University in England, but he did not feel qualified to address the sophisticated thinkers. He had no advanced degrees and he had never attended seminary. Billy confided in a close friend: "I do not know that I have ever felt more inadequate and totally unprepared for a mission." He prayed for God's help, and God used him to share the simple truth of the gospel and the cross of Christ.

Moses also felt inadequate when God recruited him for the task of telling Pharaoh to release the Israelites. Moses asked, "Who am I that I should go to Pharaoh?" (Ex. 3:11). Although Moses may have questioned his effectiveness because he was "slow of speech" (4:10), God said, "I will certainly be with you" (3:12). Knowing he would have to share God's rescue plan and tell the Israelites who sent him, Moses asked God, "What shall I say to them?" God replied, "I AM has sent me to you" (vv.13-14). His name, "I AM," revealed His eternal, self-existent, and all-sufficient character.

Even when we question our ability to do what God has asked us to do, He can be trusted. Our shortcomings are less important than God's sufficiency. When we ask, "Who am I?" we can remember that God said, "I AM." —Jennifer Benson Schuldt

Dear Lord, help me to remember that You are with me, even when I'm unsure of my own abilities. Give me the faith to believe that You can help me to do anything You ask me to do.

You need not be afraid of where you're going when you know God's going with you.

September 29
Tuesday

Color Courage

Read:
1 Corinthians 4:10-17

Imitate me, just as I also imitate Christ. —1 Corinthians 11:1

The Bible In One Year:
■ Isaiah 7–8
■ Ephesians 2

A radio ad for watches suggests that listeners buy a watch with a bright color band and then wear it with clothes of other colors. When people notice your watch because of its contrasting color, the ad says, "They'll see that you have 'color courage.' And they'll want to be like you." Something in us enjoys having others follow our example.

If you do a quick reading of 1 Corinthians 4, you might think the apostle Paul sounds a bit boastful when he says to follow his example of self-sacrifice (v.16). But a closer look at Paul's words shows why he wrote so confidently. He could ask people to imitate him because he imitated Christ (11:1), the greatest Servant of all.

The persecution he endured and the position he held in the church (4:10-17) all happened because Paul followed Jesus. When he mentioned that even if the Corinthians had 10,000 teachers he would still be their father in the faith (v.15), he was acknowledging that Jesus is the only reason people could trust his teaching.

If we want people to imitate us, we must first imitate our Lord. If we have any reason for people to follow our example—if we have any courage to point others to the Savior—it is because of Him, not us. —Anne Cetas

Joyfully following Jesus the Lord
And trusting His lead every day
Makes us examples that others can see
To follow when trials come their way. —*Sper*

Others should imitate us only as far as we imitate Christ.

September 30
Wednesday

DRINK LOTS OF WATER

READ:
John 4:7-14

The water that I shall give him will become in him a fountain of water springing up into everlasting life.
—John 4:14

THE BIBLE IN ONE YEAR:
■ Isaiah 9–10
■ Ephesians 3

Visitors to Colorado often become dehydrated without realizing it. The dry climate and intense sun, especially in the mountains, can rapidly deplete the body's fluids. That's why many tourist maps and signs urge people to drink plenty of water.

In the Bible, water is often used as a symbol of Jesus as the Living Water who satisfies our deepest needs. So it's quite fitting that one of Jesus' most memorable conversations took place at a well (John 4:1-42). It began with Jesus asking a Samaritan woman for a drink of water (v.7). It quickly progressed to a discussion of something more when Jesus said to her: "Whoever drinks of this [physical] water will thirst again, but whoever drinks of the water that I shall give him will never thirst. But the water that I shall give him will become in him a fountain of water springing up into everlasting life" (vv.13-14).

As a result of this conversation, the woman and many people in the village where she lived came to believe that Jesus was "the Christ, the Savior of the world" (v.42).

We can't live without water. Nor can we truly live now or eternally without the living water we receive from knowing Jesus Christ as our Savior. We can drink of His life-giving water today. —David McCasland

Gracious and Almighty Savior,
Source of all that shall endure,
Quench my thirst with living water,
Living water, clear and pure. —Vinal

Only Jesus, the Living Water, can satisfy the thirsty soul.

October 1
Thursday

Hubble, Zoos, and Singing Children

Read:
Psalm 148

Praise Him, all you stars of light!
—Psalm 148:3

The Bible In One Year:
- **Isaiah 11–13**
- **Ephesians 4**

What do the Hubble Space Telescope, a zoo, and singing children have in common? According to the teaching of Psalm 148, we could conclude that they all point to God's magnificent creation.

The idea that God created our world is often questioned, so perhaps it's a good time for a reminder of the praise we and all creation should heap on our heavenly Father for His magnificent handiwork.

Hubble can help us with that through its eye-popping pictures of our universe. Every one of those brilliant photos points to stars that focus attention on God's creative majesty. "Praise Him, all you stars of light!" says verse 3.

A visit to a zoo points us to the great diversity of wildlife God created. We look at verses 7 and 10 and say thank you to God for sea creatures, wild animals, insects, and birds.

And a few minutes of watching little children singing uninhibited praises to God symbolizes the truth that all people of earth should lift their voices in honor of our Creator (vv.11-13).

Stars, animals, and children: "Let them praise the name of the Lord, for His name alone is exalted" (v.13). Let's join in saying thanks for His creation. "Praise the Lord!" —Dave Branon

Praise to the Lord, the Almighty, the King of creation!
O my soul, praise Him, for He is thy health and salvation!
All ye who hear, now to His temple draw near;
Join me in glad adoration! —Neander

Creation displays God's power.

October 2
Friday

Married To Royalty

Read:
Revelation 19:6-9

The marriage of the Lamb has come, and His wife has made herself ready.
—Revelation 19:7

The Bible In One Year:
- Isaiah 14–16
- Ephesians 5:1-16

The book *To Marry an English Lord* chronicles the 19th-century phenomenon of rich American heiresses who sought marriages to British aristocracy. Although they were already wealthy, they wanted the social status of royalty. The book begins with Prince Albert, son of Queen Victoria, going to the United States to pay a social call. A mass of wealthy heiresses flood into a ball arranged for Prince Albert, each hoping to become his royal bride.

Believers in Christ don't have to just hope—they are assured of a royal marriage in heaven. John talks about it in the book of Revelation: "Let us be glad and rejoice and give Him glory, for the marriage of the Lamb has come, and His wife has made herself ready. And to her it was granted to be arrayed in fine linen, clean and bright, for the fine linen is the righteous acts of the saints" (19:7-8). Jesus is the Lamb, who is the Bridegroom talked about in that Scripture, and believers are His bride.

As the bride of Christ, we are to make ourselves "ready" for that day by striving to live close to Him now in anticipation of our future with Him in heaven. There we will "be glad and rejoice and give . . . glory" (v.7) to the King of kings and Lord of lords! —Dennis Fisher

Jesus, we look forward to that day when we will
be with You! We want to be ready, but we know
we can't live a life that is pure unless You are
in us and help us. Change us and fill us.

There is no greater privilege than to know the King of kings.

October 3
Saturday

The Gift Of Presence

Read:
John 11:14-27

Many of the Jews had joined the women around Martha and Mary, to comfort them concerning their brother. —John 11:19

The Bible In One Year:
- Isaiah 17–19
- Ephesians 5:17-33

A number of years ago, when I was a new human resource manager for a company, I attended the visitation and funeral of a long-time employee I had never met. The worker, a bricklayer, was loved by his co-workers, yet very few came to see his widow. I listened to someone trying to console her by saying that many people stay away because they are afraid of saying or doing the wrong thing and making the family more miserable.

In times of distress, however, people rarely remember what we say. What they most remember is that we were there. Familiar faces offer strength beyond description; they provide comfort for the deep feelings of loneliness setting in from the loss. This "gift of presence" is one we're all capable of offering, even if we're tongue-tied or uncomfortable.

Martha and Mary were surrounded by friends and mourners who comforted them when their brother Lazarus died (John 11:19). Then the One they most longed to see—Jesus—came and wept with them (vv.33-35). The people responded, "See how He loved him!" (v.36).

In loss of any kind, Jesus always gives His comforting presence, and we have the ability to give deeply of His compassion simply by the gift of our presence. —Randy Kilgore

O may I never fail to see
The comfort you may need from me;
And may you know that I am there
To bind our souls as grief we share. —*Kilgore*

Often the best comfort is just being there.

October 4
Sunday

Immeasurably More

Read:
Ephesians 3:14-21

He who is in you is greater than he who is in the world.
—1 John 4:4

The Bible In One Year:
- **Isaiah 20–22**
- **Ephesians 6**

It's not going to happen, Aunt Julie. You might as well erase that thought from your mind."

"I know it's unlikely," I said. "But it's not impossible."

For several years, my niece and I have had variations of that conversation regarding a situation in our family. The rest of the sentence, which I said only occasionally, was this: "I know it can happen because I hear stories all the time about how God makes impossible things happen." The part of the sentence I said only to myself was this: "But they happen only in other people's families."

Recently my pastor has been preaching from the book of Ephesians. At the end of every service we say this benediction: "Now to Him who is able to do immeasurably more than all we ask or imagine, according to His power that is at work within us, to Him be glory in the church and in Christ Jesus throughout all generations, for ever and ever! Amen" (Eph. 3:20-21 NIV).

This was the year God chose to do "immeasurably more" in my family. He replaced indifference with love. How did He do it? Beats me. But I saw it happen. And why should I be surprised? If Satan can turn love into indifference, certainly God can change indifference back into love. —Julie Ackerman Link

Lord, thank You for doing immeasurably more in our lives than we could ever imagine.
I am so thankful that You are able and often do make impossible situations possible.

God's power to restore is stronger than Satan's power to destroy.

October 5
Monday

The Value Of One

Read:
Luke 15:1-10

What man . . . having a hundred sheep, if he loses one of them, does not leave the ninety-nine in the wilderness, and go after the one which is lost? —Luke 15:4

The Bible In One Year:
- Isaiah 23–25
- Philippians 1

Only hours before Kim Haskins' high school graduation, an auto accident took the life of her father and left Kim and her mother hospitalized. The next day, Joe Garrett, Kim's high school principal, visited her at the hospital and said they wanted to do something special for her at the school. *The Gazette* (Colorado Springs) article by James Drew described the outpouring of love and support as the teachers, administrators, and classmates—deeply touched by Kim's loss—filled the high school auditorium a few days later at a graduation ceremony just for her.

Principal Garrett said, "We talk a lot in education about no child left behind. In the military, they talk about no soldier left behind. Today, this is about no graduate left behind."

Jesus underscored the importance of every person to God with three stories about something lost—a sheep, a coin, and a son (Luke 15). In each story, a person has lost something of great value. When it is found, friends and neighbors are called to celebrate and rejoice together.

The point is clear: We are all of great value to God, who offers us forgiveness and new life through Christ. And He faithfully pursues us with His love and grace. There is great joy in heaven over one sinner who repents (v.7). —David McCasland

I was lost but Jesus found me—
Found the sheep that went astray,
Threw His loving arms around me,
Drew me back into His way. —*Rowley*

Our value is measured by what God has done for us.

October 6
Tuesday

A Dangerous Challenge

Read:
2 Chronicles 20:1, 15-22

The battle is not yours, but God's.
—2 Chronicles 20:15

The Bible In One Year:
- **Isaiah 26–27**
- **Philippians 2**

While millions watched on television, Nik Wallenda walked across Niagara Falls on a 1,800-foot wire that was only 2 inches in diameter. He took all the precautions he could. But adding to the drama and danger of both the height and the rushing water below, a thick mist obscured Nik's sight, wind threatened his balance, and spray from the falls challenged his footing. Amid—and perhaps because of—these perils, he said that he "prayed a lot" and praised God.

The Israelites also praised God in the middle of a dangerous challenge. Theirs involved a large group of warriors who had gathered to fight them (2 Chron. 20:2). After humbly asking God for help, King Jehoshaphat appointed a choir to march out into battle in front of the Israelite army. The worshipers sang: "Praise the Lord, for His mercy endures forever" (v.21). When they began to sing, the Lord caused the enemy forces to attack and destroy each other.

Praising God in the midst of a challenge may mean overriding our natural instincts. We tend toward self-protection, strategizing, and worry. However, worshiping can guard our hearts against troubling thoughts and self-reliance. It reminds us of the lesson the Israelites learned: "The battle is not [ours], but God's" (v.15). —Jennifer Benson Schuldt

Lord, I praise You, for Your mercy is everlasting.
Help me to remember that every battle in
this life is Yours. The outcome belongs to
You because You are sovereign.

No matter what is in front of us,
God is always behind us.

October 7
Wednesday

Public Praise

Read:
Psalm 96

Declare His glory among the nations, His wonders among all peoples. —Psalm 96:3

The Bible In One Year:
- **Isaiah 28–29**
- **Philippians 3**

I love the YouTube video of people in a food court of a mall, who in the midst of their ordinary lives were suddenly interrupted by someone who stood up and boldly began singing the "Hallelujah Chorus." To the surprise of everyone, another person got up and joined the chorus, and then another, and another. Soon the food court was resounding with the celebrative harmonies of Handel's masterpiece. A local opera company had planted their singers in strategic places so that they could joyfully interject the glory of God into the everyday lives of lunching shoppers.

Every time I watch that video, it moves me to tears. It reminds me that bringing the glory of God into the ordinary situations of our world through the beautiful harmonies of Christlikeness is exactly what we are called to do. Think of intentionally interjecting God's grace into a situation where some undeserving soul needs a second chance; of sharing the love of Christ with someone who is needy; of being the hands of Jesus that lift up a weary friend; or of bringing peace to a confusing and chaotic situation.

As the psalmist reminds us, we have the high and holy privilege of declaring "His glory among the nations, His wonders among all peoples" (Ps. 96:3). —Joe Stowell

Thank You, Lord, for filling us with the capacity to take Your glory "public" through the way we act and react toward others. Give us the grace to interject the surprising beauty of Your wonderful ways into each encounter.

Surprise your world with the wonders of Christ shining through you!

October 8
Thursday

God Provides, But How?

Read:
Deuteronomy 24:19-22

He who tills his land will be satisfied with bread.
—Proverbs 12:11

The Bible In One Year:
- Isaiah 30–31
- Philippians 4

Outside my office window, the squirrels are in a race against winter to bury their acorns in a safe, accessible place. Their commotion amuses me. An entire herd of deer can go through our back yard and not make a sound, but one squirrel sounds like an invasion.

The two creatures are different in another way as well. Deer do not prepare for winter. When the snow comes they eat whatever they can find along the way (including ornamental shrubs in our yard). But squirrels would starve if they followed that example. They would be unable to find suitable food.

The deer and the squirrel represent ways that God cares for us. He enables us to work and save for the future, and He meets our need when resources are scarce. As the wisdom literature teaches, God gives us seasons of plenty so that we can prepare for seasons of need (Prov. 12:11). And as Psalm 23 says, the Lord leads us through perilous places to pleasant pastures.

Another way that God provides is by instructing those with plenty to share with those in need (Deut. 24:19). So when it comes to provision, the message of the Bible is this: Work while we can, save what we can, share what we can, and trust God to meet our needs. —Julie Ackerman Link

Thank You, Lord, for the promise that You will
meet our needs. Help us not to fear or doubt.
We're grateful that You're watching over us
and that our cries for help reach Your ear.

Our needs will never exhaust God's supply.

October 9
Friday

Life Without Bread

Read:
John 6:25-35

I am the bread of life.
—John 6:48

The Bible In One Year:
■ Isaiah 32–33
■ Colossians 1

In cultures with an abundance of food choices, bread is no longer a necessary part of the diet so some choose to live without it for various reasons. In the first century, however, bread was viewed as an essential staple. A diet without bread was a foreign concept.

One day a crowd of people sought out Jesus because He had performed the miracle of multiplying loaves of bread (John 6:11,26). They asked Him to perform a sign like the manna from heaven that God had provided for His people in the desert (6:30-31; Ex. 16:4). When Jesus said He was "the true bread from heaven" (John 6:32), the people didn't understand. They wanted literal daily bread. But Jesus was saying that He had been sent to be their spiritual bread; He would supply their daily spiritual needs. If they, by faith, applied and took His words and life into their very souls, they would experience everlasting satisfaction (v.35).

Jesus doesn't want to be an optional commodity in our diets; He desires to be the essential staple in our lives, our "necessary" food. As first-century Jews could never imagine life without physical bread, may we never attempt to live without Jesus, our spiritual bread! —Marvin Williams

For Further Thought

What are some ways you can let Jesus, the Bread of Life, and His words satisfy the hunger pangs of your soul today?

Only spiritual bread satisfies the hunger of the soul.

October 10
Saturday

Being A Witness

Read:
Acts 1:1-9

You shall receive power when the Holy Spirit has come upon you; and you shall be witnesses to Me. —Acts 1:8

The Bible In One Year:
- **Isaiah 34–36**
- **Colossians 2**

When I was a teen, I witnessed an auto accident. It was a shocking experience that was compounded by what followed. As the only witness to the incident, I spent the ensuing months telling a series of lawyers and insurance adjustors what I had seen. I was not expected to explain the physics of the wreck or the details of the medical trauma. I was asked to tell only what I had witnessed.

As followers of Christ, we are called to be witnesses of what Jesus has done in us and for us. To point people to Christ, we don't need to be able to explain every theological issue or answer every question. What we must do is explain what we have witnessed in our own lives through the cross and the resurrection of the Savior. Even better is that we don't have to rely on ourselves alone to do this. Jesus said, "But you shall receive power when the Holy Spirit has come upon you; and you shall be witnesses to Me in Jerusalem, and in all Judea and Samaria, and to the end of the earth" (Acts 1:8).

As we rely on the Spirit's power, we can point a hurting world to the redeeming Christ. With His help, we can witness to the life-changing power of His presence in our lives!
—Bill Crowder

I love to tell the story of unseen things above,
Of Jesus and His glory, of Jesus and His love.
I love to tell the story, because I know 'tis true;
It satisfies my longings as nothing else can do. —*Hankey*

Our testimony is the witness of what God has done for us.

October 11
Sunday

"Gorgeous Inside"

Read:
Romans 8:1-11

To be spiritually minded is life and peace. —Romans 8:6

The Bible In One Year:
- **Isaiah 37–38**
- **Colossians 3**

It's a rather nondescript house that sits on a busy thoroughfare. With no distinctive characteristics, this rather plain home is easy to ignore. But as I drove past it the other day, I noticed a "For Sale" sign in the yard. Attached to the sign was a smaller notice that happily announced: "I'm gorgeous inside." While I'm not in the market for a new house, that sign intrigued me. What could make this otherwise forgettable house gorgeous inside?

It also made me wonder: *Could that sign apply to us as followers of Jesus?* Think about it. No matter what we look like on the outside, shouldn't there be within us a beauty that reveals God's love and work in our lives?

What does the Bible say about inner beauty? We might start with Romans 7:22, which says, "In my inner being I delight in God's law" (NIV). A few verses later in Romans 8:6, Paul speaks of a Spirit-controlled mind that is characterized by "life and peace." And in Galatians, we see that letting the Spirit take charge of our inner being will build in us the "fruit of the Spirit" (5:22), a beautiful array of qualities such as love, joy, peace, patience, and kindness.

Delighting in Scripture and allowing the Spirit to work in our heart will make us look good on the inside—and will pay off in a life that honors God. —Dave Branon

Dear Lord, I pray that through the work of Your Spirit dwelling within me I will be transformed into a grand display of the fruit that will attract others to You and reflect glory back to You.

Righteousness in your heart produces beauty in your character.

October 12
Monday

I'M INVISIBLE

READ:
Isaiah 40:25-31

[The Lord] gives power to the weak.
—Isaiah 40:29

THE BIBLE IN ONE YEAR:
- Isaiah 39–40
- Colossians 4

My friend Jane said something at a work meeting and no one responded. So she repeated it and again no one responded; her co-workers just ignored her. She realized that her opinion didn't matter much. She felt disregarded and invisible. You may know what that's like as well.

The people of God felt that way as a nation (Isa. 40). Only they believed it was God Himself who didn't see or understand their daily struggle to survive! The southern kingdom had been carried away captive into Babylon, and the exiled nation complained: "My way is hidden from the LORD, and my just claim is passed over by my God" (v.27).

While Isaiah agreed that compared to God "the nations are as a drop in a bucket, and are counted as the small dust on the scales" (v.15), he also wanted the people to know that God gives power to the weak and strength to those who need it (v.29). If they waited on the Lord, Isaiah said, He would renew their strength. They would mount up with wings like eagles; they would run and not be weary (v.31).

When you're feeling invisible or disregarded, remember that God does see you and He cares. Wait on Him, and He'll give you renewed strength. —Anne Cetas

Frail children of dust, and feeble as frail,
In Thee do we trust, nor find Thee to fail.
Thy mercies how tender! How firm to the end!
Our Maker, Defender, Redeemer, and Friend. —*Grant*

Even when we don't sense God's presence,
His loving care is all around us.

October 13
Tuesday

Facing Our Past

Read:
Acts 9:20-30

**He tried to join the disciples; but they were all afraid of him, and did not believe that he was a disciple.
—Acts 9:26**

The Bible In One Year:
- Isaiah 41–42
- 1 Thessalonians 1

Chuck Colson, founder of Prison Fellowship, spent 40 years helping people hear and understand the gospel of Jesus Christ. When he died in April 2012, one newspaper article carried the headline, "Charles Colson, Nixon's 'dirty tricks' man, dies at 80." It seemed surprising that a man so transformed by faith should be identified with things he did as a politically ruthless presidential aide decades earlier before he knew the Savior.

The apostle Paul's conversion and his early Christian witness were greeted with skepticism and fear. When he began preaching that Jesus is the Son of God, people said, "Is this not he who destroyed those who called on this name in Jerusalem, and has come here for that purpose?" (Acts 9:21). Later when Paul went to Jerusalem and tried to join the disciples, they were afraid of him (v.26). In years to come, Paul never ignored his past, but spoke of it as evidence of the mercy of God (1 Tim. 1:13-14).

Like Paul, we don't need to parade our failures or to pretend they didn't happen. Instead, we can thank the Lord that through His grace and power, our past is forgiven, our present is changed, and our future is bright with hope for all He has prepared for us. —David McCasland

Transformed by grace divine,
The glory shall be Thine;
To Thy most holy will, O Lord,
We now our all resign. —*Burroughs*

Only Jesus can transform our life.

October 14
Wednesday

SEEDS & SOILS

READ:
Matthew 13:1-9

Grow in the grace and knowledge of our Lord and Savior Jesus Christ. —2 Peter 3:18

THE BIBLE IN ONE YEAR:
- Isaiah 43–44
- 1 Thessalonians 2

If you like growing pumpkins, you have probably heard of Dill's Atlantic Giant variety of premium pumpkin seeds. Developed on a family farm in Atlantic Canada, the pumpkins grown from these seeds have set records around the world. In 2011, a pumpkin grown in Quebec set a new world record at 1,818.5 pounds (825 kg). That size of pumpkin could yield almost 1,000 pieces of pie!

When news reporters asked how this pumpkin could grow to such a size, the farmer replied that it had to do with the soil. The seeds were of a special large variety, but the soil still had to be right or the pumpkin wouldn't grow properly.

The Lord Jesus used an illustration in which He compared different types of ground to a person's response to God's Word (Matt. 13). Some seeds were eaten by the birds, others started to grow but were choked by the weeds, and some grew up instantly but had no soil to further their growth. But the seeds that fell on the good soil "yielded a crop: some a hundredfold, some sixty, some thirty" (v.8).

Each of us needs to ask, "What kind of soil am I?" The Lord wants to plant His Word in our hearts so we can grow in our knowledge of Him. —Brent Hackett, RBC Canada Director

More about Jesus let me learn,
More of His holy will discern;
Spirit of God, my teacher be,
Showing the things of Christ to me. —*Hewitt*

The fruit of the Spirit grows in the soil of obedience.

October 15
Thursday

Dreams Of Childhood

Read:
Psalm 8

Out of the mouth of babes and nursing infants You have ordained strength.
—Psalm 8:2

The Bible In One Year:
■ Isaiah 45–46
■ 1 Thessalonians 3

Years ago, I asked fifth-grade students to prepare a list of questions to ask Jesus if He were to show up in person the following week. I also asked groups of adults to do the same thing. The results were startlingly different. The kids' questions ranged from adorable to poignant: "Will we have to sit around in robes and sing all day in heaven? Will my puppy be in heaven? Were the whales in or out of the ark? How's my grandpa doing up there with You?" Almost without fail, their questions were free from doubt that heaven existed or that God acts supernaturally.

Adults, on the other hand, featured a completely different line of questioning: "Why do bad things happen to good people? How do I know You're listening to my prayers? Why is there only one way to heaven? How could a loving God let this tragedy happen to me?"

For the most part, children live life unfettered by the cares and sorrows that burden adults. Their faith lets them trust God more readily. While we adults often get lost in trials and sorrows, children retain the psalmist's view of life—an eternal perspective that sees the greatness of God (Ps. 8:1-2).

God can be trusted, and He longs for us to trust Him the way children do (Matt. 18:3). —Randy Kilgore

O Father, may I find again the dreams of childhood
when thoughts of You filled me with peace
and I longed to know You more. Give me
a faith that trusts You implicitly.

An intimate walk with God lifts our eyes from today's trials and into eternity's triumphs.

October 16
Friday

Coade Stone

Read:
1 Peter 2:1-10

Coming to Him as to a living stone, rejected indeed by men, but chosen by God and precious. —1 Peter 2:4

The Bible In One Year:
- Isaiah 47–49
- 1 Thessalonians 4

Throughout London, there are statues and other items made from a unique building material called Coade stone. Developed by Eleanor Coade for her family business in the late 1700s, this artificial stone is virtually indestructible and has the capacity to withstand time, weather, and man-made pollution. Though it was a marvel during the Industrial Revolution, Coade stone was phased out in the 1840s following Eleanor's death, and it was replaced by Portland cement as a building material. In spite of that, however, there remain today dozens of examples of this sturdy, ceramic-like stone that have withstood the harsh London environment for over 150 years.

The apostle Peter described Jesus as a living stone. He wrote, "Coming to Him as to a living stone, rejected indeed by men, but chosen by God and precious, you also, as living stones, are being built up a spiritual house" (1 Peter 2:4-5). Precious in the eyes of the Father is the sacrifice of the Rock of our salvation. Christ is the enduring stone upon which the Father has built our salvation and the only foundation for meaningful life (1 Cor. 3:11).

It is only as our lives are built upon His strength that we will be able to endure the harshness of life in a fallen world.
—Bill Crowder

My hope is built on nothing less
Than Jesus' blood and righteousness;
I dare not trust the sweetest frame,
But wholly lean on Jesus' name. —*Mote*

We have nothing to fear if we stay close to the Rock of Ages.

October 17
Saturday

BARRIER-FREE LOVE

READ:
Matthew 23:37-39

O Jerusalem . . . ! How often I wanted to gather your children together, as a hen gathers her chicks under her wings, but you were not willing! —Matt. 23:37

THE BIBLE IN ONE YEAR:
- Isaiah 50–52
- 1 Thessalonians 5

Not long ago I heard the distressed chirping of a bird coming from the side of my neighbor's house. I discovered that a nest of baby birds was inside a vent covered by a screen, placing a barrier between the mother bird who was trying to feed her hungry chicks. After I told the neighbors, they removed the screen and took the nest and chicks to a safe place to be cared for.

Few things are as heartbreaking as a barrier to love. Christ, the long-awaited Messiah of Israel, experienced a barrier to His love when His chosen people rejected Him. He used the word picture of a hen and her baby chicks to describe their unwillingness to receive it: "O Jerusalem, Jerusalem . . . ! How often I wanted to gather your children together, as a hen gathers her chicks under her wings, but you were not willing!" (Matt. 23:37).

Our sin is a barrier that separates us from God (Isa. 59:2). But "God so loved the world that He gave His only begotten Son, that whoever believes in Him should not perish but have everlasting life" (John 3:16). Jesus took care of the barrier to God's love by His sacrificial death on the cross and His resurrection (Rom. 5:8-17; 8:11). Now He longs for us to experience His love and accept this gift. —Dennis Fisher

My heart is stirred whene'er I think of Jesus,
That blessed Name that sets the captive free;
The only Name through which I find salvation,
No name on earth has meant so much to me. —*Eliason*

Through His cross, Jesus rescues and redeems.

October 18
Sunday

The End?

Read:
1 Corinthians 15:50-58

But thanks be to God, who gives us the victory through our Lord Jesus Christ. —1 Corinthians 15:57

The Bible In One Year:
■ Isaiah 53–55
■ 2 Thessalonians 1

Everything in this world eventually comes to an end, which at times can be disheartening. It's the feeling you get when you read a book that's so good you don't want it to end. Or when you watch a movie that you wish would go on a little while longer.

But all things—good and bad—do come to "The End." In fact, life ultimately does come to the end—sometimes sooner than we expect. All of us who have stood by the casket of a loved one know the painful emptiness of a heart that wishes it wasn't over yet.

Thankfully, Jesus steps into the fray of terminal disappointments, and, through His death and resurrection, He interjects hope for us. In Him "the end" is a prelude to a death-free eternity, and words like "it's over" are replaced by a joy-filled "forever." Since our bodies are not an eternal reality, Paul assures us that "we shall all be changed" (1 Cor. 15:51) and reminds us that because of Christ's conquering work we can confidently say, "O Death, . . . where is your victory?" (v.55).

So let not your heart be troubled. Our sorrow is real, but we can be filled with gratitude because God "gives us the victory through our Lord Jesus Christ" (v.57). —Joe Stowell

Lord, keep our eyes and hearts fixed not on the temporary joys or disappointments but on the victorious realities of eternity. Thank You for Your death and resurrection that guarantee our forever future.

In Christ, the end is only the beginning.

October 19
Monday

How Long?

Read:
Psalm 13

How long, O Lord? Will You forget me forever? —Psalm 13:1

The Bible In One Year:
- **Isaiah 56–58**
- **2 Thessalonians 2**

For 9 long years, Saul hounded David as "one hunts a partridge in the mountains" (1 Sam. 26:20). "How long, O Lord? Will You forget me forever?" David prayed. "How long will You hide Your face from me? . . . How long will my enemy be exalted over me?" (Ps. 13:1-2).

Prolonged affliction often vexes us as well. We want a sudden solution, a quick fix. But some things can't be fixed. They can only be borne.

But we can complain to God in our troubles. We have a heavenly Father who wants us to engage with Him in our struggles. He understands His children as no one else can.

When we turn to Him with our complaints, we come to our senses. In David's case, his thoughts went back to life's certainty: God's love. David reminded himself: "I have trusted in Your mercy; my heart shall rejoice in Your salvation. I will sing to the Lord, because He has dealt bountifully with me" (vv.5-6). Sufferings may persist, but David could sing in the midst of his trials, for he was God's beloved child. That's all he needed to know.

A. W. Thorold writes, "The highest pinnacle of the spiritual life is not happy joy in unbroken sunshine, but absolute and undoubting trust in the love of God."

Even in our troubles, God's love can be trusted. —David Roper

O yes, He cares; I know He cares,
His heart is touched with my grief;
When the days are weary, the long nights dreary,
I know my Savior cares! —*Graeff*

God's love stands when all else fails.

October 20
Tuesday

Stray Hearts

Read:
Exodus 32:21-35

These people have committed a great sin, and have made for themselves a god of gold! —Exodus 32:31

The Bible In One Year:
- Isaiah 59–61
- 2 Thessalonians 3

Last fall, an expressway in my city was shut down for several hours because a cattle truck had overturned. The cattle had escaped and were roaming across the highway. Seeing this news story about stray cattle made me think of something I had recently studied in Exodus 32 about the people of God who strayed from Him.

In the divided kingdom of ancient Israel, King Jeroboam erected two golden calves for the people to worship (1 Kings 12:25-32). But the idea of worshiping hunks of gold had not originated with him. Even after escaping brutal slavery and having seen the Lord's power and glory mightily displayed, the Israelites had quickly allowed their hearts to stray from Him (Ex. 32). While Moses was on Mt. Sinai receiving the law from the Lord, his brother Aaron helped God's people stray by constructing an idol in the shape of a golden calf. The writer of Hebrews reminds us of God's anger over this idolatry and those who "go astray in their heart" (Heb. 3:10).

God knows that our hearts have a tendency to stray. His Word makes it clear that He is the Lord and that we are to worship "no other gods" (Ex. 20:2-6).

"The Lord is the great God, and the great King above all gods" (Ps. 95:3). He is the one true God! —Cindy Hess Kasper

Prone to wander, Lord, I feel it,
Prone to leave the God I love;
Here's my heart, O take and seal it,
Seal it for Thy courts above. —*Robinson*

As long as you want anything very much, especially more than you want God, it is an idol. —A. B. Simpson

October 21
Wednesday

O Glorious Day!

Read:
Matthew 27:27-31; 28:1-6

He is not here; for He is risen.
—Matthew 28:6

The Bible In One Year:
- **Isaiah 62–64**
- **1 Timothy 1**

It was the day after. My favorite team had just lost its final game and the dream of a championship was now over. It was cold out and a bit gloomy as I got in the car to go to work. None of this should have mattered much, but it was shaping up to be a blue Monday.

But then a song came on the radio that transformed my perspective. It was Casting Crowns singing "Glorious Day." "One day they led [Christ] up Calvary's mountain, one day they nailed Him to die on a tree." Nothing encouraging yet. "Suffering anguish, despised and rejected"—more bad news. But then the song describes the good news of Christ's resurrection and His victory over death.

Out of that worst of days—out of the noontime darkness on that Jerusalem hillside—has come the only true hope for mankind. Because Jesus "took the nails for me," as the song says, "He carried my sins far away." And one day He's coming back—"O glorious day!"

Perhaps today did not start out well for you. Maybe you face a host of trouble that threatens to turn this into a day of despair. Turn your attention to Jesus. Review what He did for you at Calvary and how He conquered death by His resurrection: "He is not here; for He is risen"! (Matt. 28:6). That can make any day a glorious day! —Dave Branon

Living, He loved me; dying, He saved me;
Buried, He carried my sins far away;
Rising, He justified freely forever;
One day He's coming—O glorious day! —*Chapman*

Christ's empty tomb fills us with hope.

October 22
Thursday

The Campaign

Read:
Romans 15:1-7

Let us pursue the things which make for peace and the things by which one may edify another.
—Romans 14:19

The Bible In One Year:
- **Isaiah 65–66**
- **1 Timothy 2**

Each year young people in our community participate in a "Be Nice" campaign spearheaded by a mental health organization. In one of the events in 2012, 6,000 students spelled out the words BE NICE with their bodies on their schools' sports fields. One principal said, "We want students to come to school and learn without the distraction of fear or sadness or uneasiness around their peers. We are working hard to make sure students are lifting each other up, rather than tearing each other down."

Paul desired that the people in the church at Rome would have an even higher standard of love. Both the strong and weak in the faith were judging and showing contempt for each other (Rom. 14:1-12). They despised one another as they argued about what foods were permissible to eat (vv.2-3) and what holidays they should observe (vv.5-6). Paul challenged them: "Let us pursue the things which make for peace and the things by which one may edify another" (v.19). He reminded them that their hearts should be concerned with pleasing others, not pleasing themselves. He said, "Even Christ did not please Himself" (15:3); He served.

Join the campaign that loves others despite our differences—you'll bring praise to God (v.7). —Anne Cetas

Dear Lord, I want to be a person who is kind and loving to others. Please help me to use words that will build others up and bring praise and glory to Your name.

Kindness is simply love flowing out in little gentlenesses.

October 23
Friday

Losing And Finding Our Lives In Him

Read:
Luke 9:18-27

For whoever desires to save his life will lose it, but whoever loses his life for My sake will save it. —Luke 9:24

The Bible In One Year:
■ Jeremiah 1–2
■ 1 Timothy 3

When Mother Teresa died in 1997, people marveled again at her example of humble service to Christ and to people in great need. She had spent 50 years ministering to the poor, sick, orphaned, and dying through the Missionaries of Charity in Calcutta, India.

After extensive interviews with her, British journalist Malcolm Muggeridge wrote: "There is much talk today about discovering an identity, as though it were something to be looked for, like a winning number in a lottery; then, once found, to be hoarded and treasured. Actually, . . . the more it is spent the richer it becomes. So, with Mother Teresa, in effacing herself, she becomes herself. I never met anyone more memorable."

I suspect that many of us may be afraid of what will happen if we obey Jesus' words: "If anyone desires to come after Me, let him deny himself, and take up his cross daily, and follow Me. For whoever desires to save his life will lose it, but whoever loses his life for My sake will save it" (Luke 9:23-24).

Our Savior reminded His followers that He came to give us life abundantly (John 10:10). We are called to lose our lives for Christ, and in so doing discover the fullness of life in Him. —David McCasland

"Take up thy cross and follow Me,"
I hear the blessed Savior call;
How can I make a lesser sacrifice
When Jesus gave His all? —*Ackley*

As we lose our lives for Christ,
we find fullness of life in Him.

October 24
Saturday

Re-Creation

Read:
2 Corinthians 5:12-21

Therefore, if anyone is in Christ, he is a new creation; old things have passed away; behold, all things have become new.
—2 Corinthians 5:17

The Bible In One Year:
- Jeremiah 3–5
- 1 Timothy 4

Chris Simpson's life used to be consumed by hate. After he and his wife lost their first child, he was confused and angry. He directed that anger toward various ethnic groups and covered his body with hate-filled tattoos.

After listening to his son mimic his hatred, though, Simpson knew he needed to change. He watched a Christian movie about courage and began attending church. One month later he was baptized as a follower of Jesus Christ. Simpson is now a new person and is leaving the hate behind him, which includes the painful and expensive process of having his tattoos removed.

The apostle Paul knew something about this kind of deep transformation. He hated Jesus and persecuted His followers (Acts 22:4-5; 1 Cor. 15:9). But a personal encounter and spiritual union with Christ (Acts 9:1-20) changed all of that, causing him to reevaluate his life in light of what Jesus accomplished on the cross. This union with Christ made Paul a new person. The old order of sin, death, and selfishness was gone and a new beginning, a new covenant, a new perspective and way of living had come.

Following Jesus is not turning over a new leaf; it is beginning a new life under a new Master. —Marvin Williams

For Further Thought

What is the evidence that my union with Christ has transformed my old humanity? Are there indicators that I am not the me I used to be?

Being in Christ is not rehabilitation, it's re-creation.

October 25
Sunday

Loving And Knowing

Read:
Romans 5:6-11

God demonstrates His own love toward us, in that while we were still sinners, Christ died for us. —Romans 5:8

The Bible In One Year:
■ Jeremiah 6–8
■ 1 Timothy 5

In a novel by Jonathan Safran Foer, one of the characters, speaking of New York's Empire State Building, said, "I know this building because I love this building."

That statement caused me to think about the relationship between love and knowledge. Whenever we love something, we want to know everything about it. When we love a place, we want to explore every inch of it. When we love a person, we want to know every detail of his or her life. We want to know what he likes, how she spends her time, where he grew up, who her friends are, what he believes. The list is endless. But some of us want to be loved without allowing ourselves to be known. We're afraid that we won't be loved if we are truly known.

We don't have to worry about that with God. His love is far superior to ours: "God demonstrates His own love toward us, in that while we were still sinners, Christ died for us" (Rom. 5:8). Furthermore, He makes Himself known to us. Through creation, Scripture, and Christ, God reveals His character and His love. Because God loves us in spite of our imperfections, we can safely confess our faults to Him. With God, we need not fear being known. That's why to know God is to love Him. —Julie Ackerman Link

Be still and know that He is God
For pathways steep and rough,
Not what He brings, but what He is
Will always be enough. —*Anon.*

There is no greater joy than to know that God loves us.

October 26
Monday

Healthy Ingredients

Read:
Proverbs 4:14-27

Keep your heart with all diligence, for out of it spring the issues of life. —Proverbs 4:23

The Bible In One Year:
■ Jeremiah 9–11
■ 1 Timothy 6

My wife, Martie, is a careful shopper when it comes to buying healthy and nutritious food. No matter how attractive the packaging looks, she checks the list of ingredients on the back of the box. Lots of difficult-to-pronounce words usually announce the presence of preservatives that work against good nutrition. She always puts those items back on the shelf and continues to look for labels with lists of natural food products that contribute to good health.

I've often thought that her shopping habits are a lot like what God is looking for in our lives: It's what's on the inside that counts, regardless of how attractive the outside might be. It's no wonder that the wisdom-teller of Proverbs warns us to guard what goes into our hearts, "for out of it spring the issues of life" (Prov. 4:23). Wearing the right fashions and keeping ourselves looking young are of little importance if our hearts harbor greed, hatred, grumpiness, self-pity, and other counter-productive contents.

So, ask yourself: When others get past the packaging of my life, do they experience a heart full of healthy, Christ-honoring ingredients? By putting in grace, kindness, patience, and compassion, we'll reflect the wonderful nature of Christ. —Joe Stowell

Lord, teach me to value my heart more than the externals. Grant me the wisdom to cultivate internal ingredients that will make my heart a wellspring of life to those whom I come in contact with today.

The contents in your heart are more important than the outer packaging.

October 27
Tuesday

God In The Storm

Read:
Job 37:14-24

He is excellent in power. —Job 37:23

The Bible In One Year:
- Jeremiah 12–14
- 2 Timothy 1

Early one morning the wind began to blow and raindrops hit my house like small stones. I peered outside at the yellow-gray sky and watched as trees thrashed in the wind. Veins of lightning lit the sky accompanied by bone-rattling thunder. The power blinked on and off, and I wondered how long the bad weather would continue.

After the storm passed, I opened my Bible to begin my day with reading Scripture. I read a passage in Job that compared the Lord's power to the atmospheric muscle of a storm. Job's friend, Elihu said, "God thunders marvelously with His voice" (37:5). And, "He covers His hands with lightning, and commands it to strike" (36:32). Indeed, God is "excellent in power" (37:23).

Compared to God, we humans are feeble. We're unable to help ourselves spiritually, heal our hearts, or fix the injustice we often endure. Fortunately, the God of the storm cares about weaklings like us; He "remembers that we are dust" (Ps. 103:14). What's more, God "gives power to the weak, and to those who have no might He increases strength" (Isa. 40:29). Because God is strong, He can help us in our weakness. —Jennifer Benson Schuldt

I sing the mighty power of God
That made the mountains rise,
That spread the flowing seas abroad
And built the lofty skies. —*Watts*

God is the source of our strength.

October 28
Wednesday

Wait On The Lord

Read:
Psalm 27

I waited patiently for the Lord; and He inclined to me, and heard my cry. —Psalm 40:1

The Bible In One Year:
- Jeremiah 15–17
- 2 Timothy 2

With so many instantaneous forms of communication today, our impatience with hearing a reply from others is sometimes laughable. Someone I know sent an e-mail to his wife and then called her by cell phone because he couldn't wait for a reply!

Sometimes we feel that God has let us down because He does not provide an immediate answer to a prayer. Often our attitude becomes, "Answer me speedily, O Lord; my spirit fails!" (Ps. 143:7).

But waiting for the Lord can transform us into a people of growing faith. King David spent many years waiting to be crowned king and fleeing from Saul's wrath. David wrote, "Wait on the Lord; be of good courage, and He shall strengthen your heart" (Ps. 27:14). And in another psalm he encourages us with these words, "I waited patiently for the Lord; and He inclined to me, and heard my cry. He . . . set my feet upon a rock, and established my steps" (40:1-2). David grew into "a man after [God's] own heart" by waiting on the Lord (Acts 13:22; see 1 Sam. 13:14).

When we become frustrated with God's apparent delay in answering our prayer, it is good to remember that He is interested in developing faith and perseverance in our character (James 1:2-4). Wait on the Lord! —Dennis Fisher

Sweet hour of prayer! Sweet hour of prayer!
Thy wings shall my petition bear
To Him whose truth and faithfulness
Engage the waiting soul to bless. —*Walford*

God stretches our patience to enlarge our soul.

October 29
Thursday

WONDERFUL!

READ:
Job 42:1-6

I have uttered what I did not understand, things too wonderful for me, which I did not know. —Job 42:3

THE BIBLE IN ONE YEAR:
■ Jeremiah 18–19
■ 2 Timothy 3

As our plane began its descent, the flight attendant read the long list of arrival information as if she were reading it for the thousandth time that day—no emotion or interest as she droned on about our impending arrival. Then, with the same tired, disinterested voice, she finished by saying, "Have a wonderful day." The dryness of her tone contrasted with her words. She said "wonderful" but in a manner completely absent of any sense of wonder.

Sometimes I fear that we approach our relationship with God in the same way: Routine. Bored. Apathetic. Disinterested. Through Christ, we have the privilege of being adopted into the family of the living God, yet often there seems to be little of the sense of wonder that should accompany that remarkable reality.

Job questioned God about his suffering, but when challenged by Him, Job was humbled by the wonder of his Creator and His creation. Job replied, "You asked, 'Who is this who hides counsel without knowledge?' Therefore I have uttered what I did not understand, things too wonderful for me, which I did not know" (Job 42:3).

I long for the wonder of God to take hold of my heart. Adopted by God—what a wonderful reality! —Bill Crowder

How marvelous! How wonderful!
And my song shall ever be:
How marvelous! How wonderful
Is my Savior's love for me! —*Gabriel*

Nothing can fill our hearts more than the wonder of our God and His love.

October 30
Friday

THE LAST CHAPTER

READ:
Revelation 22:6-20

Let your gentleness be known to all men. The Lord is at hand.
—Philippians 4:5

THE BIBLE IN ONE YEAR:
- **Jeremiah 20–21**
- **2 Timothy 4**

I have a friend who reads the last chapter first when she starts a new thriller. "Takes the anxiety out of reading," she claims. So with Christians: Because we know the end of the story, we can be centers of peace in the midst of utter chaos, calm in the face of disaster.

The apostle Paul calls this attitude "moderation" in Philippians 4:5 (KJV). It's a term that implies "peace under pressure." It refers to the calm and deliberate strength with which we meet the disquieting circumstances of our days. Kingdoms may fall, friends may falter, churches may fold, oceans may rise, and mountains may crumble, but we can be at peace.

How do we maintain such composure? By remembering that "the Lord is at hand" (Phil. 4:5); He is near. Our Lord is standing just outside the door ready to burst through and turn everything that's wrong right-side up. Then this world and all its troubles will become the kingdom of our Lord, and "the earth will be filled with the knowledge of the glory of the LORD, as the waters cover the sea" (Hab. 2:14).

Jesus said, "Surely I am coming quickly" (Rev. 22:20). Today could be the day! It's the very last thing He said in the very last chapter of His book. —David Roper

Lord, thank You for dispelling the fear from our lives by letting us know the end of the story. We can rest in the assurance that as Your followers we will one day be with You in Your glorious, eternal kingdom.

No doctrine is more closely linked to practical daily living than that of the Lord's return.

October 31
Saturday

Eyes Of Love

Read:
Mark 10:17-27

Then Jesus, looking at him, loved him.
—Mark 10:21

The Bible In One Year:
- **Jeremiah 22–23**
- **Titus 1**

Many people who come to Marc Salem's stage shows think he can read minds. But he makes no such claim, saying he is not a psychic or magician, but a close observer of people. He told writer Jennifer Mulson, "We live in a world that's mostly invisible to us because we're not paying attention to things . . . . I'm very sensitive to what people give off" (*The Gazette,* Colorado Springs).

It's interesting to note what Jesus saw as He met people. His encounter with a wealthy young man seeking eternal life is recorded in the gospels of Matthew, Mark, and Luke. Mark includes this telling detail, "Then Jesus, looking at him, loved him" (Mark 10:21). Some people may have seen this young man as an arrogant person (vv.19-20) while others might have envied his wealth, but Jesus looked at him with love.

We often focus on the man's sad departure and apparent unwillingness to give up his riches and follow Jesus (v.22). When the disciples wondered aloud about the difficulty of a rich man entering the kingdom of God (v.26), "Jesus looked at them and said, 'With men it is impossible, but not with God; for with God all things are possible' " (v.27).

Today, Jesus sees us through eyes of love and invites us to follow Him. —David McCasland

Down from His splendor in glory He came,
Into a world of woe;
Took on Himself all my guilt and my shame,
Why should He love me so? —Roth

God has both an all-seeing eye and all-forgiving heart.

November 1
Sunday

Loved To Love

Read:
Deuteronomy 10:12-22

What does the Lord your God require of you, but . . . to walk in all His ways and to love Him. —Deut. 10:12

The Bible In One Year:
- Jeremiah 24–26
- Titus 2

"A heart is not judged by how much you love, but by how much you are loved by others." I saw this quotation, attributed to the Wizard of Oz, on a wall plaque in a gift shop.

The Wizard of Oz may be a good story, but it's not a reliable source of spiritual information. God said something quite different. According to Him, the greatest commandment is to love—to love Him first and then others (Mark 12:29-31). Scripture says nothing about expecting to be loved in return. In fact, Jesus stated the opposite in His most famous sermon: "Blessed are you when they revile and persecute you, and say all kinds of evil against you falsely for My sake. Rejoice and be exceedingly glad, for great is your reward in heaven" (Matt. 5:11-12).

When it comes to love, the important thing we need to know is this: All love starts with God (1 John 4:19). As Moses told the Israelites, God delighted in them to love them (Deut. 10:15), and because of that they were to love others, even strangers (v.19). God's intent is that the people who receive His love will become the conduit of His love to others.

Apart from God—who Himself is love—none of us could truly love or be loved (1 John 4:7-8). —Julie Ackerman Link

"Love seeketh not her own," and so
He did not stay as God above,
But chose a manger and a cross
To show that He was Love. —*Wilmshurst*

He who does not love does not know God, for God is love. —1 John 4:8

November 2
Monday

Who's Telling The Truth?

Read:
John 8:31-47

Which of you convicts Me of sin? And if I tell the truth, why do you not believe Me?
—John 8:46

The Bible In One Year:
- **Jeremiah 27–29**
- **Titus 3**

During US presidential campaigns, television coverage of speeches and debates often include "fact checking" by analysts who compare the candidates' statements with their actual records. Are they telling the truth or manipulating the facts to their advantage?

The apostle John recorded a debate between Jesus and a group of people who believed He was making false claims about Himself. Jesus told them, "If you abide in My word, you are My disciples indeed. And you shall know the truth, and the truth shall make you free" (John 8:31-32). They told Him that they had never been in bondage to anyone and asked, "How can You say, 'You will be made free'?" (v.33).

As the debate continued, Jesus kept saying that He was telling them the truth (vv.34,40,45-46,51). Some believed Him, but others remained angry at Him and unconvinced.

In a sense, that debate goes on today. Those who oppose Jesus seek to discredit His statements and twist them into lies. Jesus says, "I am telling you the truth," and promises that He will give us a freedom we can find nowhere else.

The Bible record of Jesus' life is worth "fact checking" as we determine who we will follow. All of us have a choice to make. —David McCasland

Faith is believing, the promise is true,
Trusting in Jesus your strength to renew;
Resting so sweetly, secure on His Word,
Shielded from danger with Jesus the Lord. —*Teasley*

God's truth stands any test.

November 3
Tuesday

Be Still

Read:
Psalm 46

Be still, and know that I am God; I will be exalted among the nations, I will be exalted in the earth!
—Psalm 46:10

The Bible In One Year:
- Jeremiah 30–31
- Philemon

Eric Liddell, memorialized in the film *Chariots of Fire,* won a gold medal in the 1924 Paris Olympics before going to China as a missionary. Some years later, with the outbreak of World War II, Liddell sent his family to safety in Canada, but he remained in China. Soon Liddell and other foreign missionaries were interned in a Japanese detainment camp. After months of captivity, he developed what doctors feared was a brain tumor.

Every Sunday afternoon a band would play near the hospital, so one day Liddell requested they play the hymn "Be Still, My Soul." As he listened, I wonder if Eric pondered these words from the song: *Be still, my soul: the hour is hastening on / When we shall be forever with the Lord. / When disappointment, grief, and fear are gone, / Sorrow forgot, love's purest joys restored. / Be still, my soul: when change and tears are past / All safe and blessed we shall meet at last.*

That beautiful hymn, so comforting to Eric as he faced an illness that led to his death 3 days later, expresses a great reality of Scripture. In Psalm 46:10, David wrote, "Be still, and know that I am God." In our darkest moments, we can rest, for our Lord conquered death on our behalf. Be still, and allow Him to calm your greatest fears. —Bill Crowder

Teach me, Lord, to still my soul before You. Help
me to bear patiently the trials I face, and to
leave everything to You to direct and provide.
I know that You will always remain faithful.

God's whisper of comfort quiets the noise of our trials.

November 4
Wednesday

Leap The Wall

Read:
Romans 12:14-21

If your enemy is hungry, give him bread to eat; and if he is thirsty, give him water to drink.
—Proverbs 25:21

The Bible In One Year:
■ Jeremiah 32–33
■ Hebrews 1

Sgt. Richard Kirkland was a Confederate soldier in the US Civil War (1861–1865). When the Union's failed charge at Marye's Heights during the Battle of Fredericksburg left wounded soldiers abandoned in no-man's land, Kirkland got permission to help them. Collecting canteens, he leaped the stone wall and bent over the first soldier to lend assistance. At great personal risk, the "Angel of Marye's Heights" extended the mercy of Christ to enemy soldiers.

While few of us will face an enemy on the battlefield, those who suffer can be found all around us—people struggling against loneliness, loss, health issues, and sin. Their cries, muted by our many distractions, plead for mercy and comfort, for hope and help.

Kirkland's example of Christlike compassion put action to Jesus' command to "love your enemies" (Matt. 5:44). Paul expanded on that theme when he quotes Proverbs 25:21, "If your enemy is hungry, feed him; if he is thirsty, give him a drink" (Rom. 12:20). "Do not be overcome by evil," he instructed us, "but overcome evil with good" (v.21).

Paul's challenge compels us to emulate Sgt. Kirkland. Today is the day for us to "leap the wall" of safety to lend comfort from God to those in need. —Randy Kilgore

Father, give me the courage to reach out to those
I may not want to reach. Show Your love
through me in ways that will bring glory to You
and true peace in my corner of the world.

Kindness is in our power even when fondness is not.
—Samuel Johnson

November 5
Thursday

Good-Behavior Rewards

Read:
2 Corinthians 5:1-11

We make it our aim . . . to be well pleasing to [God].
—2 Corinthians 5:9

The Bible In One Year:
- Jeremiah 34–36
- Hebrews 2

In a children's ministry in my church, we hand out cards to the kids when we notice their good behavior. They collect the cards and receive prizes for the good choices they've made. We are trying to reinforce good behavior rather than focusing on bad behavior.

When one leader handed a card to 11-year-old Tyree, he responded, "No, thanks. I don't need one; I want to behave well, and I don't need a reward for that." For him, doing the right thing was its own reward. He definitely has good values ingrained in him, and he wants to live them out—prize or not.

As believers in Jesus, we will receive rewards one day. Second Corinthians 5:10 says that everyone will "receive the things done in the body, according to what he has done, whether good or bad." But to get a reward should not be our motivation for right living. Neither is it to earn salvation. Living out of love for God and pleasing Him should be our heart's desire.

When we love God, we make it our aim to please Him who first loved us (1 John 4:19) and to serve Him with pure motives (Prov. 16:2; 1 Cor. 4:5). The best reward will be to be with Him! —Anne Cetas

In all I think and say and do,
I long, O God, to honor You;
But may my highest motive be
To love the Christ who died for me. —*D. DeHaan*

Our desire to please God is our highest motive for obeying Him.

November 6
Friday

A Season For Everything

Read:
Ecclesiastes 3:1-8

To everything there is a season.
—Ecclesiastes 3:1

The Bible In One Year:
■ Jeremiah 37–39
■ Hebrews 3

In the 1960s, the folk-rock band The Byrds popularized the song "Turn! Turn! Turn!" It climbed to the top spot on the *Billboard* Hot 100 chart and gained worldwide popularity. People seemed captivated by the lyrics. Interestingly, though, except for the last line, those lyrics are from the Old Testament book of Ecclesiastes.

"To everything there is a season," proclaims the writer of Ecclesiastes, "a time for every purpose under heaven" (3:1). He then lists some of the seasons in human experience: birth and death, gain and loss, tears and laughter, mourning and dancing. Just as the seasons in nature change, so do the seasons in our lives. Our circumstances never stay the same for long.

Sometimes we welcome change in our lives. But often it is difficult, especially when it involves sorrow and loss. Yet even then we can be thankful that God does not change. "I am the Lord," He said through the prophet Malachi, "I do not change" (Mal. 3:6).

Because God remains the same, we can rely on Him through the shifting seasons of life. His presence is always with us (Ps. 46:1), His peace has the power to guard our hearts (Phil. 4:7), and His love provides security for our souls (Rom. 8:39). —Jennifer Benson Schuldt

A mighty fortress is our God,
A bulwark never failing;
Our helper He amid the flood
Of mortal ills prevailing. —*Luther*

God's unchanging nature is our security during seasons of change.

November 7
Saturday

Two Victories

Read:
2 Samuel 5:17-25

David inquired of the Lord.
—2 Samuel 5:19

The Bible In One Year:
- **Jeremiah 40–42**
- **Hebrews 4**

King David was up against a familiar foe. Years before as a young shepherd boy, he had faced down Goliath, the top Philistine warrior, by killing him with a well-placed stone (1 Sam. 17). Now David was king of Israel, and here come the Philistines again! They heard he was king, and they decided to attack (2 Sam. 5:17).

What do we do first when trouble is on the way? We could panic. We could plan. Or we could first do what David did—pray. "David inquired of the Lord" (v.19), and God guided the king.

David had to fight two battles with the Philistines—one at Baal Perazim and one at the Valley of Rephaim. It was a good thing he consulted God, because in these two battles there were two different strategies. In the first one, God won the battle with His power alone: "The Lord has broken through," David recorded (v.20). For the next one, God gave David an action plan, and when he carried it out, the Israelites won (vv.23-25).

Each day we face many challenges. Although there is no one-size-fits-all answer, our first action should always be to consult God. As He guides us, we can have confidence in Him. Then, whether the victory comes through His miraculous intervention or through His guidance, all the glory goes to God. —Dave Branon

Not to the strong is the battle,
Not to the swift is the race;
Yet to the true and the faithful
Victory is promised through grace. —*Crosby*

To stand up to any challenge, spend time on your knees.

November 8
Sunday

The Blessing Of Giving

Read:
Mark 12:38-44

It is more blessed to give than to receive. —Acts 20:35

The Bible In One Year:
- **Jeremiah 43–45**
- **Hebrews 5**

It made no sense for a widow to donate her last few coins to a corrupt institution in Jerusalem, where scribes who were dependent on those gifts "devour[ed] widows' houses" (Mark 12:40). But in that woman's act, Jesus saw a moving display of the proper attitude toward money (vv.41-44).

Gordon Cosby, while serving as pastor of the Church of the Saviour in Washington, DC, tells of a widow whose income was barely adequate to feed and clothe her six children. Yet every week she faithfully placed $4 in the offering plate. A deacon suggested that Cosby go to her and assure her that she could use the money instead for her family's benefit.

Cosby followed the deacon's advice—to his regret. "You are trying to take away the last thing that gives me dignity and meaning," she said. She had learned a key to giving: It can benefit the giver more than the receiver. Yes, those in poverty need financial help. But the need to give may be as important as the need to receive.

The act of giving reminds us that we live by the grace of God—like the birds and the flowers. Those creations don't worry about their future; neither should we. Giving offers us a way to express our confidence that God will care for us just as He cares for the sparrow and lily (Matt. 6:25-34). —Philip Yancey

Whatever, Lord, we lend to Thee,
Repaid a thousand-fold will be;
Then gladly will we give to Thee,
Who givest all—who givest all. —*Wordsworth*

We disarm the power of money by giving it away.

November 9
Monday

THE ROCK

READ:
Matthew 7:24-27; Ephesians 2:18-22

Jesus Christ Himself [is] the chief cornerstone. —Ephesians 2:20

On a trip to Massachusetts, my husband and I visited Plymouth Rock, an iconic symbol in the United States. It is traditionally thought to be the place where the Pilgrims, who traveled to America on the Mayflower in 1620, first set foot. While we enjoyed learning about its significance, we were surprised and disappointed that it is so small. We learned that due to erosion and people chipping off pieces, it is now just one-third its original size.

The Bible refers to Jesus as a Rock (1 Cor. 10:4), who never changes (Heb. 13:8). He is the solid Rock on which we can build our lives. The church (the body of believers) is built on a foundation with "Jesus Christ Himself being the chief cornerstone." In Him all believers are joined together (Eph. 2:20-22).

Jesus is the solid Rock we can cling to when the storms of life blow and beat against us (Matt. 7:25). Writer Madeleine L'Engle said: "It's a good thing to have all the props pulled out from under us occasionally. It gives us some sense of what is rock under our feet and what is sand."

Plymouth Rock is an interesting mass of minerals with an intriguing historical significance. But Jesus is a precious cornerstone, and those who trust in Him will always have a solid Rock to depend upon. —Cindy Hess Kasper

O build on the Rock, forever sure,
The firm and true foundation,
Its hope is the hope which shall endure—
The hope of our salvation. —*Belden*

Christ, the Rock, is our sure hope.

THE BIBLE IN ONE YEAR:
- Jeremiah 46–47
- Hebrews 6

November 10
Tuesday

Remembering Our Father's Words

Read:
Psalm 119:89-93

I will never forget Your precepts, for by them You have given me life. —Psalm 119:93

The Bible In One Year:
- **Jeremiah 48–49**
- **Hebrews 7**

Jim Davidson was climbing down Mount Rainier when he fell through a snow bridge and into a crevasse (a pitch-black, ice-walled crack in a glacier). As Jim stood bloodied and bruised in that dark ice cave, he reflected on his childhood and recalled how his father had repeatedly reminded him that he could accomplish great things if he pressed through adversity. Those words helped to sustain Jim as he spent the next 5 hours climbing out of that dark ice cave to safety with very little gear and under extremely difficult circumstances.

The psalmist seemed to climb out of his own crevasse of affliction and pain by recalling his heavenly Father's words. He admitted that if God and His Word had not sustained him with joy, he would have died in his misery (Ps.119:92). He expressed full confidence in the Lord's eternal Word (v.89) and in the faithfulness of His character (v.90). As a result of God's faithfulness, the psalmist made a commitment never to forget God's words to him because they had a central part in rescuing his life and bringing him strength.

In our darkest caves and moments of affliction, our souls can be revived by our Father in heaven when we recall and fill our minds with His encouraging words. —Marvin Williams

Thinking It Over

What crevasse of discouragement are you currently in? How can you use this time as an occasion to revive your soul by filling your mind and heart with God's Word?

Remembering God's words revives our soul.

November 11
Wednesday

Disaster Diaries

Read:
Lamentations 3:19-33

His compassions fail not. They are new every morning; great is Your faithfulness.
—Lamentations 3:22-23

The Bible In One Year:
■ Jeremiah 50
■ Hebrews 8

Yves Congar was just 10 years old when World War I began and the French town where he lived was invaded by the German army. His mother encouraged him to keep a diary, and what resulted was a lucid description of a military occupation, complete with written narrative and colored sketches. His diary recorded a disaster from a child's perspective. What he witnessed had such a profound effect on him that he felt called to bring others the hope of Christ.

Centuries earlier the prophet Jeremiah was an eyewitness to the invasion of Jerusalem by Nebuchadnezzar. He wrote down his observations in his "diary"—the book of Lamentations. Despite these distressing times, the prophet found hope in the heart of God. He wrote: "Through the LORD's mercies we are not consumed, because His compassions fail not. They are new every morning; great is Your faithfulness" (3:22-23).

At various times, we may experience or witness disasters that feel like hostile forces entering our lives. But these times of trouble do not last forever. And, like Jeremiah, our most sustaining hope is to reflect upon the faithfulness and provision of our heavenly Father. The Lord's compassions are new every morning, and His faithfulness is great! —Dennis Fisher

Great is Thy faithfulness! Great is Thy faithfulness!
Morning by morning new mercies I see;
All I have needed Thy hand hath provided—
Great is Thy faithfulness, Lord, unto me! —*Chisholm*

The best reason for hope is God's faithfulness.

November 12
Thursday

EMBARRASSING MOMENTS

READ:
John 8:1-11

Jesus said to her, "Neither do I condemn you; go and sin no more." —John 8:11

THE BIBLE IN ONE YEAR:
- Jeremiah 51–52
- Hebrews 9

The flashing lights of the police car drew my attention to a motorist who had been pulled over for a traffic violation. As the officer, ticket book in hand, walked back to his car, I could clearly see the embarrassed driver sitting helplessly behind the wheel of her car. With her hands, she attempted to block her face from the view of passersby—hoping to hide her identity. Her actions were a reminder to me of how embarrassing it can be when we are exposed by our choices and their consequences.

When a guilty woman was brought before Jesus and her immorality was exposed, the crowd did more than just watch. They called for her condemnation, but Jesus showed mercy. The only One with the right to judge sin responded to her failure with compassion. After dispatching her accusers, "Jesus said to her, 'Neither do I condemn you; go and sin no more' " (John 8:11). His compassion reminds us of His forgiving grace, and His command to her points to His great desire that we live in the joy of that grace. Both elements show the depth of Christ's concern for us when we stumble and fall.

Even in our most embarrassing moments of failure, we can cry out to Him and find that His grace is truly amazing.
—Bill Crowder

Amazing grace—how sweet the sound—
That saved a wretch like me!
I once was lost, but now am found;
Was blind, but now I see. —*Newton*

Jesus alone can supply the grace we need for each trial we face.

November 13
Friday

A PIECE OF THE PUZZLE

READ:
1 Corinthians 12:12-27

God has set the members, each one of them, in the body just as He pleased.
—1 Corinthians 12:18

THE BIBLE IN ONE YEAR:
■ Lamentations 1–2
■ Hebrews 10:1-18

At her birthday celebration, the honored guest turned the tables by giving everyone at the party a gift. Kriste gave each of us a personal note expressing what we mean to her, along with encouraging words about the person God made us to be. Enclosed with every note was one piece of a jigsaw puzzle as a reminder that each of us is unique and important in God's plan.

That experience helped me to read 1 Corinthians 12 with new eyes. Paul compared the church—the body of Christ—to a human body. Just as our physical bodies have hands, feet, eyes, and ears, all are part of a unified body. No follower of Christ can claim independence from the body, nor can one part tell another that it is not needed (vv.12-17). "God has set the members, each one of them, in the body just as He pleased" (v.18).

It's easy to feel less important than others whose gifts are different and perhaps more visible than ours. The Lord, however, wants us to see ourselves as He does—uniquely created and highly valued by Him.

You are one piece of a picture that is not complete without you. God has gifted you to be an important part of the body of Christ to bring Him honor. —David McCasland

Lord, help me not to compare myself with others
in Your family. May I seek instead to be the person
You've made me to be, and help me to use what You've
given me to bless others today.

Your life is God's gift to you;
make it your gift to God.

November 14
Saturday

On Helping Others

Read:
Leviticus 19:9-15

When you reap the harvest of your land, you shall not wholly reap the corners of your field, nor shall you gather the gleanings of your harvest. —Lev. 19:9

The Bible In One Year:
- **Lamentations 3–5**
- **Hebrews 10:19-39**

When snowstorms bury the grazing lands, ranchers must feed their herds by hand. As hay is tossed from wagons and trucks, the strongest animals bull their way to the front. Timid or sickly animals get little or no feed unless the rancher intervenes.

Workers in refugee camps and food pantries report a similar pattern. When they open their stores to those in need, the weak and timid may not make it to the front of the line. Like the ranchers, these human lifelines must take steps to ensure that their services reach the feeble, weary, and sick at the edge of society's attention.

They are carrying out a principle set forth by God long ago. In Leviticus 19, Moses instructed Israel's farmers and vintners to leave portions of their crops so the poor and the stranger could have something to eat (vv.9-10).

We too can serve as caretakers to the weak and weary. Whether we're teachers coaxing quiet students to open up, workers coming alongside a struggling co-worker, prisoners looking out for new arrivals, or parents showing attention to their children, we have ways to honor God by helping others.

As we seek to serve those in need, may the grace of God that reached us in our need move us to reach out to others in theirs. —Randy Kilgore

Father, open my eyes to those struggling to have enough food, enough love, enough hope; then open my heart to find ways to help them receive love, using my hands in service to them—and through them, to You.

By serving others, we serve God.

November 15
Sunday

Our Fearless Champion

Read:
Matthew 8:23-34

Why are you fearful?
—Matthew 8:26

The Bible In One Year:
- **Ezekiel 1–2**
- **Hebrews 11:1-19**

Falling asleep was a challenging event during my childhood. No sooner had my parents turned out the lights than the crumpled clothes I had thrown on the chair would take on the form of a fiery dragon and the thoughts of something living under my bed put me into a panic that made sleep impossible.

I've come to realize that the immobilizing power of fear is not just a childhood experience. Fear keeps us from forgiving, taking a stand at the office, giving our resources to God's kingdom, or saying no when all our friends are saying yes. Left to ourselves, we are up against a lot of fiery dragons in our lives.

In the story of the disciples in the storm-tossed boat, I'm struck by the fact that the only one who was not afraid was Jesus. He was not afraid of the storm, nor was He afraid of a crazy man in a graveyard or of the legion of demons that possessed him (Matt. 8:23-34).

In the face of fear, we need to hear Jesus ask, "Why are you fearful?" (v.26) and be reminded that He will never leave us nor forsake us (Heb. 13:5-6). There is nothing that He can't overcome and therefore nothing for Him to fear. So, next time you're haunted by your fears, remember that you can rely on Jesus, our fearless Champion! —Joe Stowell

Lord, thank You for the reminder that You will never leave us nor forsake us. When I am afraid, I know that I can rely on Your presence and power to calm my heart and overcome my fears.

In times of fear, call out to Jesus, our fearless Champion.

November 16
Monday

To Whom It Is Due

Read:
Romans 13:1-10

Render therefore to all their due: taxes to whom taxes are due, customs to whom customs, fear to whom fear, honor to whom honor. —Romans 13:7

The Bible In One Year:
■ Ezekiel 3–4
■ Hebrews 11:20-40

My husband and I live in a rural area surrounded by farms where this slogan is popular: "If you ate a meal today, thank a farmer." Farmers definitely deserve our gratitude. They do the hot, hard work of tilling soil, planting seeds, and harvesting the food that keeps us from starving to death.

But every time I thank a farmer, I also try to remember to offer praise to God, for He is the One responsible for producing the food we eat. He gives light, sends rain, and creates the energy within the seed that gives it the strength to push through the soil and produce fruit.

Although the earth and everything in it belong to God (Ps. 24:1), He has chosen humans to be its caretakers. We are responsible to use the earth's resources as He would use them—to do His work in the world (115:16). And just as we are stewards of God's physical creation, we also are stewards of His design for society. We do this by respecting those He has placed in authority, by paying taxes, by giving honor to those who have earned it, and by continuing to pay our debt of love (Rom. 13:7-8). But one thing we reserve for God: All praise and glory belong to Him, for He is the One who makes everything possible (Ps. 96:8). —Julie Ackerman Link

Sing praise to God who reigns above,
The God of all creation,
The God of power, the God of love,
The God of our salvation. —*Schütz*

God's unsearchable ways deserve our unbounded praise.

November 17
Tuesday

Hero Over Sin

Read:
1 John 1

Create in me a clean heart, O God.
—Psalm 51:10

The Bible In One Year:
- Ezekiel 5–7
- Hebrews 12

Not long ago, someone asked me a very tough question: "What is the longest you have gone without sinning? A week, a day, an hour?" How can we answer a question like that? If we're truthful, we might say, "I can't live a day without sinning." Or if we look back over the past week, we might see that we haven't confessed to God even one sin. But we would be fooling ourselves if we said we hadn't sinned in our thoughts or actions for a week.

God knows our hearts and whether we're sensitive to the convicting power of the Holy Spirit. If we really know ourselves, we take 1 John 1:8 to heart, "If we say that we have no sin, we deceive ourselves, and the truth is not in us." We certainly don't want verse 10 to be true of us, "If we say that we have not sinned, . . . His word is not in us."

A more encouraging question to ask might be: "What is God's response to our admission of sin and need for forgiveness?" The answer: "If we confess . . . , He is faithful and just to forgive us" (v.9). Jesus has taken our sin problem upon Himself by dying in our place and rising again. That's why He can create in us "a clean heart" (Ps. 51:10). My young friend Jaydon is right when he says, "Jesus is the hero over our sins." —Anne Cetas

No one can say he doesn't need
Forgiveness for his sin,
For all must come to Christ by faith
To have new life within. —*Branon*

Christ's forgiveness is the door to a new beginning.

November 18
Wednesday

Welcome Back

Read:
Nehemiah 9:7-21

You are God, ready to pardon, gracious and merciful.
—Nehemiah 9:17

The Bible In One Year:
- **Ezekiel 8–10**
- **Hebrews 13**

Jim decided to follow Christ at the age of 10. Fifteen years later his commitment had faded. He had adopted a live-for-the-moment philosophy and developed some bad habits. Then his life seemed to fall apart. He had problems at work. Three family members died almost simultaneously. Fears and doubts began to plague Jim, and nothing seemed to help—until one day when he read Psalm 121:2, "My help comes from the Lord, who made heaven and earth." These words cut through the fear and confusion in his heart. He turned back to God for help, and God welcomed him.

Jim's spiritual journey reminds me of ancient Israel's history. The Israelites had a unique relationship with God—they were His chosen people (Neh. 9:1-15). However, they spent many years rebelling and ignoring God's goodness, turning away to follow their own path (vv.16-21). Yet when they returned to Him and repented, God was "ready to pardon, gracious and merciful, slow to anger, abundant in kindness" (v.17).

These divine qualities encourage us to draw near to God—even after we have wandered away from Him. When we humbly abandon our rebellious ways and recommit ourselves to God's ways, He will show compassion and welcome us back to closeness with Him. —Jennifer Benson Schuldt

Softly and tenderly Jesus is calling,
Calling for you and for me;
See on the portals He's waiting and watching,
Watching for you and for me. —*Thompson*

God's arms of welcome are always open.

November 19
Thursday

TRAVELING COMPANION

READ:
Psalm 39

For I am a stranger with You, a sojourner, as all my fathers were. —Psalm 39:12

THE BIBLE IN ONE YEAR:
■ Ezekiel 11–13
■ James 1

I looked up the members of my seminary graduating class recently and discovered that many of my friends are now deceased. It was a sober reminder of the brevity of life. Three score and ten, give or take a few years, and we're gone (Ps. 90:10). Israel's poet was right: We're but strangers here and sojourners (39:12).

The brevity of life makes us think about our "end"—the measure of our days and how fleeting they are (v.4), a feeling that grows more certain as we draw closer to the end of our lives. This world is not our home; we're but strangers and sojourners here.

Yet we are not alone on the journey. We are strangers and sojourners with God (39:12), a thought that makes the journey less troubling, less frightening, less worrisome. We pass through this world and into the next with a loving Father as our constant companion and guide. We're strangers here on earth, but we are never alone on the journey (73:23-24). We have One who says, "I am with you always" (Matt. 28:20).

We may lose sight of father, mother, spouse, and friends, but we always know that God is walking beside us. An old saying puts it like this: "Good company on the road makes the way to seem lighter." —David Roper

My times are in my Father's hand;
How could I wish or ask for more?
For He who has my pathway planned
Will guide me till my journey's o'er. —*Fraser*

**As you travel life's weary road,
let Jesus lift your heavy load.**

November 20
Friday

Genuine Concern

Read:
Philippians 2:1-5

Let each of you look out not only for his own interests, but also for the interests of others. —Philippians 2:4

The Bible In One Year:
- Ezekiel 14–15
- James 2

On the first night at family camp, the camp director informed the families of the schedule for the week. When finished, he asked if anyone else had anything to say. A young girl stood up and made a passionate appeal for help. She shared about her little brother—a boy with special needs—and how he could be a challenge to care for. She talked about how tiring this was for her family, and she asked everyone there to help them keep an eye on him during the week. It was an appeal born out of genuine concern for her brother and her parents. As the week went on, it was great to see people pitching in to help this family.

Her appeal was a gentle reminder of how easily we can all get wrapped up in our own world, life, and problems—to the point that we fail to see the needs of others. Here's how Paul described our responsibility: "Let each of you look out not only for his own interests, but also for the interests of others" (Phil. 2:4). The next verse reminds us that this is part of the example of Christ: "Let this mind be in you which was also in Christ Jesus."

Our caring displays a Christlike concern for people who are hurting. May we rest in God's grace, trusting Him to enable us to serve others in their seasons of need. —Bill Crowder

Lord, open my eyes to the hurts, needs, and struggles
of a world that is so desperately in need of Your love.
Help me to be Your instrument to inject
that love into hurting lives.

Nothing costs as much as caring—except not caring.

November 21
Saturday

That Name

Read:
Philippians 2:5-11

God . . . has highly exalted Him and given Him the name which is above every name.
—Philippians 2:9

The Bible In One Year:
■ Ezekiel 16–17
■ James 3

Our little granddaughter Maggie and her family were back home in Missouri after visiting with us in Grand Rapids, Michigan. Her mom told us that for a few days after returning home, Maggie walked around the house happily saying, "Michigan! Michigan!"

There was something about that name that attracted Maggie. Could have been the sound of it. Could have been the enjoyable time she had. It's hard to tell with a 1-year-old, but the name "Michigan" had such an impact on her that she couldn't stop saying it.

This makes me think about another name—the name of Jesus, "the name which is above every name" (Phil. 2:9). A song by Bill and Gloria Gaither reminds us why we love that name so much. He is "Master" and "Savior." Yes, what depth of meaning there is in the names that describe our Lord! When we mention the great name of Jesus to those who need Him as Savior, we can remind them what He has done for us.

Jesus is our Savior. He has redeemed us by His blood, and we can give our lives wholeheartedly to Him. *Jesus.* Let all heaven and earth—including us—proclaim His glorious name! —Dave Branon

Jesus, Jesus, Jesus;
There's just something about that name!
Master, Savior, Jesus,
Like the fragrance after the rain. —*Gaither*

The most precious name is Jesus!

November 22
Sunday

OVERSHADOWED

READ:
Luke 1:26-38

The Holy Spirit will come upon you, and the power of the Highest will overshadow you.
—Luke 1:35

THE BIBLE IN ONE YEAR:
- Ezekiel 18–19
- James 4

The assassination of US President John F. Kennedy over 50 years ago stunned people around the globe. The day after the shooting, an article in *The Times* (London) spoke of the reverberations being felt throughout world financial markets. It carried the headline, "All Other Events Overshadowed by US Tragedy."

There are times in our lives when a death, a tragedy, or a sudden turn of events eclipses everything else. It happened to an unmarried young woman who was told that she would become the mother of the promised Messiah, God's Son (Luke 1:26-33). When she asked how this could happen, the angel Gabriel said, "The Holy Spirit will come upon you, and the power of the Highest will overshadow you" (v.35).

The impossibility in Mary's life was overshadowed not by darkness but by the brightness of God's glory and power. Her response continues to leave us in awe: "Let it be to me according to your word" (v.38).

In the coming weeks, as we read again the Christmas story and consider the birth of Jesus into our world, it's worth pondering the word *overshadowed*. It speaks so powerfully of the Lord's presence in our hearts and His ability to outshine the darkest moments. —David McCasland

I'm overshadowed by His mighty love,
Love eternal, changeless, pure,
Overshadowed by His mighty love,
Rest is mine, serene, secure. —*Ironside*

In every situation, we are overshadowed by God's mighty love and power.

November 23
Monday

Living Letters

Read:
2 Corinthians 3:1-11

Clearly you are an epistle of Christ . . . written not with ink but by the Spirit of the living God.
—2 Corinthians 3:3

The Bible In One Year:
- **Ezekiel 20–21**
- **James 5**

In November 1963, the same day that President John F. Kennedy was shot, another leader died—Clive Staples Lewis. This Oxford scholar, who had converted from atheism to Christianity, was a prolific writer. Intellectual books, science fiction, children's fantasies, and other works flowed from his pen with a strong Christian message. His books have been used by God in the conversion of many, including a politician and a Nobel Prize-winning scientist.

Some are called to tell others about Christ through their writing, but all believers are called to be "epistles," or letters of Christ, in the way we live. The apostle Paul tells us, "Clearly you are an epistle of Christ . . . written not with ink but by the Spirit of the living God" (2 Cor. 3:3).

Certainly Paul does not mean we are actually pieces of paper upon which God's message has been written. But as living "letters" we can illustrate how Jesus Christ makes a difference in how we treat others and strive to live with integrity.

Few will have the influence that C. S. Lewis did, but we are all called to bring glory to the One who loves us and has redeemed us! —Dennis Fisher

Dear Lord, You have called me to be a witness for You wherever You have placed me. Every day my life is on display. Help me to live in such a way that others will want to know You and the abundant life You offer.

We are Christ's "letters of recommendation" to all who read our lives.

November 24
Tuesday

What Time Is It?

Read:
Galatians 3:26–4:7

When the fullness of the time had come, God sent forth His Son.
—Galatians 4:4

The Bible In One Year:
- **Ezekiel 22–23**
- **1 Peter 1**

The old adage is true: Timing is everything! That's why Paul's statement, "When the fullness of the time had come, God sent forth His Son" intrigues me so much (Gal. 4:4).

A quick look at history reveals that the coming of Christ was at just the right time. Centuries earlier, Alexander the Great conquered most of the known world, bringing with him the Greek culture and language. On the heels of his demise, the Roman Empire picked up where Alexander left off and expanded the territory under the unifying influence of the culture and language of the Greeks. It was under Roman rule that the crucifixion took place, where the blood of Christ was shed for us. It was under the rule of Rome that conditions were made ready for the spread of the gospel across three continents: good roads, territorial boundaries free of "passport" restrictions, and a unifying language. The providence of God had put all the pieces in place for the perfect time to send His Son.

God's timing is perfect in everything. While you are waiting, perhaps wondering why God doesn't seem to be acting on your behalf, remember that He's working behind the scenes to prepare His moment of intervention at just the right time. Trust Him. He knows what time it is. —Joe Stowell

Lord, in Your infinite wisdom and power, You work behind the scenes to prepare all things for just the right time. Teach me to wait well and to trust You to know when the fullness of time has come.

Teach us, O Lord, the disciplines of patience, for to wait is often harder than to work. —Marshall

November 25
Wednesday

Spiritual Plagiarism

Read:
John 1:1-18

The Word became flesh and dwelt among us, and we beheld His glory, the glory as of the only begotten of the Father, full of grace and truth. —John 1:14

The Bible In One Year:
- Ezekiel 24–26
- 1 Peter 2

When I teach English composition, I require students to write in class. I know that in-class writing is their own work, so in this way I become familiar with each student's writing voice and am able to detect if they "borrow" a bit too heavily from another writer. Students are surprised to learn that their writing voice—which includes what they say as well as how they say it—is as distinctive as their speaking voice. Just as the words we speak come from our hearts, so do the words we write. They reveal who we are.

We become familiar with God's voice in much the same way. By reading what He has written, we learn who He is and how He expresses Himself. Satan, however, tries to make himself sound like God (2 Cor. 11:14). By using God's words in a slightly altered fashion, he comes up with convincing arguments for things that are untrue. For example, by convincing people to do things that simulate godliness, such as trusting in an outward regimen of self-discipline rather than Christ's death for salvation (Col. 2:23), Satan has led many astray.

God went to extremes to make sure we'd recognize His voice. He not only gave us His Word, He gave us the Word made flesh—Jesus (John 1:14)—so that we will not be easily deceived or misled. —Julie Ackerman Link

Instill within my heart, dear Lord,
A deep desire to know Your Word,
I want to learn to hear Your voice
That I may make Your will my choice. —D. DeHaan

Your Word is very pure;
therefore Your servant loves it. —Psalm 119:140

November 26
Thursday

REAL LOVE

READ:
1 Corinthians 13:1-8

[Love] bears all things,
believes all things,
hopes all things,
endures all things.
Love never fails.
—1 Corinthians 13:7-8

THE BIBLE IN ONE YEAR:
■ Ezekiel 27–29
■ 1 Peter 3

A few years ago, my friend's mother was diagnosed with Alzheimer's disease. Since then, Beth has been forced to make tough decisions about her mom's care, and her heart has often been broken as she watched her vibrant and fun-loving mom slowly slipping away. In the process, my friend has learned that real love is not always easy or convenient.

After her mom was hospitalized for a couple of days last year, Beth wrote these words to some of her friends: "As backwards as it may seem, I'm very thankful for the journey I am on with my mom. Behind the memory loss, confusion, and utter helplessness is a beautiful person who loves life and is at complete peace. I am learning so much about what real love is, and even though I probably wouldn't have asked for this journey and the tears and heartache that go with it, I wouldn't trade it for anything."

The Bible reminds us that love is patient and kind. It is not self-seeking or easily angered. It "bears all things, believes all things, hopes all things, endures all things" (1 Cor. 13:4-7).

Real love originated with our Father, who gave us the gift of His Son. As we seek to show His love to others, we can follow the example of Christ, who laid down His life for us (1 John 3:16-18). —Cindy Hess Kasper

Teach me to love, this is my prayer—
May the compassion of Thy heart I share;
Ready a cup of water to give,
May I unselfishly for others live. —*Peterson*

Real love is helping others for Jesus' sake even if they can never return the favor.

November 27
Friday

Place Of Water

Read:
Psalm 42:1-5

The water that I shall give him will become in him a fountain of water springing up into everlasting life.
—John 4:14

The Bible In One Year:
■ Ezekiel 30–32
■ 1 Peter 4

East Africa is one of the driest places on earth, which is what makes "Nairobi" such a significant name for a city in that region. The name comes from a Masai phrase meaning "cold water," and it literally means "the place of water."

Throughout history, the presence of water has been both life-giving and strategic. Whether a person lives in a dry climate or a rainforest, water is a nonnegotiable necessity. In a dry and barren climate, knowing where to find the place of water can mean the difference between life and death.

Our spiritual life also has certain nonnegotiable elements. That is why Jesus, upon encountering a spiritually thirsty woman at a well, declared to her that He alone could provide living water. He told her, "Whoever drinks of the water that I shall give him will never thirst. But the water that I shall give him will become in him a fountain of water springing up into everlasting life" (John 4:14).

Like the deer mentioned in Psalm 42:1-2 who pants for water, our souls thirst for God and long for Him (63:1). We desperately need the sustenance that comes only from Jesus Christ. He is the source of living water that refreshes our hearts. —Bill Crowder

Rivers of living water,
Rivers of life so free,
Flowing from Thee, my Savior,
Send now the rivers through me. —Wood

Jesus is the fountain of living water.

November 28
Saturday

How To Enjoy Things

Read:
Ecclesiastes 5:13-20

As for every man . . . to receive his heritage and rejoice in his labor—this is the gift of God.
—Ecclesiastes 5:19

The Bible In One Year:
- **Ezekiel 33–34**
- **1 Peter 5**

In his book *Daring To Draw Near,* Dr. John White writes that several years earlier God had made it possible for him to acquire a lovely home with many luxuries. His feelings about the house fluctuated dramatically.

When he reminded himself that it was a gracious gift from God, he felt joy and thanksgiving. But when he would begin to compare it with those of his friends, he would feel proud because he had such a fine house and his joy would evaporate. His home would actually become a burden. All he could see were the many hedges and trees to care for and the endless odd jobs to do. White said, "While vanity clouds my eyes and burdens my heart, gratitude clears my vision and lightens my load."

The writer of Ecclesiastes saw God at every turn in the enjoyment of material things. The power to eat the fruits of our labors and even the strength to receive and rejoice in them is from Him (5:18-19).

From beginning to end, all of life is a continuous gift-giving by God. We deserve nothing. He owes us nothing. Yet He gives us everything. If we remember this, we need not feel selfish or guilty. Whatever material blessings we have are a gift from our gracious God. —Dennis J. DeHaan

Ten thousand thousand precious gifts
My daily thanks employ;
Nor is the least a cheerful heart,
That tastes those gifts with joy. —Addison

God, who has given so much to us, gives one more thing—a grateful heart. —Herbert

November 29
Sunday

FIRST IMPRESSIONS

READ:
1 Samuel 16:1-7

For man looks at the outward appearance, but the LORD looks at the heart.
—1 Samuel 16:7

THE BIBLE IN ONE YEAR:
- Ezekiel 35–36
- 2 Peter 1

As I shopped for groceries one day, I was perceived as a thief by one person and a hero by another.

As I exited the supermarket, an employee said, "Excuse me, Sir. There are too many unbagged items in your cart." This is evidently a strategy used by shoplifters. When he saw that they were products too big to be bagged, he apologized and sent me on my way.

In the parking lot, a woman glanced at my gold embroidered sportsman's cap. Mistaking it for a military hat, she said, "Thank you for defending our country!" Then she walked away.

The supermarket employee and the woman in the parking lot had each formed hasty conclusions about me. It's easy to form opinions of others based on first impressions.

When Samuel was to select the next king of Israel from the sons of Jesse, he too made a judgment based on first impressions. However, God's chosen was not any of the older sons. The Spirit told Samuel, "Do not look at his appearance or at his physical stature" (1 Sam. 16:7). God chose David, the youngest, who looked least like a king.

God can help us view people through His eyes, for "the LORD does not see as man sees; . . . the LORD looks at the heart" (v.7). —Dennis Fisher

If we could view through eyes of faith
The people we meet each day
We'd quickly see God's gracious hand
In all who come our way. —*D. DeHaan*

First impressions can often lead to wrong conclusions.

November 30
Monday

ATTENDING TO OUR WORDS

READ:
Psalm 66:10-20

Certainly God has heard me; He has attended to the voice of my prayer.
—Psalm 66:19

THE BIBLE IN ONE YEAR:
■ Ezekiel 37–39
■ 2 Peter 2

A week after C. S. Lewis died in 1963, colleagues and friends gathered in the chapel of Magdalen College, Oxford, England, to pay tribute to the man whose writings had fanned the flames of faith and imagination in children and scholars alike.

During the memorial service, Lewis' close friend Austin Farrer noted that Lewis always sent a handwritten personal reply to every letter he received from readers all over the world. "His characteristic attitude to people in general was one of consideration and respect," Farrer said. "He paid you the compliment of attending to your words."

In that way, Lewis mirrored God's remarkable attention to what we say to Him in prayer. During a time of great difficulty, the writer of Psalm 66 cried out to God (vv.10-14). Later, he praised the Lord for His help, saying, "Certainly God has heard me; He has attended to the voice of my prayer" (v.19).

When we pray, the Lord hears our words and knows our hearts. Truly we can say with the psalmist, "Blessed be God, who has not turned away my prayer, nor His mercy from me!" (v.20). Our prayers become the avenue to a deeper relationship with Him. At all times, even in our hours of deepest need, He attends to our words. —David McCasland

My Savior hears me when I pray,
Upon His Word I calmly rest;
In His own time, in His own way,
I know He'll give me what is best. —*Hewitt*

We always have God's attention.

December 1
Tuesday

GOD WAITING

READ:
John 14:1-6

The Lord is not slack concerning His promise, . . . but is longsuffering toward us, not willing that any should perish but that all should come to repentance.
—2 Peter 3:9

THE BIBLE IN ONE YEAR:
- **Ezekiel 40–41**
- **2 Peter 3**

During the Christmas season we wait. We wait in traffic. We wait in checkout lines to purchase gifts. We wait for family to arrive. We wait to gather around a table filled with our favorite foods. We wait to open presents lovingly chosen.

All of this waiting can be a reminder to Christians that Christmas is a celebration of waiting for something much more important than holiday traditions. Like the ancient Israelites, we too are waiting for Jesus. Although He already came as the long-awaited Messiah, He has not yet come as ruler over all the earth. So today we wait for Christ's second coming.

Christmas reminds us that God also waits . . . He waits for people to see His glory, to admit that they are lost without Him, to say yes to His love, to receive His forgiveness, to turn away from sin. While we wait for His second coming, He waits for repentance. What seems to us like God's slowness in coming is instead His patience in waiting (2 Peter 3:9).

The Lord is waiting to have a relationship with those He loves. He made the first move when He came as baby Jesus and the sacrificial Lamb. Now He waits for us to welcome Him into our lives as Savior and Lord. —Julie Ackerman Link

God is waiting in the silence
As the world goes rushing by;
Will not someone stop and listen,
Answer quickly, "Here am I"? —*Smith*

God patiently keeps His promises.

December 2
Wednesday

INTEGRITY LEAGUE

READ:
Psalm 26

He who walks with integrity walks securely. —Proverbs 10:9

THE BIBLE IN ONE YEAR:
■ Ezekiel 42–44
■ 1 John 1

We call it the Integrity League, but it's really just a bunch of guys who get together at lunchtime to play basketball. We call fouls on ourselves, attempt to avoid angry outbursts, and simply try to keep everything fair and enjoyable. We are competitive and we don't like to lose—but we all agree that integrity and honesty should control the atmosphere.

Integrity. Scripture clearly indicates the importance of this trait. And we honor the God of our lives when we practice it.

Through His Word, God has given us clear reasons to "walk in . . . integrity" (Ps. 26:11). A person who has integrity has the security of a quiet life unknown to the one who "perverts his ways" (Prov. 10:9). The follower of God who lives with integrity is preserved by his confidence in God, for that person waits for God's intervention in his life instead of running ahead of Him (Ps. 25:21). And the one who practices integrity will be given guidance and clear direction (Prov. 11:3).

Why should we care about life's "Integrity League"? Because obeying God this way shows that we trust Him with our lives and that we want to shine His great love on others. —Dave Branon

Dear Father, help my word be true. Help my
actions be honest. Help my life to
reflect Your holiness and shine God's light
for all to see. Help me to live with integrity.

Integrity is Christlike character in workclothes.

December 3
Thursday

One Stretch

Read:
1 John 2:24–3:3

Behold what manner of love the Father has bestowed on us, that we should be called children of God!
—1 John 3:1

The Bible In One Year:
- Ezekiel 45–46
- 1 John 2

For years, Sarah had low-back pain that continued to worsen. Her doctor sent her for physical therapy, and she was given 25 stretches to do every day. The pain lessened but not completely. So the doctor ordered x-rays and sent her to another therapist, who instructed her to discontinue the other therapist's stretches and do only one stretch a day as needed. Surprisingly, the one simple stretch worked the best.

Sometimes the simplest truths are the best. When asked to summarize in one sentence his whole life's work in theology, Karl Barth responded: "Jesus loves me!" Some say he added, "This I know, for the Bible tells me so."

God's love for us is evident. He gave His Son to rescue us from ourselves. Christ died on the cross, taking our burden of sin. Then He rose again, giving us new life in Him. Amazing love! As John tells us: "Behold what manner of love the Father has bestowed on us, that we should be called children of God!" (1 John 3:1).

Jesus' love for us isn't a Band-Aid or a cure-all for all of life's problems, of course. But it is the one truth we can always depend on to give purpose to life and peace with God. —Anne Cetas

I am so glad that our Father in heaven
Tells of His love in the Book He has given;
Wonderful things in the Bible I see—
This is the dearest, that Jesus loves me. —*Bliss*

The wonder of it all—
just to think that Jesus loves me.

December 4
Friday

Eureka Stone

Read:
Matthew 13:44-50

The kingdom of heaven is like treasure hidden in a field, which a man found and hid; and for joy over it he goes and sells all that he has and buys that field.
—Matthew 13:44

The Bible In One Year:
- **Ezekiel 47–48**
- **1 John 3**

In 1867 on a farm in South Africa, 15-year-old Erasmus Jacobs saw a stone glistening in the sun. The shining rock was eventually reported to a neighbor, who wanted to buy it from the family. Not knowing its value, Erasmus' mother told the neighbor, "You can keep the stone, if you want it."

Eventually, a mineralogist determined the stone to be a 21.25 carat diamond and worth a great sum. It became known as the "Eureka Diamond." (The Greek word *eureka* means "I found it!") Soon the fields near the Jacobs' farm soared in value. Underneath the land was one of the richest diamond deposits ever discovered.

Jesus said that the value of being part of God's kingdom is like treasure: "The kingdom of heaven is like treasure hidden in a field, which a man found and hid; and for joy over it he goes and sells all that he has and buys that field" (Matt. 13:44).

When we put our faith in Christ, a spiritual "eureka moment" arrives. God gives us forgiveness in His Son. It is the greatest treasure that could ever be found. Now all of life can begin to center on the value of becoming a joyous member of His eternal kingdom. It's our joy to share that valuable discovery with others. —Dennis Fisher

How we need a keen awareness
Of the joys God wants to share!
Priceless treasures found in Jesus—
We are rich beyond compare! —D. DeHaan

God's kingdom is a treasure meant to be shared.

December 5
Saturday

Get Your "Wanter" Fixed

Read:
Philippians 4:4-13

I have learned in whatever state I am, to be content.
—Philippians 4:11

The Bible In One Year:
- Daniel 1–2
- 1 John 4

When my wife was a young girl in Austin, Texas, Carlyle Marney was her family's neighbor, pastor, and friend. One of his off-hand remarks about being content became one of her family's enduring expressions: "Dr. Marney says, 'We just need to get our wanter fixed.' "

It's so easy to want more than we need and to become more focused on getting than on giving. Soon, our desires dictate our choices.

When the apostle Paul wrote to the followers of Jesus in the city of Philippi, he told them, "I have learned in whatever state I am, to be content . . . . I have learned both to be full and to be hungry, both to abound and to suffer need" (Phil. 4:11-12). Paul was saying, in effect, "I've had my 'wanter' fixed." It's important to note that Paul was not born with contentment. He *learned* it in the difficult circumstances of everyday life.

During this season of the year, when shopping and buying often take center stage in so many countries and cultures, why don't we decide to focus on being satisfied in our present circumstances? It may sound difficult, but Paul, when talking about learning to be content said, "I can do all things through Christ who strengthens me" (v.13).
—David McCasland

Help us, Lord, to learn contentment when life is rough. Protect us from believing the lie that having more will bring us happiness. May we be content with what You have given.

Contentment begins with having fewer wants.

December 6
Sunday

More Than Enough

Read:
Psalm 103:1-11

[The Lord] crowns you with lovingkindness and tender mercies.
—Psalm 103:4

The Bible In One Year:
- Daniel 3–4
- 1 John 5

When I entertained a large group in my home, I feared that the menu I planned wouldn't be enough to serve all the guests. I shouldn't have worried though. Several friends unexpectedly brought additional items and all of us were able to enjoy the surprise surplus. We had more than enough and were able to share out of the abundance.

We serve a God of abundance who is consistently "more than enough." We can see God's generous nature in the way He loves His children.

In Psalm 103, David lists the many benefits our Father bestows on us. Verse 4 says that He redeems our life from destruction and crowns us with lovingkindness and tender mercies.

The apostle Paul reminds us that God "has blessed us with every spiritual blessing" and "is able to do exceedingly abundantly above all that we ask or think" (Eph. 1:3; 3:20).

Because of His great love, we are called children of God (1 John 3:1), and His grace gives us "sufficiency in all things" that we "may have an abundance for every good work" (2 Cor. 9:8).

God's love and grace, spilled over into our lives, enables us to share them with others. The God of power and provision is always the God of "more than enough"! —Cindy Hess Kasper

Praise, my soul, the King of heaven;
To His feet your tribute bring.
Ransomed, healed, restored, forgiven,
Evermore His praises sing. —*Lyte*

We always have enough when God is our supply.

December 7
Monday

Christmas Lights

Read:
Matthew 5:13-16

The people who sat in darkness have seen a great light, and upon those who sat in the region and shadow of death Light has dawned.
—Matthew 4:16

The Bible In One Year:
- Daniel 5–7
- 2 John

In December each year, a neighborhood of 13 families near where we live sets up a dazzling display of 300,000 Christmas lights. People drive for miles and wait in line for hours to see the flashing, colorful lights and hear the music that is programmed to go with it. The sound-and-light display is so elaborate that it requires a network of 64 computers to keep everything synchronized.

When I think about these holiday lights, I am reminded of the Light that makes Christmas a holiday for many—a single Light so bright that it illuminates the whole world with truth, justice, and love. This Light—Jesus—is everything that the world is longing and looking for (Isa. 9:2,6-7). And He has told His followers to display His light so that others will see and glorify God (Matt. 5:16).

Imagine if Christians worked as hard at shining and synchronizing the light of God's love as the families of that neighborhood work when they illuminate their street with Christmas lights. Perhaps then the people still living in darkness would make an effort to see this great Light. When Christians work together to display God's love, the gospel will shine more brightly and attract more people to Jesus—the Light of the world. —Julie Ackerman Link

O to be filled with His life divine;
O to be clothed with His power and might;
O to reflect my dear Savior sublime—
Always to shine as the saints in light! —Anon.

Our witness for Christ is a light in a dark world.

December 8
Tuesday

Serious Fear

Read:
Luke 2:8-20

Do not be afraid, for behold, I bring you good tidings of great joy. —Luke 2:10

The Bible In One Year:
- **Daniel 8–10**
- **3 John**

After weeks of preparation by the children's choir, the night had finally arrived for our annual Christmas musical in 1983. The costumed children began filing into the auditorium when suddenly we heard a ruckus at the back door. My wife and I turned to look and saw our own little Matt. Sobbing loudly and with a look of sheer terror on his face, he had a death grip on the door handle. He refused to enter the auditorium. After much negotiating, the director finally told him he didn't have to go on stage. Instead, Matt sat with us, and soon his fears began to subside.

Although we don't usually identify Christmas as a time of fear, there was plenty of it on the night of Christ's birth. Luke says, "Behold, an angel of the Lord stood before them, and the glory of the Lord shone around them, and they were greatly afraid" (Luke 2:9). The sight of the angelic messenger was more than the shepherds could process. But the angel reassured them: "Do not be afraid, for behold, I bring you good tidings of great joy which will be to all people" (v.10).

In a world full of fear, we need to remember that Jesus came to be the Prince of Peace (Isa. 9:6). We desperately need His peace. As we look to Him, He will ease our fears and calm our hearts. —Bill Crowder

Hail, the heaven-born Prince of Peace!
Hail the Sun of righteousness!
Light and life to all He brings,
Risen with healing in His wings. —*Wesley*

God incarnate is the end of fear. —F. B. Meyer

December 9
Wednesday

The Good And The Bad

Read:
Jonah 4

The Lord God prepared a plant [for] shade . . . [and] a worm, and it so damaged the plant that it withered. —Jonah 4:6-7

The Bible In One Year:
- **Daniel 11–12**
- **Jude**

The story of the rebellious prophet Jonah shows us how God desires to use both blessings and trials to challenge us and change us for the better. Five times in the book of Jonah it says that the Lord prepared circumstances for him—both good and bad.

In Jonah 1:4 we read that the Lord sent a storm. It says He "sent out a great wind on the sea, and there was a mighty tempest on the sea." After the mariners discovered that Jonah was the reason for this storm, they threw him overboard (1:15). Then God "prepared a great fish to swallow Jonah" to save him from drowning (1:17).

Later in the book we read that "the Lord God prepared a plant" to shade Jonah (4:6). Then we see that God prepared a worm to kill the vine as well as a scorching wind and sun to beat down upon him (4:7-9). These circumstances were used to reveal Jonah's rebellious attitude. Only after that revelation could God directly confront Jonah's heart problem.

As we face different situations, we should remember that God is sovereign over both the blessings and the troubles that come our way. He desires to use everything to build our character (James 1:1-5). He uses both good and bad to transform us and guide us on our journey. —Dennis Fisher

The Maker of the universe
Knows every need of man,
And made provision for that need
According to His plan. —*Crane*

The Lord gives and takes away. Blessed be the Lord.

December 10
Thursday

A Giving Competition

Read:
2 Corinthians 9:6-15

Thanks be to God for His indescribable gift!
—2 Corinthians 9:15

The Bible In One Year:
- **Hosea 1–4**
- **Revelation 1**

A television commercial I enjoy at Christmastime shows two neighbors in a friendly competition with each other to see who can spread the most Christmas cheer. Each keeps an eye on the other as he decorates his house and trees with lights. Then each upgrades his own property to look better than the other's. They then start competing over who can give the most extravagantly to other neighbors, running around cheerfully sharing gifts.

God's people aren't in a competition to see who can give the most, but we are called to be "ready to give, willing to share" (1 Tim. 6:18). The apostle Paul instructed the church at Corinth: "Let each one give as he purposes in his heart, not grudgingly or of necessity; for God loves a cheerful giver" (2 Cor. 9:7).

At Christmastime, as we share gifts with others, we remember the generosity of God toward us—He gave us His Son. Ray Stedman said, "Jesus set aside His riches and entered into His creation in a state of poverty in order to enrich us all by His grace."

No gift-giving could ever compete with the Lord's extravagance. We thank God for the indescribable gift of Jesus! (v.15). —Anne Cetas

Sing praise to the Father, Creator and King,
Whose mercy has taught us a new song to sing;
Who made us, and loved us though rebels and lost,
And planned our redemption at infinite cost. —*Clarkson*

No gift is greater than the gift of Christ Himself.

December 11
Friday

HOPE FOR SKEPTICS

READ:
Isaiah 55:6-13

So shall My word be that goes forth from My mouth; it shall not return to Me void, but it shall accomplish what I please.
—Isaiah 55:11

THE BIBLE IN ONE YEAR:
- **Hosea 5–8**
- **Revelation 2**

As a workplace chaplain, I'm privileged to be in conversation with many different people. Some are skeptics of the Christian faith. I've discovered three major hurdles that keep them from trusting in Christ for salvation.

The first barrier, surprisingly, isn't an unwillingness to believe that God exists; instead some doubt that they're important enough for God's attention. Second, some believe they are unworthy of His forgiveness. People are often their own harshest judges. The third hurdle? They wonder why God is not communicating with them if He is out there.

Let's work backward through the hurdles to see what God's Word says. First, God doesn't play head games. He promises that if we read His Word, He will make sure it accomplishes His purpose (Isa. 55:11). In other words, if we read it we will discover that God *is* communicating with us. This is precisely why the Bible speaks so often of His grace and mercy toward all (v.7). His willingness to forgive surpasses our own. Once we learn that we can hear God in the Bible and once we see the emphasis on His mercy, it becomes easier to believe we have His attention when we cry out to Him.

God's story is amazing. It can give hope for all of us. —Randy Kilgore

There can be times when one's mind is in doubt,
Times when one asks what the faith is about;
But we can believe Him, we know that He cares—
Our God is real, as the Bible declares. —*Fitzhugh*

Honest skepticism can be the first step to a strong faith.

December 12
Saturday

Costume Or Uniform?

Read:
Romans 13:11-14

Put on the Lord Jesus Christ, and make no provision for the flesh, to fulfill its lusts.
—Romans 13:14

The Bible In One Year:
- **Hosea 9–11**
- **Revelation 3**

Eunice McGarrahan gave an inspiring talk on Christian discipleship in which she said, "A *costume* is something you put on and pretend that you are what you are wearing. A *uniform,* on the other hand, reminds you that you are, in fact, what you wear."

Her comment sparked memories of my first day in US Army basic training when we were each given a box and ordered to put all our civilian clothes in it. The box was mailed to our home address. Every day after that, the uniform we put on reminded us that we had entered a period of disciplined training designed to change our attitudes and actions.

"Cast off the works of darkness," the apostle Paul told the followers of Jesus living in Rome, "and . . . put on the armor of light" (Rom. 13:12). He followed this with the command to "put on the Lord Jesus Christ, and make no provision for the flesh, to fulfill its lusts" (v.14). The goal of this "casting off" and "putting on" was a new identity and transformed living (v.13).

When we choose to follow Christ as our Lord, He begins the process of making us more like Him each day. It is not a matter of pretending to be what we aren't but of becoming more and more what we are in Christ. —David McCasland

O to be like Thee, O to be like Thee,
Blessed Redeemer, pure as Thou art!
Come in Thy sweetness, come in Thy fullness;
Stamp Thine own image deep on my heart. —*Chisholm*

Salvation is free, but discipleship will cost you your life. —Dietrich Bonhoeffer

December 13
Sunday

LASTING REWARDS

READ:
1 Corinthians 9:24-27

Bodily exercise profits a little, but godliness is profitable for all things. —1 Timothy 4:8

THE BIBLE IN ONE YEAR:
- Hosea 12–14
- Revelation 4

Ukrainian gymnast Larisa Latynina held the record of 18 Olympic medals. She won them in the 1956, 1960, and 1964 Olympics. The 48-year-old record was surpassed when Michael Phelps swam for his 19th gold in the 4 x 200-meter free-style relay in the 2012 London Games. "[Latynina] kind of got lost in history," the publisher of the *International Gymnast* magazine said. When the Soviet Union broke up, "we had forgotten about her."

Paul, the apostle, reminds us that sometimes hard work is forgotten. Athletes subject their bodies to great discipline as they train to win perishable medals for their effort (1 Cor. 9:25). But it is not just that the medals are perishable. Over time, people's memory of those achievements dim and fade. If athletes can sacrifice so much to achieve rewards on the earth, rewards that will eventually be forgotten, how much more effort should followers of Christ exert to gain an imperishable crown? (1 Tim. 4:8).

Athletes' sacrifice and determination are rewarded with medals, trophies, and money. But even greater, our Father in heaven rewards the discipline of His children (Luke 19:17).

God will never forget our service done out of love for Him who first loved us. —C. P. Hia

I thank You, Lord, for the opportunities to use the gifts You have given me for Your service today. Help me to do so in obedience, expecting nothing more than Your "well done" as reward.

Sacrifice for the kingdom is never without reward.

December 14
Monday

A New Force

Read:
Luke 2:25-35

My eyes have seen Your salvation which You have prepared before the face of all peoples.
—Luke 2:30-31

The Bible In One Year:
- Joel 1–3
- Revelation 5

When Matteo Ricci went to China in the 16th century, he took samples of religious art to illustrate the Christian story for people who had never heard it. They readily accepted portraits of Mary holding the baby Jesus, but when he produced paintings of the crucifixion and tried to explain that the God-child had come to be executed, his audience reacted with revulsion and horror. They couldn't worship a crucified God.

As I thumb through my Christmas cards, I realize that we do much the same thing. In our celebrations and observances, we may not think about how the story that began at Bethlehem turned out at Calvary.

In Luke's account of the Christmas story, only one person—the old man Simeon—seems to grasp the mysterious nature of what God has set in motion. "This Child is destined for the fall and rising of many in Israel, and for a sign which will be spoken against," he told Mary, and then he made the prediction that a sword would pierce her own soul (2:34-35).

Simeon knew that though on the surface little had changed—Herod still ruled, Roman troops still occupied Israel—underneath, everything had changed. God's promised redemption had arrived. —Philip Yancey

One day they led Him up Calvary's mountain,
One day they nailed Him to die on the tree;
Suffering anguish, despised and rejected,
Bearing our sins, my Redeemer is He! —Chapman

The cradle without the cross misses the true meaning of Christ's birth.

December 15
Tuesday

Canceled Christmas

Read:
Luke 2:36-38

Joseph and His mother marveled at those things which were spoken of [Jesus].
—Luke 2:33

The Bible In One Year:
■ Amos 1–3
■ Revelation 6

We felt as if our Christmas was being canceled last year. Actually, our flight to see family in Missouri was canceled due to snow. It's been our tradition for quite a few years to celebrate Christmas with them, so we were greatly disappointed when we only got as far as Minnesota and had to return home to Michigan.

On Sunday, in a message we would have missed, our pastor spoke about expectations for Christmas. He caught my attention when he said, "If our expectations for Christmas are gifts and time with family, we have set our expectations too low. Those are enjoyable and things we're thankful for, but Christmas is the celebration of the coming of Christ and His redemption."

Simeon and Anna celebrated the coming of Jesus and His salvation when Joseph and Mary brought Him to the temple as a baby (Luke 2:25-38). Simeon, a man who was told by the Spirit that he would not die before he saw the Messiah, declared: "My eyes have seen Your salvation" (v.30). When Anna, a widow who served God, saw Jesus, she "spoke of Him to all those who looked for redemption in Jerusalem" (v.38).

We may experience disappointments or heartache during the Christmas season, but Jesus and His salvation always give us reason to celebrate. —Anne Cetas

How wonderful that we on Christmas morn
Though centuries have passed since Christ was born,
May worship still the Living Lord of men,
Our Savior, Jesus, Babe of Bethlehem. —*Hutchings*

Jesus is always the reason to celebrate.

December 16
Wednesday

Living Backward

Read:
Matthew 16:21-28

Whoever loses his life for My sake will find it.
—Matthew 16:25

The Bible In One Year:
- Amos 4–6
- Revelation 7

The Chicago River is unusual because it flows backward. Engineers reversed its direction over a century ago because city-dwellers were using it as a dump. Dishwater, sewage, and industrial waste all funneled into the river, which emptied into Lake Michigan. Since the lake supplied drinking water for the city, thousands grew sick and died before city authorities decided to redirect the river to flow backward, away from the lake.

When we look at the earthly life of Jesus, it may seem backward from what we would expect. As the King of glory, He came to earth as a vulnerable infant. As God in the flesh, He endured accusations of blasphemy. As the only sinless man, He was crucified as a criminal. But Jesus lived on earth according to God's will (John 6:38).

As followers of Christ, to clothe ourselves with Jesus' attitudes and actions may appear "backward." Blessing our enemies (Rom. 12:14), valuing godliness over wealth (1 Tim. 6:6-9), and taking joy in hardship (James 1:2) seem to oppose worldly wisdom. Yet, Jesus said, "Whoever loses his life for My sake will find it" (Matt. 16:25).

Don't worry if living your life sometimes means operating in reverse. God will give you the strength to honor Him, and He will propel you forward. —Jennifer Benson Schuldt

Dear God, please give me the strength to go
against the flow of this world. Help me to resist
what is wrong in Your eyes and to act in ways
that please You, for the glory of Your name.

Clothing ourselves with Jesus' attitudes and actions shows His presence in our lives.

December 17
Thursday

Love And Support

Read:
Philippians 4:10-18

I thank my God . . . for your fellowship in the gospel from the first day until now.
—Philippians 1:3,5

The Bible In One Year:
■ Amos 7–9
■ Revelation 8

I received this note from a friend serving in an orphanage in a developing country: "Yesterday, as I was sitting at my office desk, I noticed a trail of ants on the floor. As I followed it, I was shocked to see that thousands of ants had blanketed the walls of our office building—inside and out. They swarmed everything. Fortunately, one of the workers . . . set to work. Less than an hour later, the ants were gone."

After telling this insect story, my friend wrote, "So, how was your day at work?" Sometimes we need reminders of the needs of those who have left behind the comforts and conveniences of home. God calls each of us to different paths of service, and some paths are bumpy. Working in an office that is overrun by ants doesn't appeal to anyone, but my friend is not there for the perks.

She and many other believers have had their hearts captured by Christ and think that abandoning "essential" comforts and conveniences is a small thing to do to honor Him who loves us. They need our support in the way Paul depended on his friends in Philippi—for fellowship (Phil. 1:5), for finances (4:16), and for care (4:18). When we encourage our friends who have left their familiar environments to serve God elsewhere, we show our love for the One who sent them. —Dave Branon

Dear Lord, give me wisdom to know which of Your workers in the fields of the world need my help. Show me how my family can surround them with encouragement and support.

The glory of life is to love, not to be loved; to give, not to get; to serve, not to be served.

December 18
Friday

Not All Empty

Read:
Psalm 107:1-9

He satisfies the longing soul, and fills the hungry soul with goodness.
—Psalm 107:9

The Bible In One Year:
- Obadiah
- Revelation 9

Our granddaughter Julia spent the summer working in an orphanage in Busia, Uganda. On the final day of her internship, she went to the children to tell each one goodbye. One little girl named Sumaya was very sad and said to her, "Tomorrow you leave us, and next week the other aunties [interns] leave."

When Julia agreed that she was indeed leaving, Sumaya thought for a minute and exclaimed, "But we will be all empty. None of you will be left!" Again, Julia agreed. The little girl thought a few moments and replied: "But God will be with us, so we won't be all empty."

If we are honest with ourselves, we know that "all empty" feeling. It is an emptiness that friendship, love, sex, money, power, popularity, or success can never assuage—a longing for something indefinable, something incalculably precious but lost. Every good thing can remind, beckon, and awaken in us a greater desire for that elusive "something more." The closest we get is a hint, an echo in a face, a painting, a scene . . . . And then it is gone. "Our best havings are wantings," said C. S. Lewis.

We were made for God, and in the end, nothing less will satisfy us. Without Him, we are all empty. He alone fills the hungry with good things (Ps. 107:9). —David Roper

Dear Lord, fill me with Your goodness and love.
I desire nothing in heaven and earth but You.
Without You, I have nothing. Thank You for the
abiding satisfaction that we can find in You.

God cannot give us a happiness and peace apart from Himself because it is not there. —C. S. Lewis

December 19
Saturday

THE SON IS GIVEN

READ:
Luke 1:26-33

For unto us a Child is born, unto us a Son is given. —Isaiah 9:6

THE BIBLE IN ONE YEAR:
- Jonah 1–4
- Revelation 10

One of my favorite portions of Handel's *Messiah* is the joyous movement "For unto us a Child is born," from the first part of the oratorio. I especially love how the chorus rises to the phrase, "Unto us a Son is given." Those words, of course, are taken from Isaiah 9:6, "For unto us a Child is born, unto us a Son is given." Handel's majestic music soars with adoration for the Son who came to us in human flesh that first Christmas.

The New Testament clarifies even further who this Son is. In Luke 1, the angelic messenger appeared to Mary and identified the Christ-child in four ways. He would be the son of Mary, making Him fully human (1:31). He would be the Son of the Highest, which made Him fully divine (1:32). He would also be the Son of David, giving Him royal lineage (1:32). And He would bear the title of Son of God (1:35), giving Him equality with the Father in all things. All of the roles the Messiah was called to fill are made possible in these distinct expressions of His Sonship.

As we worship Him this Christmas, may our celebrations be filled with joy and wonder at the fullness of what it means. Our heavenly Father has given us His perfect, sufficient Son. O come, let us adore Him! —Bill Crowder

Yea, Lord, we greet Thee, born this happy morning,
Jesus, to Thee be all glory given;
Word of the Father, now in flesh appearing;
O come, let us adore Him, Christ the Lord. —*Wade*

God's love became incarnate at Bethlehem.

December 20
Sunday

Taking Refuge

Read:
Proverbs 18:1-10

The name of the Lord is a strong tower;
the righteous run to it and are safe.
—Proverbs 18:10

The Bible In One Year:
- **Micah 1–3**
- **Revelation 11**

In the medieval world, farmers would care for their crops until an enemy appeared on the horizon. Then they would flee with their families to their fortified city for protection from the marauders.

The city of Carcassonne has been a refuge for generations. Built in the 5th century BC, this stone fortress has provided protection for Romans, Gauls, Visigoths, Franks, and French. Its sprawling size and majestic watchtowers and battlements gave confidence to those hiding inside its protective walls.

As believers, we can take refuge in the presence of the living God. The book of Proverbs tells us: "The name of the Lord is a strong tower; the righteous run to it and are safe" (Prov. 18:10). "The name of the Lord" refers to God's character—abounding with faithfulness, power, and mercy. The term *safe* means "set on high out of danger."

We all face threats at times that make us want to run for cover. Some seek security in material wealth or relationships. But the Christ-follower has a more secure refuge. Because of who God is and what He can do for us, our best protection ultimately rests in Him. If you are facing a threat today, go to the Lord, who is a strong tower. You will find refuge in His care. —Dennis Fisher

In the times of greatest struggle,
When the angry billows roll,
I can always find my Savior,
Christ, the Refuge of my soul. —*Woodruff*

In good times and bad, God is our safe resting place.

December 21
Monday

Light And Shadow

Read:
Isaiah 9:1-7

The people who walked in darkness have seen a great light; those who dwelt in the land of the shadow of death, upon them a light has shined.
—Isaiah 9:2

The Bible In One Year:
- **Micah 4–5**
- **Revelation 12**

Art historian Seymour Slive described the great Dutch artist Rembrandt (1606–1669) as the master of light and shadow, a compelling storyteller on canvas. Rembrandt's painting *The Adoration of the Shepherds* portrays the darkened stable in Bethlehem where two shepherds kneel beside the manger while other people stand farther away. One man holds a lantern, but the brightest light shines not from his lantern but from the Christ-child, illuminating those who have gathered close to Him.

Seven centuries before Jesus' birth, Isaiah used an image of light and shadow to foretell the coming of a Savior for Israel: "The people who walked in darkness have seen a great light; those who dwelt in the land of the shadow of death, upon them a light has shined. . . . For unto us a Child is born, unto us a Son is given" (Isa. 9:2,6).

Each person may see a different story in Rembrandt's painting, but perhaps each of us is represented somewhere in that stable. Are we kneeling in worship, standing back in hesitation, or hiding from the light that has penetrated our darkness?

Christmas invites us to step out of the shadows of darkness and to allow the light of Christ to shine into our hearts.
—David McCasland

Observing God's love from afar
Is only a passing delight;
But when we experience Christ's presence,
Our darkness is turned into light. —*Hess*

Faith in Christ is not a leap into the dark; it's a step into the Light.

December 22
Tuesday

Christmas Wonder

Read:
1 Chronicles 16:7-13

Remember His marvelous works which He has done.
—1 Chronicles 16:12

The Bible In One Year:
- **Micah 6–7**
- **Revelation 13**

After my first semester in seminary, my family was given airline tickets to fly home for Christmas. The night before our flight, we realized we had less than $20 for the trip. Parking, transportation, and other incidentals were certain to cost more than $20. Heartsick, we resolved to pray about it. Though our children were small (6 and 2), we included them in the prayer time.

As we were praying, we heard footsteps in the hallway of the apartment building, and then "whisk"—the sound of an envelope sliding under the door. Inside the envelope was an anonymous gift of $50.

The wonder reflected on our 6-year-old daughter's face matched the wonder in our own hearts. Here was a mighty God writing His name on a little girl's heart by hearing and answering our prayer in the same instant. And so we, like the psalmist David, could "talk of all His wondrous works!" (1 Chron. 16:9).

So it was that first Christmas night, when a mighty, all-knowing, all-powerful God wrote His name on the heart of humanity, stunning us with the generosity of forgiveness and the joy of unconditional love. The birth of Christ is the answer to our most fervent prayers for love and forgiveness. Can you feel the wonder? —Randy Kilgore

Lord, restore to me the wonder of Christmas,
felt most keenly when I first met Jesus;
for I long to tell the story with all the
joy it brought me that day.

A wonder-filled life is ours when we know the Christ of Christmas.

December 23
Wednesday

God With Us

Read:
Matthew 1:18-25

Behold, the virgin shall be with child, and bear a Son, and they shall call His name Immanuel, which is translated, "God with us." —Matthew 1:23

The Bible In One Year:
- **Nahum 1–3**
- **Revelation 14**

His presence in the room was obvious. Everyone else was dressed rather formally. He had on a pair of jeans, a T-shirt, and a weathered baseball cap. I couldn't help but notice him as I addressed students that day in a seminary chapel in Bucharest, Romania. I have no idea why he didn't conform to the norms of seminary attire, but I do remember his name.

At the close of the meeting he came up to introduce himself. When I asked him his name, he answered, "Immanuel." I was surprised by his answer and asked if he knew what that meant; he unashamedly replied, "Yes—'God with us!'"

I've often thought about that young man and how he stood out in the crowd. Just as Jesus came to bring the presence of God into our world—"Immanuel . . . God with us" (Matt. 1:23)—so too we are called to bring His presence into our world. Jesus made that clear when He said, "As the Father has sent Me, I also send you" (John 20:21).

This Christmas, we can give the gift of God's likeness through us. When our lives reflect the God who lives in us, we can be different from the world, and that difference can bless others with the transforming presence of His love and grace. —Joe Stowell

His Spirit fill my hungering soul,
His power all my life control;
My deepest prayer, my highest goal,
That I may be like Jesus. —*Chisholm*

The gift of God's presence through you is your gift to the world.

December 24
Thursday

One Silent Night

Read:
Luke 2:1-14

Behold, I bring you good tidings of great joy which will be to all people. —Luke 2:10

The Bible In One Year:
- Habakkuk 1–3
- Revelation 15

Simon had emigrated from the Netherlands to the United States. His wife, Kay, and all three of their children had been born in the US. Then Jenny married Roberto from Panama. Bill married Vania from Portugal. And Lucas married Bora from South Korea.

On Christmas Eve, as the family gathered for a celebration, they began singing "Silent Night" in their native tongues—a sweet sound indeed for the Lord of the earth to hear as they celebrated the birth of His Son.

Two thousand years ago, the silence of a quiet night ended abruptly when an angel told the shepherds a baby had been born: "Behold, I bring you good tidings of great joy which will be to all people" (Luke 2:10). Then a multitude of angels began praising God, saying, "Glory to God in the highest, and on earth peace, goodwill toward men!" (v.14). Christ the Lord, the Savior of the world, was born!

God's gracious gift, His Son, which was announced on that long-ago silent night, is still available to everyone—"every tribe and nation" (Titus 2:11-14; Rev. 5:9-10). "For God so loved the world that He gave His only begotten Son, that whoever believes in Him should not perish but have everlasting life" (John 3:16). —Cindy Hess Kasper

Silent night! holy night! Shepherds quake at the sight;
Glories stream from heaven afar,
Heavenly hosts sing Alleluia—
Christ the Savior is born! Christ the Savior is born! —*Mohr*

Heaven's choir came down to sing when heaven's King came down to save.

December 25
Friday

Christingle

Read:
1 John 1:1-7

That was the true Light which gives light to every man coming into the world. —John 1:9

The Bible In One Year:
- **Zephaniah 1–3**
- **Revelation 16**

In the Czech Republic and other places, the Christmas celebration includes "Christingles." A Christingle is an orange, representing the world, with a candle placed in the top of it to symbolize Christ the light of the world. A red ribbon encircles the orange, symbolizing the blood of Jesus. Four toothpicks with dried fruits are placed through the ribbon into the sides of the orange, representing the fruits of the earth.

This simple visual aid vividly represents the purpose behind Christ's coming—to bring light into the darkness and to redeem a broken world by shedding His blood.

In John's account of Christ's life, the disciple describes Jesus as the Light of the world. He wrote of Christ: "That was the true Light which gives light to every man coming into the world" (John 1:9). Not only did Christ the Light come to penetrate our world's darkness, but He is also "The Lamb of God who takes away the sin of the world!" (v.29).

Think of it! The baby of Bethlehem became the living, risen Christ who has rescued us from our sin. And so John instructs us to "walk in the light as He is in the light" (1 John 1:7). May all who have experienced His rescue find in Jesus the peace of walking in His light. —Bill Crowder

Yet in thy dark streets shineth
The everlasting Light;
The hopes and fears of all the years
Are met in Thee tonight. —*Brooks*

The newborn Christ-child became the Light of the world and the Lamb of God.

December 26
Saturday

Be Present

Read:
Job 2:3-13

They sat down with him on the ground seven days and seven nights, and no one spoke a word to him, for they saw that his grief was very great. —Job 2:13

The Bible In One Year:
- **Haggai 1–2**
- **Revelation 17**

After 20 children and 6 staff members were murdered in a Connecticut school, the entire nation was stunned that such a horrific thing could happen. Everyone focused on the tragedy and the questions surrounding it: What kind of person would do such a thing, and why? How can we prevent it from happening again? How can we help the survivors? Amid the chaos, an unlikely group moved in and made a difference.

From Chicago came dogs—specially trained golden retrievers that offered nothing except affection. Dogs don't speak; they simply offer their presence. Children traumatized by the violence opened up to them, expressing fears and emotions they had not spoken to any adult. Tim Hetzner of Lutheran Church Charities said, "The biggest part of their training is just learning to be quiet."

As we learn from the book of Job, people in grief do not always need words. Sometimes they need someone to sit silently with them, to listen when they need to speak, and to hug them when their sorrow turns to sobs.

God may not intervene to change circumstances and He may not explain suffering, but He comforts us through the presence of other believers (Col. 4:8). —Julie Ackerman Link

He's with us in the valley,
Amid the darkest night
He tells us in our sorrow;
Faith will give way to sight. —*D. DeHaan*

Listening may be the most loving and Christlike thing you do today.

December 27
Sunday

The Challenge Of Confinement

Read:
Jeremiah 29:4-14

Grow in the grace and knowledge of our Lord and Savior Jesus Christ. —2 Peter 3:18

The Bible In One Year:
■ Zechariah 1–4
■ Revelation 18

At the age of 86, Ken Deal concluded more than 3 decades of volunteer jail and prison ministry with a final Sunday sermon. His message to the inmates was about serving the Lord while incarcerated. Many of the examples he used came from prisoners, some serving life sentences. In a place everyone wants to leave, he encouraged them to grow and to share the good news of Jesus Christ with others.

After the people of Judah were taken captive by King Nebuchadnezzar and deported to Babylon because of their disobedience to God, the prophet Jeremiah sent them this message from the Lord: "Build houses and dwell in them; plant gardens and eat their fruit. Take wives and beget sons and daughters; and take wives for your sons and give your daughters to husbands . . . that you may be increased there, and not diminished" (Jer. 29:5-6).

We may face some limiting circumstance today. Whether it is the result of our failure, or through no fault of our own, we can "go" through it or seek God's strength to "grow" through it. The challenge of every confinement is to increase rather than decrease; to grow and not diminish. The Lord's goal is to give us "a future and a hope" (v.11). —David McCasland

I know, Lord, that You can use the circumstances
I am in for my good. Change me, and grow
me in my knowledge of You and intimacy
with You. Give me Your strength.

A limited situation may afford the soul a chance to grow.

December 28
Monday

THE PRESENTATION

READ:
Colossians 1:21-23

He has reconciled . . . to present you holy, and blameless, and above reproach in His sight.
—Colossians 1:21-22

THE BIBLE IN ONE YEAR:
- **Zechariah 5–8**
- **Revelation 19**

My wife, Martie, is a great cook. After a long day I often look forward to the smell of spicy aromas that promise a tasty feast. Not only does she know how to prepare a meal, but she is also a master at the presentation. The colors of the food on the plate, beautifully arranged in a harmony of meat, white puffy rice, and vegetables welcome me to pull up my chair and enjoy her handiwork. But the food was not so attractive before she got her hands on it. The meat was raw and squishy, the rice was hard and brittle, and the vegetables needed to be scrubbed and trimmed.

It reminds me of the gracious work Jesus has done for me. I am well aware of my frailty and propensity to sin. I know that in and of myself I am not presentable to God. Yet when I'm saved, Jesus makes me a new creation (2 Cor. 5:17). He takes me just as I am and makes me just as I should be—"holy, and blameless, and above reproach" (Col. 1:22). He presents me to our Father as a thing of beauty worthy to be in His presence.

May His transforming work on our behalf stimulate us to live up to the presentation and to be humbly grateful to Christ for His finishing work in our lives! —Joe Stowell

Let the beauty of Jesus be seen in me—
All His wonderful passion and purity!
O Thou Spirit divine, all my nature refine,
Till the beauty of Jesus be seen in me. —*Orsborn*

Jesus takes us as we are and makes us what we should be.

December 29
Tuesday

Letter To A Child

Read:
3 John

I have no greater joy than to hear that my children walk in truth.
—3 John 4

The Bible In One Year:
- **Zechariah 9–12**
- **Revelation 20**

Even at the end of his life, C. S. Lewis showed an interest in the spiritual nurture of younger believers. Although in ill health, he took time to respond to the letter of a child named Philip. Complimenting the boy's fine written expression, Lewis said he was delighted that Philip understood that in the Narnia Chronicles the lion Aslan represented Jesus Christ. The next day, Lewis died at his home in the Kilns, Oxford, England, one week before his 65th birthday.

The apostle John, in his later years, sent a letter to his spiritual children. In it we see the joy of a mature believer encouraging his spiritually younger disciples to keep walking in the truth and following Christ.

John wrote, "I have no greater joy than to hear that my children walk in truth" (3 John 1:4). Short by New Testament standards, John's letter demonstrates the joy that comes in nurturing and watching the next generation's spiritual growth.

Encouraging spiritual understanding in the next generation should be the pursuit of mature believers. Sending a note of appreciation, giving a word of encouragement, praying, or offering sound advice can all be ways of helping others on their spiritual journey with God. —Dennis Fisher

To help another in Christ to grow
You have to pay a price
It takes the giving of yourself
And that means sacrifice. —*D. DeHaan*

The journey is better with someone who knows the way.

December 30
Wednesday

Mixed Emotions

Read:
Revelation 21:1-7

Even in laughter the heart may sorrow, and the end of mirth may be grief.
—Proverbs 14:13

The Bible In One Year:
- **Zechariah 13–14**
- **Revelation 21**

For Marlene and me, "mixed emotions" precisely describes our wedding. Don't take that the wrong way. It was a wonderful event that we continue to celebrate more than 35 years later. The wedding celebration, however, was dampened because Marlene's mom died of cancer just weeks before. Marlene's aunt was a wonderful stand-in as the "mother of the bride," but, in the midst of our happiness, something clearly wasn't right. Mom was missing, and that affected everything.

That experience typifies life in a broken world. Our experiences here are a mixed bag of good and bad, joy and pain—a reality that Solomon expressed when he wrote, "Even in laughter the heart may sorrow, and the end of mirth may be grief" (Prov. 14:13). The merry heart often does grieve, for that is what this life sometimes demands.

Thankfully, however, this life is not all there is. And in the life that is to come, those who know Christ have a promise: "God will wipe away every tear from their eyes; there shall be no more death, nor sorrow, nor crying. There shall be no more pain, for the former things have passed away" (Rev. 21:4). In that great day, there will be no mixed emotions—only hearts filled with the presence of God! —Bill Crowder

Peace! peace! wonderful peace,
Coming down from the Father above,
Sweep over my spirit forever, I pray,
In fathomless billows of love. —*Cornell*

For the Christian, the dark sorrows of earth will one day be changed into the bright songs of heaven.

December 31
Thursday

In His Grip

Read:
Romans 8:31-39

I press on, that I may lay hold of that for which Christ Jesus has also laid hold of me.
—Philippians 3:12

The Bible In One Year:
- Malachi 1–4
- Revelation 22

When we cross a busy street with small children in tow, we put out our hand and say, "Hold on tight," and our little ones grasp our hand as tightly as they can. But we would never depend on their grasp. It is our grip on their hand that holds them and keeps them secure. So Paul insists, "Christ Jesus has also laid hold of me" (Phil. 3:12). Or more exactly, "Christ has a grip on me!"

One thing is certain: It is not our grip on God that keeps us safe, but the power of Jesus' grasp. No one can take us out of His grasp—not the devil, not even ourselves. Once we're in His hands, He will not let go.

We have this assurance: "I give them eternal life, and they shall never perish; neither shall anyone snatch them out of My hand. My Father, who has given them to Me, is greater than all; and no one is able to snatch them out of My Father's hand" (John 10:28-29).

Doubly safe: Our Father on one side and our Lord and Savior on the other, clasping us in a viselike grip. These are the hands that shaped the mountains and oceans and flung the stars into space. Nothing in this life or the next "shall be able to separate us from the love of God which is in Christ Jesus our Lord" (Rom. 8:39). —David Roper

Father, I thank You for the nail-pierced hands
that reached out in love and took me by my hand.
You have led me by Your right hand throughout life.
I trust You to hold me and keep me safe to the end.

The One who saved us
is the One who keeps us.

The Forgiveness of God

Society is troubled when crime goes unpunished. For the murder of a child, we want the guilty to pay. This demand for justice is deeply rooted. The God of the Old Testament established the principle of eye-for-eye, life-for-life justice in a setting of legal witnesses and due process (Deut. 19:21).

How then can this same God pardon a sinner? How can justice be satisfied except by punishment of the guilty? There is only one other possibility. Other than ourselves, the only one who can be held responsible is the One who gave us the freedom to sin. Like a parent who gives freedom to a nearly grown child, God gave us the freedom, the time, and the capacity to sin. Is it possible for Him to offer to pay for our damages?

According to the Bible, that's exactly what God did. At great cost to Himself, He paid the price for our sin.

Was this a veiled admission of divine guilt? Was God allowing for the possibility He had been wrong to give us moral capacity and freedom of choice? Is this why He put in motion a ritual system of sacrifice that would end up costing Him inexpressible pain? No. The last book of the Bible shows that for all eternity, the choirs of heaven will declare God holy in all He is and does (Rev. 4:8). Throughout all eternity, heaven will show that God was right in giving us freedom to sin. Eternity will show His wisdom in letting us discover the wages of sin and the terrible consequences of our willful disobedience.

Throughout all eternity, heaven will also honor the justice and mercy of the Creator who lovingly chose to bear the burden of our rebellion.

The payment for our sin came at heaven's expense. In an act of unparalleled self-sacrifice, God built a two-lane bridge of mercy and justice over the chasm of sin separating us from Him. On earth, Roman executioners drove nails into the hands and feet of God's only Son. In heaven, a Father suffered as no human father has ever suffered. When it was finished, God accepted the sacrifice as sufficient payment for our sin.

Justice was satisfied. In the eternal moments and infinite agony of the Son who cried, "My God, My God, why have You forsaken Me?" (Matt. 27:46), the Creator Himself became sin for us (2 Cor. 5:21).

Three days later, Christ rose bodily from the dead. By the miracle of resurrection He showed heaven's acceptance of His sacrifice. An endless river of mercies began flowing from the cross on which He died. A legal foundation had been laid for the doctrine of justification by faith. According to the apostle Paul, God is just (righteous) to justify (declare righteous) all who come to Christ in faith. In Romans 3, he wrote:

> *By the deeds of the law no flesh will be justified in His sight, for by the law is the knowledge of sin. But now the righteousness of God apart from the law is revealed, being witnessed by the Law and the Prophets, even the righteousness of God, through faith in Jesus Christ, to all and on all who believe. For there is no difference; for all have sinned and fall short of the glory of God, being justified freely by His grace through the redemption that is in Christ Jesus, whom God set forth as a propitiation by His blood, through faith, to demonstrate His righteousness, because in His forbearance God had passed over the sins that were previously committed, to demonstrate at the present time His righteousness, that He might be just and the justifier of the one who has faith in Jesus (vv.20-26).*

Some Common Questions

We should not be surprised if we continue to have questions about the forgiveness of God. We may very well have troubling questions about God's forgiveness and our own unrelenting guilt.

What if I don't feel forgiven by God? Most of us struggle with feelings of guilt and shame. Long after we have confessed our sins to God, we are apt to feel unforgiven. We might fear that we have been rejected by God.

When feelings of guilt hound us, we need to remind ourselves that our forgiveness does not depend on how we feel.

Forgiven people can feel like they are hanging by a thread over the fires of hell. Forgiven people can be oppressed by the accuser of our souls (Satan), who stirs up old emotions the way we stir up the embers of a dying fire. But those emotions are not telling us the truth about the forgiveness of God.

Forgiveness is something God does. It is not rooted in our own emotions. It doesn't depend on whether we forgive ourselves. Forgiveness is what God does in the books of heaven when He marks "canceled" over our debt of sin. We are forgiven when He declares us legally acquitted, regardless of how we might be feeling at the moment.

It is vital to realize that the forgiveness of God is something He does. Let's look at eight pictures of God's forgiveness from the Old Testament. Author David B. Kennedy notes:

1. God bags up our sins to throw them away. "My offenses will be sealed up in a bag" (Job 14:17 NIV).

2. God blows away the sin barrier. "I have swept away your offenses like a cloud, your sins like the morning mist" (Isa. 44:22 NIV).

3. God takes away our sins. "As far as the east is from the west, so far has He removed our transgressions from us" (Ps. 103:12 NIV).

4. God treats our sin like a vanquished foe. "You will tread our sins underfoot" (Mic. 7:19 NIV).

5. God puts our sins out of His sight. "You have put all my sins behind your back" (Isa. 38:17 NIV).

6. God puts our sins out of His mind. "I will . . . remember their sins no more" (Jer. 31:34 NIV).

7. God cancels the debt of our sin. "I, even I, am he who blots out your transgressions" (Isa. 43:25 NIV).

8. God removes sin's stain and restores purity. "Though your sins are like scarlet, they shall be as white as snow" (Isa. 1:18 NIV).

Why does the Bible say God will not forgive us if we don't forgive one another? Jesus said:

If you forgive men their trespasses, your heavenly Father will also forgive you. But if you do not forgive men their trespasses, neither will your Father forgive your trespasses (Matt. 6:14-15).

The answer is in the context. Jesus was not teaching lost people how to be saved. He was teaching His own disciples how to stay in good family relationship with the Father.

By comparing this Scripture with other passages, we must conclude that Jesus was referring to an unwillingness to love those who have harmed us, and an unwillingness to forgive those who have repented of the wrong they have done (Luke 17:3-4). What He will hold against us (in a family sense) is our determination to withhold from others the kindness and forgiveness that He has shown to us. He has adopted us as sons and daughters. This is a "family issue," not a factor that could determine our eternal destiny.

Does this mean we should always forgive others unconditionally? No. Like so many other principles of Scripture, there is a time to forgive and a time not to forgive. While we are always to love others unconditionally (by seeking their good), Jesus Himself teaches us to forgive people when they acknowledge their wrongs (Matt. 18:15-17; Luke 17:1-10).

We do not love well when we allow our brothers or sisters to knowingly harm us without holding them accountable.

But doesn't God forgive us unconditionally? Aren't we to forgive others as He has forgiven us? When the apostle told us to "be kind to one another, tenderhearted, forgiving one another, even as God in Christ forgave you" (Eph. 4:32), he made it clear that we are to pattern our forgiveness after God's forgiveness of us.

God does not forgive unconditionally. First He grants legal pardon to those who meet the condition of acknowledging their sin and believing in His Son. Then He extends family forgiveness to those sons and daughters who confess their sin and seek to be restored to the Father (1 John 1:9).

If we have been forgiven by God, why won't people let us forget the past? Being forgiven by God does not release us from the natural consequences of our sins. Crimes against the state must be subjected to legal due process. Acts against individuals deserve restitution. God's forgiveness doesn't qualify former embezzlers to be entrusted with other people's money, nor does it give us reason to entrust children to someone with a history of molesting. This is wisdom.

The Effects of Guilt

When we sin and refuse to come to Christ for forgiveness, our guilt may express itself in a number of different ways. For instance, before David repented of the terrible sins of adultery and murder, he experienced physical, emotional, and spiritual anguish. In Psalm 32:3-4, describing how his guilt affected him, he wrote these words:

> *When I kept silent, my bones grew old through my groaning all the day long* [emotional]. *For day and night Your hand was heavy upon me* [spiritual]; *my vitality was turned into the drought of summer* [physical].

David's entire life was affected by his guilt. It touched him physically, emotionally, spiritually, and relationally. But he cried out to God, found the assurance of forgiveness, and was able to enjoy life again—damaged but hopeful.

Would David have been more honorable not to seek God's forgiveness? Would he have been more respectful of his victim's survivors to refuse any mercy? Would self-condemnation and suicide have been a more noble course of action? Only if there is no life beyond the grave. Only if the rest of us were not sinners. Only if a forgiven person has nothing to offer. Only if God doesn't love us enough to long for our restoration. But as the Scriptures show, God loves sinners.

God's Forgiveness Equals Our Guilt

Because of the unlimited scope of Christ's death on the cross, we have received forgiveness not only for past sins, but for all sins—past, present, and future.

Once-for-all. The moment we trust Christ as Savior, we are given immunity from punishment. The issue is settled: Our case is closed and God will not open the files of our guilt again. As the courts of earth honor the principle of double jeopardy, so heaven will not judge twice those whose sins have been punished in Christ.

The wonderful truth of justification is that God by His own authority acquits us. While He doesn't "make" us righteous, He "declares" righteous those who have appealed to the death of Christ as payment for their sin.

Does this mean we are no longer accountable for our wrongs? No. We are still subject to natural and legal consequences. We can still lose rewards and a "well done" at the judgment seat of Christ, where our Lord will hold us accountable as His children. But those of us who are in Christ will never be condemned for our sin.

In essence, God says to the one who trusts Christ, "Your sins have been paid for. My Son died for you. Therefore, in Him you stand righteous before Me. You are forgiven of all your sin in a once-for-all transaction!"

Complete. The forgiveness God offers is comprehensive. It is complete and final—not just until the next inevitable sin. This is why in another letter Paul could quote Psalm 32:1-2 when he wrote: "Blessed are those whose lawless deeds are forgiven, and whose sins are covered; blessed is the man to whom the Lord shall not impute sin" (Rom. 4:7-8).

Forgiven. Think about a young, struggling mountain climber trudging up a steep trail with a large backpack. The burden is heavy. Then an experienced climber lifts the load off his back and shoulders it himself. The young hiker feels revitalized and free. The word forgiven means "to lift off, to carry away."

Covered. When we trust in Christ, our sins are removed forever. The Greek word translated "covered" in Romans 4:7 means to "cover over completely, to obliterate." They are gone forever.

Not imputed. The word impute means "to charge to an account." God charges to our account the righteousness of Christ. He will not hold our sins against us. They will not affect our standing in heaven.

If you have never known the forgiveness of God, it can be yours right now. All that remains is for you to personally choose to trust in the One who has done so much for you. He died on the cross to pay the penalty for our sins. He offers forgiveness and an eternal place in the family of God.

Look up these New Testament references to be assured of what God has promised:

- John 3:16; 5:24; 6:47; 7:38; 11:25; 20:31
- Acts 13:48; 16:31
- Romans 1:16; 4:3; 5:1; 10:11

Growing In Christ

Once we have trusted Christ as our Savior, how do we grow in our relationship with Him? Jesus is called the "Good Shepherd" because He leads and watches over those who follow Him. He said: "My sheep hear My voice, and I know them, and they follow Me" (John 10:27).

But how do we hear the Shepherd? Our sensitivity to His voice depends on communication in four areas.

God talks to us. As we read the Bible, He speaks to us through His own words and self-revelation (2 Tim. 3:16).

We talk to God. As we receive understanding from Him, we respond to Him with the affections and needs of our hearts (John 15:7).

We talk with our new family. As we connect with others who share our faith in Christ, we experience mutual encouragement and motivation to love as we ourselves have been loved (Heb. 10:24-25).

We talk with others about Christ. Christ desires for us to be His representatives to those who have not yet believed (Matt. 4:19). One of the best ways to do this is to show honest concern for them. If they see our changed life and see that we are genuinely interested in them, they are more likely to be curious about the difference they see in us.

No two believers have an identical relationship with the Savior, but a genuine believer will have a desire to listen to God, to respond to Him, to fellowship with other believers, and to witness to those who do not yet know Christ.

As you walk the Christian journey, let God creatively guide your path to a growing relationship with Him.

TOPIC INDEX

TOPIC DATE

TOPIC DATE

RBC MINISTRIES OFFICES
IBERO-AMERICA & CARIBBEAN REGION

For more information on RBC Ministries resources, contact us at the office nearest you listed below.

ARGENTINA
Ministerios RBC, Casilla de Correo 23, Sucursal Olivos, B1636AAG Olivos, Buenos Aires
Email: argentina@rbc.org • PH: (011) 15 5467-4008

BRAZIL
Ministérios RBC, Caixa Postal 4190, 82501-970, Curitiba/PR
Email: brazil@rbc.org • PH: (+55) 41 3257-4028

COLOMBIA
Ministerios RBC, Apartado Postal 21, Fusagasugá, Cundinamarca
Email: colombia@rbc.org • PH: (+57) 1 873 6476

GUYANA
RBC Ministries, PO Box 101070, Georgetown
Email: guyana@rbc.org • PH: (+592) 231 6704

HONDURAS
Ministerios RBC, Apartado Postal 30082, Toncontín
Email: honduras@rbc.org • PH: (+504) 2213 1277

JAMAICA W.I.
RBC Ministries, 10 Hagley Park Plaza, PO Box 139, Kingston 10
Email: jamaica@rbc.org • PH: (+1-876) 926 5552

MEXICO
Ministerios RBC, Apartado Postal 91-48, C.P. 02431, Azcapotzalco, Mexico D.F.
Email: mexico@rbc.org • PH: (+52-55) 2877 0255

PERU
Ministerios RBC, Casilla de Correos 14-425, Lima
Email: peru@rbc.org • PH: (+51) 1 221-8530

PORTUGAL
Ministérios RBC, Rua da Cinquenta 59, 4500-712, Nogueira da Regedoura
Email: portugal@rbc.org • PH: (+351) 22 4896232

SPAIN
Ministerios RBC, Apartado de correos 33, 36950 Moaña, Pontevedra
Email: spain@rbc.org • PH: (+34) 986 31 80 85

TRINIDAD & TOBAGO W.I.
RBC Ministries, PO Box 4938, Tunapuna
Email: trinidad@rbc.org • PH: (+1-868) 645-7402

USA
RBC Ministries, PO Box 2222, Grand Rapids, MI 49501-2222
Email: usa@rbc.org • PH: (+1-616) 974-2210

For a detailed listing of all our offices, go to **www.rbc-addresses.info**

For more information about our resources, write to **brazil@rbc.org**, or visit us online at **www.rbc.org**